Beyond the Rhetoric:

Politics, the Economy and Social Policy in Northern Ireland

edited by Paul Teague

LAWRENCE AND WISHART
LONDON

Lawrence and Wishart Limited
39 Museum Street
London WC1A 1LQ

First published 1987
Reprinted 1988 (twice)

© Lawrence and Wishart, 1987

Each essay © the author

Photoset in North Wales by
Derek Doyle & Associates, Mold, Clwyd

Printed in Great Britain
at the University Printing House, Oxford

Contents

Acknowledgements

I owe a great many debts to people who have helped me produce this book. First and foremost are my debts to the contributors who participated in this project with considerable enthusiasm. Stephen Hayward and Jeff Skelley at Lawrence and Wishart proved to be both patient and constructive. Chris Brewster, my colleague at Cranfield Institute of Technology, was a constant source of encouragement and advice, and Sarah Willett provided secretarial assistance which was second to none. Finally the patience and resilience of two close friends, Brian McCaffery and Carol Larratt, were taxed to the limits. Without the assistance of all these people I doubt if this book would have materialised.

Chronology

1968

October   The Civil Rights Association's first march in Derry ends in violence.

November   O'Neill's Unionist government attempts to appease the growing opposition to its rule by announcing a package of reforms, but these are widely regarded as inadequate.

1969

April   The continuing Civil Rights campaign and the general increase in civil disorder and violence force O'Neill to resign; he is replaced as Prime Minister by James Chichester-Clark.

Bernadette Devlin is elected as 'Independent Unity' MP for Mid-Ulster.

June   Unemployment in Northern Ireland is recorded at 35,202.

August   After severe rioting in Belfast, Derry and other places, the British army is brought into the province.

After a period of internal tension, the Republican movement and IRA split into two factions, the Marxist-inclined Officials and the more traditionally nationalist Provisionals.

September   As a result of pressure from Westminster, the RUC is reorganised, the 'B' Specials are disbanded and new electoral laws introduced.

1970

April   The Ulster Defence Regiment is established to replace the 'B' Specials.

May   Jack Lynch, Taoiseach in the Republic, dismisses

Charles Haughey and Neil Blaney from his Fianna Fáil Cabinet after allegations are made concerning their involvement in a gun-running plot.

June Ian Paisley is elected to Westminster as MP for North Antrim.

The fragmented constitutionalist nationalist opposition agrees at a conference to combine and form a new political party, the SDLP.

Unemployment in Northern Ireland falls to 32,174.

1971

March James Chichester-Clark resigns as Premier and is succeeded by Brian Faulkner.

June Unemployment in Northern Ireland rises to 37,749.

July The SDLP withdraws from Stormont after the Unionist government refuses an inquiry into shooting by the army of two men in Derry.

August In the face of mounting and widespread IRA bombing and shooting attacks, internment without trial is introduced; as a response, the Civil Rights Association launches a campaign of civil disobedience.

December In what is widely regarded as the start of the backlash from the Protestant paramilitaries, fifteen people die in an explosion at a Catholic public house – McGurk's Bar – in Belfast.

1972

January Thirteen people are shot dead by the Parachute Regiment during a Civil Rights march in Derry; the incident becomes known as 'Bloody Sunday'. The following weekend in Newry more than 100,000 people attend the Civil Rights Association's largest ever rally.

February Seven people, five of them civilians, die when the Official IRA explodes a car bomb outside a Parachute Regiment Officers' Mess in Aldershot.

March The Provisional IRA is widely condemned after nine people die and many hundreds are injured in a series of explosions in Belfast, the bombing of the Abercorn Restaurant producing the worst casualties.

The British government announces the dissolution of devolved government at Stormont and the establishment of a system of Direct Rule for the province.

May The Official IRA calls a ceasefire.

June The Provisional IRA also announces a ceasefire, but this lasts less than three weeks.

Unemployment in Northern Ireland rises to 39,577.

July Two weeks after ending their ceasefire, the Provisionals kill nine people when 22 bombs explode in Belfast ('Bloody Friday').

December Two people are killed and 80 injured in Dublin when two bombs explode outside the Dáil.

1973

March A referendum is held to ascertain whether Northern Ireland citizens want to remain within Britain; an overwhelming 'yes' vote is recorded, but many nationalists boycott the poll, regarding the result as a foregone conclusion.

The Provisional IRA brings its campaign to England and explodes two car bombs in London, killing one man and injuring 180.

The British government publishes a White Paper, proposing an Assembly elected by proportional representation.

June Members are elected to the new Assembly.

Unemployment in Northern Ireland falls to 29,655.

July The Assembly opens amidst noisy scenes caused by extreme Loyalists.

December At a conference held in Sunningdale an agreement is reached between Brian Faulkner and the SDLP to establish a power-sharing executive in the province; a Council of Ireland, involving government ministers from Britain, Southern Ireland and the province is also agreed on.

1974

January   The new power-sharing executive takes office.
The Unionist Party's ruling body – the Ulster Unionist Council – rejects the Council of Ireland proposed in the Sunningdale agreement; as a result, Brian Faulkner resigns as leader of the Unionist Party, and is replaced by Harry West.

February   The Unionist bloc splits into two camps, the pro-Faulknerite Ulster Unionist Party and the United Ulster Unionist Coalition (UUUC), an umbrella organisation covering all strands of Unionism opposed to the power-sharing Assembly.
In the Westminster General Election, the UUUC wins eleven seats while the Faulknerite Unionists fail to win one seat.

May   The Loyalist Ulster Workers' Council calls a strike against the Assembly which has immediate effect – power cuts and mass walk-outs bring industry to a standstill; during the strike, 29 people are killed by car bombs in Dublin and Monaghan.
With the strike causing widespread disruption, the Unionist members of the Executive resign; the British government announces the immediate resumption of Direct Rule.

June   Unemployment in Northern Ireland falls to 26,868.

October   James Molyneaux is elected leader of the UUUC group of MPs.

November   The Provisional IRA kills 21 and injures 184 when it plants bombs in two Birmingham pubs.

December   The Provisionals announce a Christmas ceasefire.

1975

February   After initial uncertainty the Provisional IRA calls a general ceasefire; Incident Centres, manned by Provisional Sinn Fein members, are set up to monitor the ceasefire.

April   A violent feud costing eight lives erupts on both sides of the border when a group calling itself the Irish Republican Socialist Party (IRSP) announces that it has split from the Official Republican movement; its military wing becomes known as the Irish National Liberation Army.

May   Elections are held to the Northern Ireland Convention which is intended to negotiate a future political arrangement for the province; the Convention opens with the UUUC stating its refusal to share power with the SDLP.

June   Unemployment in Northern Ireland rises to 37,582.

September   The Ulster Volunteer Force, a Protestant paramilitary, kills twelve people in sectarian attacks.

October   The Provisional IRA attacks members of the Republican Clubs (the political wing of the Official IRA), killing five and injuring 30.
              The ceasefire which has held for nine months breaks down; the Provisionals almost immediately launch a bombing campaign on the British mainland.

December   After the last detainees are released, internment is officially ended.
              The IRA unit which has carried out the bombings in Britain is captured after a seven-day siege in Balcombe Street, London.

1976

January   Early in the month five Catholics are killed in sectarian attacks by Protestant paramilitaries; the following day ten Protestants are killed by the IRA on their way home from work.
              The Irish Congress of Trade Unions launches its 'Better Life For All' campaign in response to the sectarian murders.

March   The British government announces the formal dissolution of the Convention after the political parties have failed to agree on a single substantial point.

June   Unemployment in Northern Ireland reaches 53,954, a post-war record.

August   The death of three children in an incident involving the IRA and the army leads to the establishment of the Peace People; the organisation's first rally attracts 20,000 people.

Merlyn Rees, Secretary of State for Northern Ireland, announces the phasing out of special category (political) status prisoners.

September   The European Commission on Human Rights declares that Britain was guilty of torturing detainees in 1971, but that internment had been justified.

October   Gerry Adams is jailed for three years for membership of the Provisional IRA.

1977

January   The British government announces plans to strengthen the role of the RUC in the province's security – this is interpreted by some analysts as the beginning of 'Ulsterisation'.

March   Brian Faulkner is killed in a riding accident.

Fermenting antagonisms within the UUUC reach their climax when the Official Unionist Party decides to boycott it.

May   An organisation called the Ulster Unionist Action Committee (UUAC) calls for a strike to protest against security policy, and demands a return of devolved government, but the protest is widely regarded as a failure.

June   Unemployment in Northern Ireland reaches 59,654.

July   Four people are killed and eighteen injured when a feud erupts between the Provisional and Official IRA.

October   Betty Williams and Mairead Corrigan, founders of the Peace People, are awarded the 1976 Nobel Peace Prize.

1978

January   A major report by the Fair Employment Agency concludes that Catholics suffer more unemployment than Protestants.

	The European Court of Justice holds that interrogation techniques used on internees did not amount to torture, but were inhuman and degrading.
February	An IRA fire bomb attack on the Le Mons Restaurant kills twelve people.
June	Unemployment in Northern Ireland reaches 64,658.
August	Roy Mason, the Secretary of State for Northern Ireland, announces a major new international investment project making sports cars – the De Lorean project.
November	The SDLP departs from a long-standing policy and votes that British withdrawal is 'desirable and inevitable', and calls for a conference involving both the British and Irish governments and the two communities in Northern Ireland.

1979

March	Airey Neave, the Conservative spokesman on Northern Ireland, is killed in an INLA car bomb attack.
	The Bennett Committee investigating RUC interrogation methods concludes that some suspects had been abused while in custody.
May	In the Westminster General Election, the Paisleyite DUP gains two seats from the OUP in Belfast.
June	Ian Paisley (DUP), John Hume (SDLP) and John Taylor (OUP) are elected to fill Northern Ireland's three seats in the European Parliament.
	Unemployment in Northern Ireland falls to 62,763.
August	On the same day the IRA kills 18 British Paratroopers in an ambush near Warrenpoint, Northern Ireland, and Lord Mountbatten in Sligo, Southern Ireland.
October	The Secretary of State, Humphrey Atkins, announces that he is inviting the four main political parties – OUP, DUP, SDLP and Alliance – to a Stormont conference to discuss a political settlement; the OUP immediately turns down the invitation.
November	At its annual conference, the SDLP votes to reject

the invitation to attend the Atkins talks; this leads the party's leader, Gerry Fitt, to resign; shortly afterwards John Hume is elected as his successor.

December   Charles Haughey is appointed to succeed Jack Lynch as the leader of Fianna Fáil.

The SDLP party leadership reverses its conference decision and decides to attend the Atkins Conference.

1980

January   The Constitutional Conference opens at Stormont, but is put into immediate jeopardy as the DUP and SDLP disagree over the agenda.

March   The Conference adjourns indefinitely after the discussions reach a deadlock.

May   Mrs Thatcher and Mr Haughey meet at 10 Downing Street. The communiqué agreed by the two promises closer political co-operation and refers to the 'unique relationship' between the two countries.

June   The European Commission of Human Rights rejects the case brought on behalf of H-Block prisoners in the Maze Prison who were on the 'dirty protest', a campaign for political status which has been running for more than two years.

Unemployment in Northern Ireland rises to 73,031.

October   Seven H-Block prisoners begin a hunger strike in support of political status.

December   A communiqué after a meeting between Mr Haughey and Mrs Thatcher in Dublin announces the establishment of a joint study group in a wide range of subjects; Haughey calls it 'an historic breakthrough'.

After one IRA prisoner becomes critically ill, the H-Block hunger strike is called off.

1981

January   Bernadette McAlliskey (formerly Devlin) and her husband are shot and seriously injured, and are only saved by the quick arrival of British troops.

March	Frank Maguire, MP for Fermanagh and South Tyrone, dies.
April	The DUP holds three late-night rallies to show that there is an 'army of Ulster men' ready to fight to maintain Northern Ireland's existing constitutional status.

A new H-Block hunger strike in support of political status begins when Bobby Sands, the IRA's commander inside the Maze, goes on strike; Sands wins the Fermanagh and South Tyrone by-election. |
| *May* | Four hunger strikers – Bobby Sands, Francis Hughes, Patsy O'Hara and Gerald McCreash – die. |
| *June* | Two H-Block prisoners, are elected to the Dáil in the Republic's General Election, which results in the return of a Fine Gael/Labour coalition.

Official Unionist Westminster MP, the Revd Robert Bradford, is killed by the IRA.

Unemployment in Northern Ireland rises to 103,833. |
| *July* | Two more hunger strikers (Hurson and McDonnell) die. |
| *August* | Four more hunger strikers (Docherty, Lynch, McElwee, Devine) die.

Owen Carron of Provisional Sinn Fein is returned as MP for Fermanagh and South Tyrone in the by-election following Bobby Sands' death. |
| *September* | The Labour Party Conference adopts a special study group's report on Northern Ireland which declares that Irish unification should be the long-term aim of the party.

James Prior replaces Humphrey Atkins as Secretary of State for Northern Ireland. |
| *October* | After the intervention of the families of hunger strikers, the fast is called off by the prisoners; a negotiated compromise is then reached between the prisoners and the prison authorities. |

November   An Anglo-Irish Council, consisting of Ministers from Britain and Southern Ireland, is set up to discuss matters of mutual interest.

1982
February   Mr Haughey and his Fianna Fáil Party are elected to government in the Irish General Election.
March   The British government launches yet another initiative to establish devolved government in the province (Prior's rolling devolution plan).
June   Unemployment in Northern Ireland rises to 116,071.
July   The Southern Irish government attacks the plans for a Northern Ireland Assembly for not including an Irish dimension.
October   The elections to the Northern Ireland Assembly are held; Provisional Sinn Fein contests elections for the first-time and causes a stir when it achieves 30 per cent of the nationalist vote; the SDLP also contests the election but refuses to take its seats.
               The De Lorean factory, opened with so much fanfare, closes after months of speculation.
November   Major protests are made by nationalist politicians over what they see as 'a shoot to kill' policy being operated by the security forces, particularly in the Armagh area.
               A Fine Gael/Labour coalition government under Garret FitzGerald regains power in a snap General Election in the South; earlier, FitzGerald has made clear his intention to make the South a more pluralist society.
December   Seventeen people are killed by a bomb planted by the INLA in the 'Droppin' Well' public house in Derry.

1983
April   The first mass 'supergrass' trials take place amidst considerable publicity.
               The All Ireland Forum, consisting of all

constitutionalist nationalist parties from both sides of the Border, is established with the aim of establishing a commonly agreed policy on the constitutional question.

The Goodyear multinational closes its production plant and research centre at Craigaron with the loss of 1750 jobs.

May The Official Unionist Party quits the Assembly following an INLA attack on a Protestant congregation at Dartley, Co. Armagh, which leaves five dead.

June Unemployment in Northern Ireland falls to 113,411.

September 38 Republican prisoners escape from the Maze prison in a mass break-out.

A referendum to make abortion (already illegal) in breach of the Constitution in the South is sponsored by religious groups and passed overwhelmingly.

1984

March Gerry Adams, leader of Provisional Sinn Fein, is wounded in a gun attack.

April The All Ireland forum report is published: it outlines three possible scenarios for the future government of Northern Ireland – joint sovereignty, a federal Ireland, and a united Ireland.

June Lear Fan, the American multinational, closes its plant in the province with the loss of 500 jobs; unemployment in Northern Ireland rises to 118,897.

The European Parliament passes a resolution calling for a halt to the use of plastic bullets.

August Douglas Hurd replaces James Prior as Secretary of State for Northern Ireland.

September Thatcher rejects the three options put forward by the All Ireland Forum.

October Several leading Conservatives are killed when the IRA bombs the Brighton hotel in which Margaret Thatcher is staying.

1985

June	Unemployment in Northern Ireland rises to 121,392.
July	Fierce clashes break out between Loyalists and the RUC during an Orange Order march in Portadown.
November	After months of highly secret negotiations, Thatcher and FitzGerald sign the Anglo-Irish Agreement at Hillsborough.
	Over 100,000 attend a Unionist rally against the Agreement in Belfast.
	Charles Haughey denounces the Agreement as a sell-out in a Dáil Speech.

1986

January	Fifteen parliamentary by-elections are held in Northern Ireland after sitting Unionist MPs resign their seats in protest against the Anglo-Irish Agreement; Unionists want the by-elections to be seen as a mini-referendum on the issue, but their plans backfire somewhat when the SDLP gains one seat.
February	Unionist councillors in the province announce that they will refuse to set rates as part of the Loyalist campaign against the Anglo-Irish Agreement.
	A report on the Kincora Children's Home which investigated cases of alleged sexual abuse of children by public figures leaves open the question of whether an official cover-up took place.
March	A day of action organised by the major Unionist parties involves widespread violence and intimidation.
April	The homes of RUC personnel are attacked by Loyalist extremists.
May	The New York State legislature passes an Act aimed at supporting investment in US companies which generate employment policies favouring Catholic workers in Northern Ireland.
June	A referendum to change the Constitution in the

South and make divorce legal is overwhelmingly defeated.

The Northern Ireland Assembly is dissolved.

John Stalker, then Deputy Chief Constable of Greater Manchester, is removed from heading the investigation into allegations that the RUC had been operating a shoot-to-kill policy.

Unemployment in Northern Ireland rises to 125,888.

July   The US Senate ratifies the Anglo-American Extradition Treaty which effectively puts an end to the United States being used as a 'safe haven' by the IRA.

November   Unionist demonstrations on the first anniversary of the Anglo-Irish Agreement end in violence.

1987

March   Charles Haughey is elected as Taoiseach in a general election in the South; concern on the part of constitutionalist nationalists in the North and the British government that Haughey might undermine the Agreement proves to be unfounded.

In what is widely regarded as a surprise initiative, the UDA publishes a document calling for Unionist politicians to reach a power-sharing agreement with the SDLP.

A bloody internal feud leaves twelve members of the INLA dead.

April   Increased security measures are announced following a significant increase in IRA attacks.

May   Nine Provisional IRA members killed by British forces at Loughall, Co. Tyrone.

June   Enoch Powell loses his seat to the SDLP in the Westminster General Election, while Gerry Adams retains his with a reduced majority.

Paul Teague

Introduction

Since the outbreak of violence in the late 1960s more than 5,000 publications have appeared about the 'Northern Ireland crisis'. At a glance, then, it may seem that few original words can now be written on the subject, but the simple fact that this book has been brought out means that neither the editor nor the contributors believe this to be the case. Indeed, one of the main motivating influences for this collection of essays was a deep dissatisfaction with a major segment of the existing literature, namely, left-wing writings on the crisis. More often than not these works are simply designed to uphold or entrench predetermined positions.[1] As a result the developed analyses are either partial or superficial; many, moreover, are written with an uncompromising and at times vindictive pen.[2]

This book departs from this trend. Although some of the authors have firmly held political convictions, they have examined features of the current political and economic situation in the province in a rigorous and comprehensive manner. The outcome is a set of detailed and closely argued essays. Furthermore, no one political line is followed or promoted in the book: the main different viewpoints on the left are all represented. Of course this means that the book does not develop a specific strategy for the province, but this is hardly the present imperative. What is more important at the moment is a full and open debate about future policy towards Northern Ireland. It is our hope that this collection of essays will help initiate this debate.

The book is in two parts. The first examines the nature of politics in the province since the signing of the Anglo-Irish Agreement, the second examines the other crisis – economic stagnation – an area which has received little attention. An assessment of the impact of the Anglo-Irish Agreement on politics in the province is now timely. Despite being a lightweight policy document and being dismissed at the outset as being insignificant, the Agreement has broken the relative calm that had emerged in the province in the wake of the hunger strikes.[3] Unionist mobilisation against the Agreement has been intense, surprising even those who predicted such a reaction. The sectarian murder gangs have reappeared on the streets of Belfast, and harassment and intimidation is now once again a daily experience.

The Agreement has also made a telling impact on formal politics. The Official Unionist Party has been thrown into turmoil. The leadership of the party, afraid of being eclipsed by the Paisleyite Democratic Unionists and unsure of what policy direction to promote, has taken the unprecedented step of refusing to hold public press conferences. Within the party marked divisions have emerged between a pro-integrationist group (those who want full political integration of Northern Ireland with Great Britain) and a devolutionist faction (those who prefer some form of devolved government in the province). The integrationists appear to be in the majority at present, but with a significant floating centre remaining, it is by no means certain that they will become the dominant view. The Democratic Unionist Party responded to the Agreement by launching a strategy of permanent opposition. The aim has been to make the province ungovernable until the Agreement is either repealed or smashed. But this strategy is looking increasingly ineffectual as the British government has seen off all forms of opposition mounted by the DUP militants and its allies. As a consequence, frustration has mounted in the ranks of extreme Unionism, leading to its campaign of opposition taking on a more pronounced paramilitary character, and for important figures in its ranks to moot the possibility of an independent Ulster.

At the same time, the political battle has got underway for the 'hearts and minds' of the nationalist community. The SDLP has attempted to reap the maximum amount of political capital from the Agreement. It has not shied away from the glory of getting Thatcher and FitzGerald to go to Hillsborough and sign what the party declares as a historic landmark. And while certain elements of the party have expressed disquiet at the few tangible initiatives resulting from the Agreement, the overall mood is still one of confidence that this intended lifeline will stop the SDLP from going under. For its part, Provisional Sinn Fein has responded to the Agreement in a low key manner. Gerry Adams and others of the 'new leadership' have been able to keep the IRA on the bridle – there has been no significant increase in IRA violence since the signing of the Agreement. It appears that Adams has been content with consolidating his position within Sinn Fein, and further building up the latter's support base in the nationalist community. If this assessment is correct, then the assumption of the Provisionals must be that local community-oriented action by Sinn Fein councillors will be more successful in winning nationalist votes than the 'high politics' strategy played by the SDLP. Clearly the battle between the SDLP and Provisional Sinn Fein has just begun, and it is by no means certain which will be the winner.

The Agreement has even put strains on the non-sectarian parties. The mainly middle-class Alliance Party initially split on religious lines on the issue. The rift was only contained by the adoption of a policy calling for the speedy establishment of a power-sharing assembly as urged by the Agreement. The response of the Workers' Party has been uncertain. At the outset the party gave a guarded welcome to the Agreement, but its present policy argues for its suspension should the political parties in the province agree to enter into meaningful talks on devolved government. An uneasy relationship appears to exist in the organisation at the moment between those who wish to see a firm Irish dimension in any future political arrangement for the province and those who do not.

The Agreement has therefore had a far-reaching impact: the polarisation of politics around fixed and deep-seated positions has been broken. A more uncertain environment has emerged with parties unsure of what political line to follow. Of course, this new situation will have strong reverberations in Westminster: having ruptured the Direct Rule system in which 'normalisation' was gathering momentum, the onus is on the British government to be the architect of a new more sustainable political arrangement. The politics of the province after the

Accord make this a daunting task. But failure to do so will once again cast the British as the villains of the piece. In other words the Anglo-Irish Agreement has sharpened the focus on what long-term policy strategy should be followed for the province.

It is important that the left take this opportunity not only to put forward its policy alternatives for Northern Ireland, but also to appraise the appropriateness of existing views on the subject as these are looking increasingly unconvincing. There are three policy perspectives towards the 'Ulster crisis' on the left at present. The first is the uncompromising call for the immediate withdrawal of troops and for steps to be taken for the reunification of Ireland. Those who hold this position reject any exercise in reappraising policy options as a dubious reformist strategy. They regard possible changes in the political environment in the province as nothing but a new veneer on the central problem – British imperialist dominance over Northern Ireland. It is a highly rigid position with the priority on retaining ideological purity rather than being sullied by the murky waters of *realpolitik*. Because of this its suitability as a policy stance must be questioned. It is even in sharp contrast to the recently developed active ground-level strategy of the Provisionals in which the emphasis is placed on the careful choice of issues on which to engage the British government and other opponents, and the astute avoidance of terrains which could result in costly political failures.

At the same time, however, the main counter position, the democratic alternative, is now also being exposed as having serious shortcomings. This position is based primarily on the policies espoused by the mainstream socialist organisations in Ireland – the Workers' Party, sections of the Communist Party and progressive elements in the trade unions. These organisations view sectarianism as the main problem that has to be tackled in Northern Ireland. To this end they argue for democratic institutions and legislation (devolved government and a Bill of Rights), and for the establishment of democratic political alliances to challenge the dominance of the two main political blocs of nationalism and Unionism. This is a seductive position, but it has its problems. The main deficiency is that the case for the democratic alternative is argued at a high level of generality. Major questions remain unanswered: in what ways, for example, would a democratic devolved government be different from the old Stormont Unionist regime? Would essentially legalistic mechanisms be sufficient to stop the re-emergence of widespread discrimination? Moreover, the present deep entrenchment of people within either Unionist or nationalist blocs holds out little prospect for a third democratic alliance being successful. In the prevailing climate the call for democratic politics is highly laudable, but unfortunately it is little more than that.

A third position which can be referred to as the harmonisation strategy has recently been taking shape inside the Labour Party. Since 1981 the party's researchers have been attempting to put flesh on the Conference resolution which declared that it should work towards a united Ireland. While many specific aspects of the strategy remain opaque, the thinking behind it has emerged clearly. It is that a whole series of actions should be introduced to harmonise large areas of the economy and the polity both sides of the border under new single administrative units. One example is the proposal for a standardised social security system with payments being made from Dublin. The underlying logic is that this and other similar initiatives will gradually foster a new all-Ireland identity. The strategy has been criticised for not taking full account of the significant political and administrative barriers which stand in its way, and for being exceedingly reductionist in thinking that deep-seated loyalties can be changed by a series of essentially technocratic actions. There is much substance to these criticisms; as things stand, the harmonisation strategy appears to be insufficiently thought out to deal with the complexities of the Northern Ireland crisis.

It appears, therefore, that the left's policy perspectives on the crisis are deficient in several important respects. What is required therefore is not simply an analysis of politics in the province in the wake of the Anglo-Irish Agreement, but also an examination of what revisions are necessary to these perspectives. These are the themes of the first part of this book. The first essay is by Brendan O'Leary, who begins with an examination of the constitutional significance of the Agreement. This is necessary because so many contradictory claims have been made about its status that there is now widespread confusion about what was actually signed at Hillsborough on 15 November 1985. An assessment is then made of the motivating influences which led the British and Irish governments to sign the Agreement. Amongst the factors identified are the 'accommodationist crusade' by FitzGerald in the Republic of Ireland, the convergence of the 'internal' and 'external' tracks of British policy-making in the province, the desire on the part of both Prime Ministers to be acknowledged as history-makers, and the political lobbying of John Hume and the SDLP. The essay concludes by suggesting that although few tangible results have emerged from the Agreement, the Labour Party should wholeheartedly embrace it as the most effective mechanism to bring about a power-sharing assembly (the author's preferred policy option). More controversially, O'Leary argues that the Labour Party should abandon its support for a United Ireland, and organise within the province.

The second essay is by Paul Bew and Henry Patterson, two writers who are the leading academic exponents of the 'democratic alternative' political strategy. At the heart of their many writings is the argument that the stereotypical caricature of Unionism as a homogeneous bloc made up of reactionary dupes is highly misleading. They suggest that a large faction of Unionist opinion would support some form of democratic devolved government provided the constitutional status of the province was secured. Only when this status is threatened, their argument goes, does Unionism become a united and more often than not a reactionary force. This thinking permeates their analysis of the impact of the Anglo-Irish Agreement. The British and Irish governments are criticised for leaving Unionist politicians out of the background discussions and for having a simplistic view of Protestant politics. They argue that the Unionist reaction was entirely predictable and, moreover, suggest that although the Unionists' campaign of opposition will be unable to deliver a knock-out blow, it will be sufficiently strong to render impossible any progress towards the political aims of the Agreement. Given this possibility of prolonged political stalemate, coupled with the re-emergence of the sectarian murder gangs, Bew and Patterson argue that it is now timely to reassess the Agreement.

Bill Rolston in the following chapter approaches the problem from the opposite angle – the impact of the Agreement on nationalist politics in the province. Rolston traces the motivation for signing the 'Hillsborough Accord' to the political battle which emerged in the nationalist bloc between the SDLP and Provisional Sinn Fein in the early 1980s. He argues that the Agreement is a lifeline to the SDLP, albeit a precarious one since it is all that stands between the party and decline. As the Agreement has not yet produced any significant political results it is suggested that the political precipice lurches that much closer for the SDLP. But Rolston's conclusion goes even further than this, for he argues that significant reforms are virtually impossible. He poses the question of how major reforms can be made to the UDR without dismantling the entire security philosophy and policy of the British government. Of course the implication of all this is that the Agreement will fail in its declared aim of marginalising Provisional Sinn Fein, thereby intensifying the political pressure on the SDLP.

One of the most overlooked issues in existing studies of the Northern Ireland crisis is the role of the Irish Republic in the whole affair. The conventional view appears to be that political parties and voters in the South are in favour of Irish unity and would be willing to make the necessary sacrifices in support of a policy aimed at reuniting both parts of the island. This view is challenged by Peter Mair in the fourth essay in the political section of the book. Mair argues that owing to a shift from territorial to economic nationalism, the main political parties, along with the majority of Irish voters, are not interested in seriously pursuing the goal of Irish unity. They are now more concerned with mainstream political issues – the state of the economy, unemployment, education and welfare and so on. From this analysis Mair suggests that any strategy to reunite Ireland could be faced with the unexpected opposition from Southern Irish voters as well as the inevitable resistance from Northern Unionists.

Alongside this new uncertain political environment in the province, the 'other crisis' – economic decay – has continued unabated. Apart from a few notable exceptions, the scale and nature of the economic problems in Northern Ireland have not been examined fully. This is self-evidently a shortcoming, for although a political solution is not dependent on economic renewal, it is hard to conceive of any new political initiative without a major programme aimed at reversing the present economic decline. Yet in the absence of a clear understanding of the Northern Ireland economy, and in particular of the problems presently bedevilling it, a question mark must hang over the potential of any such programme. The second part of the book attempts to redress these inadequacies by examining the peculiarities and problems of the Northern Ireland economy.

The first essay is by Bob Rowthorn, one of the few academic economists who has seriously analysed the economic crisis in the province. Rowthorn's thesis is that the crisis is now so chronic that the Northern Ireland economy now resembles, in analogy, a workhouse economy – an economy in which most of the population are preoccupied with servicing and controlling each other, taking imports from the outside world without exporting anything in return. He then shows that even this precarious situation exists only by virtue of the British subvention to the province without which there would be an economic disaster. In his conclusion, Rowthorn suggests that economic decline will only be arrested when a lasting peaceful settlement is reached to the current political conflict.

The following essay by Frank Gafikin and Mike Morrissey examines the relationship between politics and poverty in the province. They argue that the ability of the two main political blocs, nationalism and Unionism, to integrate poverty related issues with more fundamental aspects of their ideological perspectives is the main reason why little or no political discourse on purely poverty-based matters has emerged in Northern Ireland. From this starting point, they go on to show, in considerable detail, how Northern Ireland is by far the most deprived region in the UK. The essay concludes, however, on an optimistic note by suggesting that, if the Anglo-Irish Agreement can ride out the protestations aimed against it, a more favourable environment may be created for positive action to be taken against poverty.

I have written the next essay that examines multinational companies in the Northern Ireland economy. It is suggested that during the past thirty years or so there have been two phases to international investment in the province. In the first phase, foreign firms played a leading role in reviving the province's faltering manufacturing base. In the second phase, however, the economy-wide benefits from the multinationals have lessened due to these companies either withdrawing from or boycotting the province. I go on to argue that despite the lacklustre performance of outside companies in the economy, it is important that the industrial development agencies continue with some form of inward investment activity, and conclude by suggesting that as a model of industrial development the policy of attracting investment should be replaced with a strategy designed to create a national dynamic economy within Ireland.

The penultimate essay is by Liam O'Dowd who focuses on developments in the service economy in the province. The essay clearly shows that if it were not for the expansion of public service employment during the 1970s the Northern Ireland economy would have collapsed. But O'Dowd also points out that in the area of private producer services, which have considerable value-added and employment creation potential, the province fared particularly badly in comparison with other UK regions. He also addresses the politically sensitive question of the impact of service employment on the spatial and occupational disadvantages of Catholics in Northern Ireland, and concludes that while the expansion in service sector employment has not remedied the relative disadvantage of Catholics in the province, it has prevented it from widening.

The final essay is by David Canning, Barry Moore and John Rhodes. By using a statistical method known as shift-share analysis, they provide a detailed account of the changes that have occurred in the province's labour market since the 1950s.[4] The picture they develop coincides with the popular perception of declining manufacturing employment being compensated by the growth of service based jobs. They suggest that this and other related developments mean that the Northern Ireland economy is now in a weak and vulnerable state. To revitalise the economy a two-pronged strategy is put forward. Its first component, which is essentially short-term, is to increase public sector employment in the province so as to reduce the numbers unemployed; the second part of the strategy is to implement a longer-term programme aimed at rejuvenating the manufacturing base in the province. It is only through action at these two levels, the authors conclude, that Northern Ireland will avoid becoming still poorer and more dependent on Britain.

There remains one important point. As mentioned earlier, this is a pluralist book: the contributors approach the Northern Ireland crisis, whether it is the economic or political one, from differing perspectives. It should be reported that all those involved in this project have done so with considerable eagerness and enthusiasm. There was full recognition that promoting a full and open debate on Northern Ireland would lead to a wider appreciation of the crisis which is unfortunately missing at present. Perhaps if a similarly co-operative attitude was adopted at the level of formal politics, the opportunity for a lasting peace would be greater, and the need for a book like this would not exist.

Notes

[1] A recent example of this trend is Andrew Boyd's *Have the Trade Unions Failed the North?*, Dublin 1985. In this book Boyd accuses the trade unions of openly complying with sectarian employment practices and British imperialism more generally. He suggests that if the trade unions would have adopted a militant nationalist stance then a major blow would have been struck against imperialism. In his efforts to make this point he portrays the potential of trade union action in a manner which most serious students of industrial relations would, quite frankly, find amazing.

[2] A good example of this is Anthony Barnett's article in the 1982 *Socialist Register*.

[3] See the round-table discussion between Henry Patterson, Bob Rowthorn and Clare Short, *Marxism Today*, January 1986. Although the participants have quite different viewpoints on Northern Ireland, they were unanimous in suggesting that the Agreement would only make a marginal impact on politics in the province.

[4] Shift-share analysis allows insights to be made into changes in a region's labour market by breaking that down into three different components, namely, national share, industry mix and regional share. National share indicates the employment change that would have occurred if a region's employment growth rate had equalled the national (UK) growth rate over the study period. Industry mix shows the amount of regional employment growth attributable to the region's initial industrial mix: that is, it reflects a region's mix of fast and slow growth industries. Finally, regional share indicates whether a region's industries performed better or worse than the national average for each industry. These three components give an entire series of 'actual minus expected' data. For analytical purposes the industry mix and regional share figures are the more interesting, because they relate regional changes to developments at the national level.

Brendan O'Leary

The Anglo-Irish Agreement: Meanings, Explanations, Results and a Defence

Rhetorical reaction to the Anglo-Irish Accord was predictable. Irish ultra-nationalists interpreted the Accord as an imperialist manoeuvre, targeted against the self-styled 'armalite and ballot box' school of national liberation. Gerry Adams of Sinn Fein (SF) condemned the agreement for 'copper-fastening partition'.[1] Ulster Unionists saw the Accord as a victory for the Provisional IRA, the pay-off for a war of sectarian attrition, a milestone in the liquidation of their cherished union. Ian Paisley, at the Democratic Unionist Party (DUP) conference, asserted that the Accord 'rode to victory on the back of IRA terrorism'.[2] These polarised interpretations are as incompatible as they are individually implausible.

Four major political questions provoked by the Accord signed by the Prime Ministers of the Republic of Ireland and the United Kingdom on 15 November 1985 are addressed in this essay. Firstly, what is the constitutional significance of the Accord? Secondly, why was the Accord signed? This essay assesses the value of three ways of explaining major state decisions.[3] Thirdly, what have been the consequences of the Accord? Finally, there is the political evaluation question: how should the British and Irish democratic left respond to the Hillsborough concordat? Should we condemn it, support it, or as the stale cliché has it, 'offer our critical support'? This essay unashamedly offers critical support for Margaret Thatcher and Garret FizGerald.

11

Meanings: What is the Anglo-Irish Agreement?

The Accord is best understood negatively: it is not three things which it is alleged to be. It is not joint authority, the equal sharing of sovereignty of Northern Ireland by two separate states. Contrary to Unionist rhetoric, Peter Barry, the Irish Minister for Foreign Affairs at the time, did not become joint governor of Northern Ireland and neither has his successor assumed that role.[4] The Accord is not a complete acceptance by the British government of one of the proposals made by the New Ireland Forum which reported in May 1984.[5] The articles of the Accord do not give London and Dublin equal responsibility for all aspects of the government of Northern Ireland. As Article 2 states:

> There is no derogation from the sovereignty of the Irish government or the United Kingdom government, and each retains responsibility for the decisions and administration of government within its own jurisdiction.

There is no case for those who contend that the UK government's action represents a formal erosion of the Act of Union of 1801, as a judge ruled in January 1986 in the High Court against a Unionist claim to the contrary.

Neither does the Accord 'put the Unionists on notice that reunification of Ireland will inevitably be enacted on an as yet undetermined date', as one constitutional lawyer has asserted.[6] The first clause of the agreement simply repeats the often expressed policy of successive British governments since the abolition of the Stormont parliament in 1972 and enshrined in Section 1 of the Northern Ireland Constitution Act of 1973, that Irish unification will not take place without the consent of a majority of the people of Northern Ireland (Article 1a). There is nothing new about the 'notice' being given to the Unionists about their constitutional status with regard to the Irish Republic, and indeed the Accord is a formal recognition by the current Irish government of the rectitude of the British constitutional guarantee. If there is a 'notice' of constitutional significance embedded in the Accord, it is that the Unionist identity has been downgraded to equality with the nationalist identity in the internal affairs of Northern Ireland. Lastly, the

Accord does not represent the *de jure* abandonment of the Irish Republic's constitutional claim to Northern Ireland as Sinn Fein and other ultra-nationalists allege. Articles 2 and 3 of the Irish Constitution read as follows:

> Article 2: The national territory consists of the whole island of Ireland, its islands and the territorial seas.
> Article 3: Pending the re-integration of the national territory and without prejudice to the right of parliament and government established by this Constitution to exercise jurisdiction of the whole of that territory, the laws enacted by that parliament shall have the like area and extent of application as the laws of Saorstát Eireann[7] and the like extra-territorial effect.

As the Accord can legitimately be interpreted as an agreement over how the national territory might be 're-integrated' it is not in violation of the letter of the Irish Constitution. Article 1c of the Accord states that 'if in the future a majority of the people of Northern Ireland clearly wish for and formally consent to the establishment of a united Ireland' then the two governments will introduce enabling legislation. However, ultra-nationalists are correct to emphasise that the Accord represents the *de facto* abandonment of Irish unification as a policy goal of Fine Gael (FG) and the Irish Labour Party (ILP) for the foreseeable future, which is not the same as 'in perpetuity' as Tom King bluntly suggested on 3 December 1985 when the ink on the Accord was still fresh.[8]

If the Accord is not joint authority, neither a notice to Unionists of eventual reunification, nor the formal abandonment of territorial irredentism by the Irish Republic, then what is its significance? Firstly, it is the formalisation of inter-state co-operation; secondly it is formal notice that whilst the Unionist guarantee remains, Unionists have no veto on policy formulation within Northern Ireland; and finally, it is the formalisation of a strategy which binds the Irish Republic to a constitutional mode of reunification which is almost unfeasible. Let us take these points in turn. First, the Accord is the formalisation of inter-state co-operation because the Inter-Governmental Conference (IGC) which it established is solely a consultative body. The IGC has no executive authority or capacity, no recognisable instruments of state (taxation and coercion), and has no formal policy implementation function.

The IGC represents little more than the institutionalisation of the talks which the two governments have been having in the Anglo-Irish Inter-Governmental Council since 1980. (In the communiqué which accompanied the Accord it was stated that British and Irish ministers had met on over twenty occasions in the previous year, a clear sign of the extent of existing collaboration as much as proof of the impending agreement.) The IGC is a policy-formulation forum which the Secretary of State for Northern Ireland can choose to concur with, take into consideration or ignore. The policy arenas open to the two governments in the IGC are spelt out in Article 2a of the Accord: '(i) political matters; (ii) security and related matters; (iii) legal matters, including the administration of justice; (iv) the promotion of cross-border co-operation'. The possible agenda is thus extremely wide-ranging. Article 6 of the Accord elaborates these four fields, and specifically entitles the Irish government to discuss the work of the Standing Advisory Commission on Human Rights (SACHR), the Fair Employment Agency (FEA), the Equal Opportunities Commission (EOC), the Police Authority for Northern Ireland (PANI) and the Police Complaints Board (PCB). These five agencies are the fruit of British attempts to reform Northern Ireland, and a direct input from the Irish government is clearly intended as a confidence-building measure for the Catholic population.

The Accord signifies the formal end of Unionist supremacy within Northern Ireland: Unionism without an Ulster Unionist veto on the structure of the union or policy-making within the union. The Unionists are denied formal access to policy formulation unless they take advantage of the possibilities for devolution which are built into the Accord. The Assembly set up under James Prior's rolling devolution proposals in 1982 was not mentioned in the Accord, and its subsequent demise in June 1986 in the face of continued SDLP abstention and Unionist abuse of its facilities to attack the Accord came as no surprise.[9] Unless the Ulster Unionists accept an agreed form of devolution the British government will act as representative for Unionism in the Inter-Governmental Conference. On the other hand, the Northern Ireland minority can have its grievances articulated in the IGC without agreed devolution, through the offices of the

Irish government. The fact that the Accord gives the Irish Republic a *de jure* interest in the affairs of a minority within another state border is symbolic affirmation of the legitimacy of the minority's complaints about the government and politics of Northern Ireland, both before and after 1972.[10] Before the signing of the Accord the official British position blamed all the discreditable features of Northern Ireland upon Unionist hegemony in the period of devolved government (1920-72), but the British signature affirms that Direct Rule (1972-85) has not reformed Northern Ireland.[11] The Accord explicitly recognises that an Irish dimension and agreed devolution (Article 4) are necessary to complete the reform of Northern Ireland. Since these arguments have been dominant in the SDLP from its inception, it is plain why the Accord symbolically establishes the constitutional equality of the Northern Ireland minority. Ian Paisley made the point graphically when he suggested that the Accord has made John Hume the 'uncrowned King of Northern Ireland'.[12]

The Accord signifies the end of a united front amongst constitutional Irish nationalists. It has crystallised divisions which have long been apparent. Fine Gael, the ILP, and the new party in the Irish Republic, the Progressive Democrats (PD) support the Accord, whereas Fianna Fáil (FF) opposes it. Within Northern Ireland the SDLP supports the Accord, whereas the small Irish Independence Party (IIP) rejects it. Since the Accord was signed, FF has shown signs of wanting to support a revamped IIP against the SDLP in Northern Ireland.[13] Consequently FF and the IIP now represent the brand of constitutionalist nationalism which simply disagrees with the IRA and SF over means rather than ends, whereas most sections of the SDLP, FG and ILP are making the reform of Northern Ireland a higher priority than any putative unification. This fissure between constitutionalist nationalists, if permanent, is of potentially immense significance on both sides of the border. The SDLP has its nationalist flank protected from criticism by SF and the IIP because of the Irish dimension in the Accord, and therefore is freer to bargain for the reform of Northern Ireland. The consequences for the politics of the Irish Republic are also far-reaching, as Mair's essay in this volume illustrates.

Three final points should be made about the constitutional significance of the Accord. It is not permanent, and envisages renewal after three years. The Accord does not form part of the domestic law of the United Kingdom, and thus the manner in which the British government manages the IGC is not amenable to judicial regulation. Finally, the Accord is a framework which permits other constitutional settlements to be built on top of it: it is compatible with substantial, albeit necessarily agreed, devolution (Article 4b and 4c); alternatively, it could be the basis for joint authority, as envisaged by the New Ireland Forum or the Kilbrandon Inquiry of November 1984.[14] However, to repeat, the Hillsborough agreement does not currently amount to joint authority.

Explanations: Why was the Accord Signed?

The communiqué which accompanied the Accord declared that the promotion of reconciliation was its main objective. What are we to make of this claim? Was the signing of the Accord prompted by more ignoble intentions? Was it, in the words of disgruntled Unionists, 'a mixture of the vilest cunning on the one hand, and the most enormous stupidity on the other'?[15] There are three ways of explaining the signing of the Accord which are worthy of serious attention.

The first approach suggests that the Accord was the outcome of a clear rational strategy reached by the British and Irish governments in pursuit of mutually acceptable goals. This approach underpins several markedly different interpretations of why the Accord was signed: one, the anti-imperialist perspective, sees it as an attempt to redefine and reconstitute British domination in Ireland; another sees it as a clever and calculating way of establishing power-sharing in the province; the final explanation sees the Accord in a light similar to that presented by the British and Irish governments – as a framework for establishing peace and security in the province. These different scenerios are examined in turn below.

Imperialist manoeuvres?

The anti-imperialist school assumes that the Northern Ireland conflict is caused by British imperialism and will only cease with the latter's termination.[16] Adherents to this view see the Accord as an attempt by the British state, fearful of what James Prior once described as the threat of an Irish Cuba off the British mainland, to re-establish its hegemony in Ireland by obtaining the consent of the 'comprador' government of the twenty-six counties to the continuation of British rule in Northern Ireland, and indeed to direct British intervention in the affairs of the twenty-six counties. To these ends the Accord was explicitly conceived to de-mobilise the radical nationalist movement built by Sinn Fein in the wake of the hunger strikes of 1980-81, to restore the social base and credibility of the SDLP and to cement the conditions for a military and political counter-offensive against the IRA. Promises of symbolic gestures towards nationalist sentiment were traded by the British government in return for the Irish government's support for Britain's real objectives: a security agreement on extradition, a Europe-wide offensive against terrorists and the Irish government's support for an assault on the American havens of support for Republicans.

Such an account is to be found in the Sinn Fein press, *An Phoblacht/Republican News*, and is echoed by some sections of the British ultra-left. The analysis presupposes clear and well defined objectives for the Accord: the maintenance of British rule in Ireland, the incorporation of the Irish Republic into NATO and the repression of Sinn Fein and the IRA. The circumstantial evidence for the anti-imperialist school includes symbolic British attempts to appease the SDLP, the Irish government's decision to join the European Convention on the Suppression of Terrorism, EEC defence arrangements which seem to violate the Republic's traditional conceptions of neutrality and the co-ordinated efforts by Thatcher and Reagan to ensure that the US Senate pass an extradition treaty against the opposition of a well-organised Irish-American lobby. There can be no doubt about such evidence, only about its significance.

There are fundamental problems with this analysis. The Irish Republic is implausibly portrayed as a puppet-state rather than as one of the most independent of small capitalist nation-states. No rigorous rationale is provided for why the British state, let alone British capital, should be so concerned to maintain Northern Ireland as part of Britain.[17] Northern Ireland is not a good source of surplus value, and it is no longer tied by aristocratic lineage networks to the dominant echelons of British society. The Unionist political movements no longer form a key component of mainland Conservatism. The importance of the province as a military training ground is much disputed by British army officers, and its geo-political significance in the era of thermonuclear warfare is negligible, despite the arguments advanced by the Troops Out Movement, Tony Benn, Sean MacBride and the odd British general. Northern Ireland's principal exploitative value seems to be as a testing ground for experiments in public and social administration. And with the notable exceptions of repressive law and military policing, its use as a testing-ground is not as detrimental to the general citizenry as one might suspect.[18]

Fear of an Irish Cuba exists amongst the more paranoid sections of the British administrative and political class, but there is little evidence that such paranoia has been paramount in British policy-making. The Provisionals and their fellow travellers have a vested interest in exaggerating the mortal threat which Sinn Fein poses to the British state, but there is no reason why the serious left should accept such claims. The British state exists in Northern Ireland because of past imperialism, and British policy-makers display the customary arrogance and ignorance of their imperialist precursors. But, these observations do not mean that the present conflict in Northern Ireland is an artefact of current British imperialism. Successive British governments have not left Northern Ireland because they have respected the wish of the overwhelming majority of Northern Irish Protestants to remain British citizens, because the Irish Republic's governments since the 1950s have never seriously wanted the British to withdraw, and because neither state has wanted the submerged civil war to become a full-scale holocaust.

The anti-imperialist explanation of the Accord falls at the first hurdle because it has an implausible conception of British objectives, based on an outmoded and falsely applied theory of imperialism. It also lacks a well developed account of the evolution of the Irish state. But the failings of this explanation are best illustrated by its incomprehension of Ulster Loyalist reaction to the Accord, which holds that the Protestant reaction to the Accord is either wholly irrational, or based upon a misperception of devious Albion. Both of these readings are sectarian and false. The Loyalists are not stupid. The Accord presents them with painful dilemmas, ends their supremacy within Northern Ireland and threatens their interpretation of the Union if not in the way that the IRA would prefer. Other than Sinn Fein supporters, the only personality to have consistently maintained an interpretation of the Accord as an imperialist plot is Enoch Powell who regards the Anglo-Irish Agreement as part of American expansionism.[19] It is rather strange that the Left only takes Powell seriously when he shares its most far-fetched conspiracy theories.

From voluntary to coercive power-sharing?

This interpretation of the Accord portrays it as an attempt to coerce the Unionists into accepting a new version of the Sunningdale agreement of 1973-74. British policy-making between 1972 and 1975 was in favour of voluntary power-sharing in a devolved regional government in Northern Ireland, and was marked by a willingness to concede an Irish dimension to assuage minority grievances. The Sunningdale agreement had some features of what political scientists call the consociational model of liberal democracy which is considered appropriate for societies with deeply divisive non-class cleavages.[20] A power-sharing executive in which a cross-bloc majority – Faulkner's Unionists, the SDLP and the Alliance (APNI) – composed the government, was the pre-eminent feature. More widely however, political representation, civil service composition and the allocation of public funds were to be made on a proportional basis. Why did the Sunningdale settlement fail? Its Irish dimension, the Council of Ireland, created a furore amongst Unionists opposed to power-sharing (35.5 per cent of the total electorate of 1973), and left Faulkner without the backing of his party as the experiment began. The British General Election of February 1974 then intervened at a critical stage in the experiment. The plurality electoral rule meant that anti-Sunningdale Unionists were able to rout Faulkner Unionists, and obtain 51 per cent of the popular vote and eleven of the twelve Northern Ireland seats at Westminster.

Whilst poll evidence showed that strong Protestant support for the experiment had dropped after the general election to 28 per cent of their bloc,[21] the SDLP's discontent at internment and repression meant that it was neither willing nor able to save Faulkner by making concessions over the Council of Ireland. Finally, the new Labour government proved spineless during the Ulster Workers Council (UWC) strike which led to the collapse of the Executive. More generally, the Sunningdale settlement's fate showed that the conditions for voluntary power-sharing were not present. There was no multiple balance of power amongst the blocs, and there was asymmetry between the majority of the Unionist bloc's attitudes towards power-sharing and that of the majority of the nationalist bloc. Moreover, the blocs were fragmenting just when their cohesion was essential to facilitate power-sharing. The political élites of the nationalist, and especially the Unionist bloc, were not sufficiently autonomous from their supporters to bargain and make concessions, even if they wanted to, because they had good reason to fear being outflanked by opposing groups favouring their bloc's version of 'no surrender'.[22] These features of Northern Ireland precluded voluntary power-sharing.

It is possible to understand the Accord as an attempt to create the conditions for power-sharing to work by coercing key fractions of the Unionist bloc to accept some version of the 1973-74 settlement as the lesser of several evils. On the one hand the Accord confronts the Unionists with an Irish dimension, the Inter-Governmental Conference, of far greater political salience than the Council of Ireland proposed in 1973. But on the other hand the Accord offers Unionists devolution as a mechanism for removing the agenda-setting scope of the IGC provided they are prepared to accept agreed devolution – which would mean power-sharing because the SDLP cannot settle for anything less. The unpalatable choices which the Accord puts before the Unionist bloc – which are discussed below – look designed to divide them, and to create a fraction sufficiently significant and autonomous to do business with the SDLP and the APNI after ultra-loyalism has been tried and defeated. Unlike 1973-74, the Unionist ultras are being given the initiative to do what they will first, in the hope that their defeat will create a new and more stable Faulkner-style grouping. Thatcher's remarks in her famous interview in Belfast certainly lend credence to such an interpretation: 'The people of Northern Ireland can get rid of the Inter-Governmental Conference by agreeing to devolved government.'[23] This interpretation of the Accord makes sense. The political education of the British and Irish élites since 1973 must have persuaded them that a voluntary internal settlement was impossible as long as important fractions of Unionists outside the APNI have no selective incentives to induce them to accept power-sharing, and as long as the SDLP have felt threatened from the Provisionals and other extreme nationalists.

But the interpretation is, unfortunately, implausible if it is understood as a deliberately conceived rational policy in which all costs and benefits were calculated and all permutations of possible consequences known in advance. To take one counter-example, according to civil servants, the scale and depth of Unionist opposition to the Accord was not anticipated by the Northern Ireland Office or the relevant Cabinet ministers in the UK.[24] Likewise Garret FitzGerald was startled by the reaction of moderate Unionists to the Accord. These surprised reactions of officials from both states are not those of people implementing a well defined and elaborately worked out rational policy. As a result, whilst the consequences of the Accord may eventually conform to the pattern expected as if the British and Irish policy-makers did plan coercive power-sharing, the reasons for the signing of the Accord do not wholly conform to this rational policy-making scenerio.

The establishment of peace and security?

The British and Irish governments highlighted peace, reconciliation and security as their principal objectives when presenting the Accord to their respective societies. Could it be the case that both governments were truly motivated by these objectives? The British government has constantly underlined the security dimensions of the Accord to both dissident Conservatives and the Ulster Unionists. Increased cross-border security liaison, the Republic's accession to the Suppression of Terrorism convention and the American extradition Bill have figured prominently in British rhetoric. Embarrassing incidents like the Glenholmes affair[25] and the emergence of 'Stalkergate'[26] have not stopped both governments claiming early successes from the increased harmonisation of the intelligence and resources of the RUC and the Garda Síochána. However, as the table below makes apparent, there was no overwhelming case for a security offensive on the part of the British and Irish states prior to the signing of the Accord. The most intense phase of political violence was in the early 1970s, during the collapse of Stormont and the failure of the Sunningdale settlement.

Table 1: Political Murders in Northern Ireland 1969-84

	Catholic Civilians	IRA, INLA, etc.	Protestant Civilians	UVF, UDA etc.	Local security forces	British security forces
1969	7	1	6	0	1	0
1970	8	5	8	0	2	0
1971	62	17	31	0	16	43
1972	166	65	74	10	42	107
1973	75	32	50	8	21	58
1974	95	17	50	4	24	27
1975	104	17	69	18	18	13
1976	124	14	95	5	40	14
1977	33	6	19	6	30	16
1978	9	7	21	0	19	12
1979	17	5	14	0	30	38
1980	20	4	19	1	19	12
1981	27	16	15	3	33	11
1982	20	9	18	4	21	20
1983	n/a	n/a	n/a	n/a	28	5
1984	n/a	n/a	n/a	n/a	19	9

Source: *New Ireland Forum*, Dublin 1984, and Northern Ireland Office press releases.

Since the mid-1970s the IRA has altered its organisation and switched its military strategy. Economic targets have been abandoned to concentrate on attacking local security forces. The reasons for this change were the comparative success of British security policy in the mid-1970s, and the Provisionals' need for a strategy less likely to alienate their own social base. A cell structure and attacks on local security forces served both goals. The consequence has been a dramatic fall-off in civilian deaths. The policy of Ulsterisation (the replacement of the British army by the RUC) has also led to a considerable reduction in the numbers of British Army personnel killed since the mid-1970s. The brunt of the IRA's strategy is now carried by local security forces (the RUC, the UDR, and on occasions, prison officers), but their fate does not cause the same concern to British policy-makers as civilian or Army deaths. It is perfectly sensible to suggest that British strategists had achieved their goal of 'acceptable levels of violence' within Northern Ireland before the signing of the Accord. But the high-risk initiative embarked upon at Hillsborough puts Catholic civilians at risk, has caused ferocious conflicts of loyalty within the RUC and the UDR, and compels the British into increasing the Army presence.

On the Irish side, the Accord left the Fine Gael-ILP coalition government exposed to Fianna Fáil charges of violating the Republic's sovereignty, giving retrospective recognition to RUC cross-border pursuits, and abandoning a well established constitutional freedom for the protection of political exiles. When one recalls that Haughey's deft playing of the 'green card' over RUC cross-border incursions in the 1982 Irish general election caused severe damage to Fine Gael, there are reasons for suggesting that the security dimensions of the Accord were not in the short-run rational interests of the Irish government. Furthermore, as John Taylor of the OUP pointed out with sublime subtlety, the prospects of bombs on the streets of Dublin have risen greatly since the Accord was signed.[27] Finally, the Irish government's presence at the Inter-Governmental Conference binds it against making wholesale criticisms of the RUC and the UDR. Its desire for the RUC to stand firm in the summer of 1986 restrained it from making political capital over the Stalker affair.[28]

No one in either government believed that the Accord would bring immediate peace and reconciliation, but the prelude to the Accord did not help matters. The exclusion of the Unionists from participation in the negotiation of the agreement, whilst entirely practical, made their opposition all the stronger. In the short run the Accord has undoubtedly exacerbated rather than ameliorated the existing levels of polarisation, raised sectarian attacks on Catholics, induced Protestant assaults on the RUC and encouraged the IRA to reap the whirlwind. There is also evidence that both the British and Irish governments have been genuinely surprised by the levels of animosity towards the Accord amongst the Unionists, and by the apparent intransigence of John Hume to those 'feelers' which some Unionists have made towards the SDLP.[29]

To summarise, if both governments believed their own rhetoric, they miscalculated the scale of short-run conflict which the Accord would produce. But it should be added that on the conventional security front, their administrators' advice suggested that the Accord would worsen the security front, at least for the time being.

The three interpretations outlined above of why the Accord was signed are all crucially defective. They either impute too much cohesion and clear-headed foresight to the respective policy-makers, or assume incredible naïvety on questions of security and the prospects for peace.

The Institutional Approach

The institutional approach analyses the reasons for the Accord in an entirely different light, and suggests that diplomatic or political initiatives are rarely launched by a government or governments pursuing a fully developed and coherent master plan. Instead such initiatives are the product, for the most part, of the workings of state institutions – the way they perceive problems, and the manner in which they define solutions to them. Thus from the point of view of the institutional approach, the Accord, far from being a radical departure on the part of the British and Irish governments, was, in fact, the outcome of the policies and actions of state institutions and agencies in the two countries. The plausibility of this approach is examined below.

On the British side the state agencies involved in the prelude to the Accord were the Foreign Office, the Northern Ireland Office (NIO), the Cabinet Office (the Overseas and Defence Committee chaired by Margaret Thatcher), and, according to press briefings, the pertinent intelligence services. Whilst the Northern Irish NIO officials were not influential, the NIO's British officials certainly were. Interviews have established a most interesting jargon amongst NIO officials for dealing with Northern Ireland. Since the early 1970s they have developed what they call 'internal' and 'external' tracks. The internal track tells them to pursue policies to encourage the broadest possible agreement within Northern Ireland for an internal settlement. The external track tells them to pursue the maximum feasible good relations with the Irish Republic and the USA on the Ulster crisis, and to ensure minimum feasible international embarrassment.[30] The jargon of internal and external tracks captures the basic thrust of British policy-making, or more strictly, the administrative advice of the NIO, since 1972. The Accord has both these tracks built into it – agreed devolution and good relations with the Irish Republic. Consequently, apart from timing and formality, the Accord is consistent with the 'broad thrust' of British policy-making in the province. The Accord made sense to the British because it fitted their existing definitions of the 'problem' and their pre-established policies for managing it. Such an interpretation makes better sense of the facts than the coercive power-sharing scenario precisely because it does not assume a comprehensive master plan on the part of the British government.

On the Irish side, since the partial success of the modernisation programmes embarked upon in the late 1950s and early 1960s, the standard modes of defining the Northern Ireland question have altered, amongst both administrators and the policy élite. The legitimation of the Irish state is altering from the assertion of national sovereignty through cultural autonomy from the UK, to achieving support through the material prosperity of advanced industrial capitalism. Irish state officials, outside the ranks of Fianna Fáil, have come to define Northern Ireland as a problem for the stability of their state, as a threat to their programmes of modernisation, and as an anachronism rather than a question of burning injustice or uncompleted national revolution. Thus the Northern Ireland conflict is primarily managed by them through two strategic methods. Firstly, playing the role of guardian of the Northern Ireland minority rather than prospective ruler of Ulster Unionists (advocating reform and power-sharing within Northern Ireland and using the international stage to proclaim this guardian role). And secondly, increasing co-operation with the British state, through the EEC and other forums, to contain the conflict ('unique relationships amongst these islands', and 'interdependence is not dependence' provide the bureaucratic codes here). The Accord again fits neatly with these well established routines, and also makes better sense of the facts than the other interpretations. Fianna Fáil, not having made the full transition from a party of cultural nationalism to a party of economic nationalism, is the only major organisation yet to accept in its rhetoric these decisive alterations in the foreign policy routines of the Irish state. But in practice, FF governments have both initiated such changes and furthered them.

The institutional approach explanation is plausible. Ensconced in the vacillations of personalities and crisis episodes, behind the zig-zags in British policy postures highlighted by Bew and Patterson,[31] buried under the rapid turnover in Irish governments during 1980-82, and indeed behind the aberration of Thatcher's reaction to the New Ireland Forum proposals ('Out! Out! Out!'), compatible strategies for managing the Northern Ireland conflict have developed amongst the agencies of both states. With the Thatcher and FitzGerald administrations both in mid-term, and determined to make a symbolic initiative, 1985 proved to be the opportune moment for the cementing of the two states' approaches. It was also timely because memories of the hunger strikes of 1980-81 and the Irish Republic's studied neutrality during the Falklands/Malvinas war in 1982 were fading.

Other Contributory Factors

But the institutional approach, despite its considerable merits, does not fully explain why the Accord came about. Other factors such as political symbolism, the role of key personalities – Thatcher, FitzGerald and Hume – and party manoeuvres must also be taken into account. The symbolic dimensions of a major initiative and agreement appealed to both Prime Ministers. FitzGerald claims to have entered politics to solve the Northern Ireland problem and to hasten the secularisation and pluralisation of the Irish Republic. The rationality of Thatcher's political project is always greatly exaggerated on the Left, but she has displayed a penchant for tackling head-on what are perceived to be the major unresolved crises of the British state, and a preparedness to break through existing conventional wisdom and inertia.[32] Escape from death at Brighton also concentrated Thatcher's mind on the Northern Irish question in a way the IRA did not anticipate. Her commitment to the Accord is 'total' according to NIO officials. There seems little doubt that both leaders not only enjoyed the symbolism of a major initiative but shared a similar resolution to embark upon a 'leap in the dark', a propensity few of their predecessors have displayed.

The Accord was good domestic politics in both states. The Irish Coalition enjoyed a brief renewal of support and enjoyed overwhelming approval for the Accord in opinion polls. Such a response was anticipated. The split in Fianna Fáil, its opposition to the Accord in the Dáil, and the formation of the Progressive Democrats were unexpected, and briefly enjoyed, bonuses. The Conservative government counted on and received all-party support in the Commons and thrived on playing the role of acting in the national interest until the Westland affair besmirched its reputation. However, successive governments have shown Northern Ireland does not matter electorally (unless one MP or TD can affect the stability of the executive), and as the Accord comes under pressure for producing few immediate tangible results, much more radical initiatives might be acceptable to both the British and Irish electorates. As a result some contend that both leaders' preoccupation with symbolic politics have set in train a policy fiasco which could defeat their respective objectives.

Whatever the truth of these contentions, the decisive actor in the politics of the signing of the Accord, has been the SDLP and its leader John Hume. Content that the British and Irish premiers obtain whatever short-run glory on offer, the SDLP leader has been reticent about his role in the Accord. But as the instigator of Anglo-Irish discussions and the New Ireland Forum, as the leader who advocated abstaining from Prior's Assembly on the grounds that a boycott would produce something more, as an actively consulted advisor to the Irish government during the negotiations, Hume has contributed more than any other political leader towards the Accord. Ulster Unionists are far more aware of this fact than the Republic's or

British mainland commentators who have vied to credit the Accord to Cabinet Secretaries, Foreign Affairs or Office staff, ambassadors, Thatcher or FitzGerald. To Ulster Unionists, Hume is the evil genius behind the Accord. Hume has always said that agreed devolution is acceptable to the SDLP provided that it is part of a broader Anglo-Irish process. The SDLP's welcome for the Accord and its willingness to give both the RUC and the British government some trust confirm both its prior interest in the Accord and its willingness to exploit it to maximum advantage within the nationalist bloc. These facts explain why Hume has been condemned by the OUP, the DUP, SF and even the Workers' Party as the villain behind the agreement. There is some plausibility in the charge that the Accord was made to save the SDLP from Sinn Fein, but there is also truth in the Unionist charge that the Accord was the SDLP's minimum price for abandoning abstentionist politics.

Thus, on current evidence it seems best to conclude that the Accord was signed because of the confluence of well established institutional strategies, symbolic politics and jockeying for position on the part of the SDLP. Hume's description of the Accord as a 'framework' rather than a political blueprint is correct, but he also knows that it is a framework potentially weighted in favour of SDLP solutions. These conclusions are at odds with most ultra-left analyses of British and Irish policy-making on Northern Ireland. They are also at odds with the two sophisticated left-wing analyses of the character of British direct rule since 1972 relevant to explanations of the Accord. The first, that of O'Dowd and his associates, argues that British policy-making has *reproduced* rather than *reformed* sectarian relations in Northern Ireland, and implicitly regards the British state as functionally structured to do so.[33] These authors have a functionalist account of the state, which they deploy to 'explain' policy outputs. The second theory, put forward by Bew and Patterson, contends that the *unintended* consequences of British policy-making have been to exacerbate sectarian conflict between Catholics and Protestants.[34] This second view is more theoretically and empirically sophisticated, unspoiled by the functionalist fallacies of much Marxist thought.[35] The logical extrapolation of Bew and Patterson's position is to suggest that the Accord may end up reinforcing sectarian relations, but that the Hillsborough agreement itself must be explained by the decisions of politicians and administrators who genuinely thought themselves to be engaged in a process designed to weaken sectarianism. By contrast, this essay contends, in conclusion, that the unintended consequences of the Accord will, and should be, the coercion of key fractions of the Unionist bloc to accept some form of power-sharing thereby creating conditions for the eventual dissolution of sectarianism.

Interim Results

The most significant results of the Accord so far have been its own survival, the regular inter-ministerial meetings, the institutionalisation of an administrative Secretariat at Maryfield in Belfast, and striking evidence of attempts to harmonise their statements by both governments. As yet it is impossible to assess objectively the consequences of formal increases in police co-operation. The major move on the Irish side has been to sign the Convention on the Suppression of Terrorism, but that was specifically promised in the communiqué accompanying the Accord. The British have so far reciprocated with two very minor changes – ensuring that Irish citizens will have the same rights in Northern Ireland which they enjoy in the UK and facilitating the use of the Irish language in street-naming.

The most conflictual items on the policy agenda are obvious: the demand for a code of conduct for the RUC; the existence and character of the almost wholly Protestant UDR; the idea of an entrenched Bill of Rights; the symbolic demand for the repeal of the Flag and Emblems Act of 1954; and, the indefensible administration of justice by Diplock (no-jury, one judge) courts and 'supergrass' trials. On all of these items movement so far has been confined to chairs, helicopters and press-briefings. The Irish government has promised that major changes in the administration of justice will be forthcoming, signalling to the nationalist minority that it should wait until Unionist civil disobedience ends before it can obtain its just deserts. The British government, while willing to move on the RUC's code of conduct, has remained adamant on the retention of the UDR, has shown little willingness to give on a minor reform of the

Diplock courts (three judges instead of one) and is procrastinating in the face of Unionist opposition to the Accord.

The bind that the British government faces can be expressed simply. To display to the Unionists that the IGC does not amount to joint authority, the Secretary of State for Northern Ireland must show himself capable of ignoring Irish representations at its deliberations. But to show the Irish government that the IGC is worthwhile, he must make concessions to nationalist feelings. However, he must present any concessions that he does make as measures he would have taken without Irish intervention. The Secretary of State is thus obliged to zig-zag. To date King has chosen to show that the IGC is operational, and will not be suspended or postponed, but has refused rapid reforms in order to ease his most visible difficulty, managing Unionist discontent. Apart from his statement on the Union's perpetual existence and 'misleading' Barry over the Stalker inquiry, the Irish government has shown comprehension, even empathy, for the complex logic of King's position.

Given the number of political uncertainties surrounding the Accord, it is too precarious exactly to predict its future, but two broad scenarios are proffered. The first is the benign scenario which envisages the British and Irish governments waiting until Loyalist mobilisation against the Accord tails off. At this point, it is hoped that a split will emerge in the Unionist camp, with a sufficiently large fraction prepared to bargain with the SDLP on power-sharing. Militant Unionists may make a half-cocked bid for independence, but this will only work to hasten a deal between the SDLP and moderate Unionists. In short, the benign scenario predicts short-run protest followed by an internal settlement incorporating power-sharing and an Irish dimension.

The second, malign, scenario is that the whole Unionist bloc will unite in an unstoppable drive towards independence, sparking off the long heralded repartition and civil war. However the malign scenario is improbable both because it forgets that both governments can put an end to a Unionist uprising either by force, or by repudiating the agreement. Consequently the risks of allowing the benign scenario to play itself are worth taking.

Should the Accord be Supported by the Left?

This author wants the Accord to work, that is, for it to result in an internal power-sharing settlement within Northern Ireland, with an Irish dimension. But, why should the British Left support the Accord? After all, the standard orthodoxies of the Labour Left are either to support Irish unification and adopt an ultra-nationalist stance which tails Sinn Fein,[36] or to take a class-based line like the Workers' Party or Militant, and adopt a *de facto* Unionist position on partition whilst arguing for democratic reforms (Workers' Party line) or a common economic class-based revolutionary strategy (Militant line). These positions exemplify the two standard faults in socialist analyses of national questions. One, the romantic nationalist line, swallows national self-determination rhetoric, identifies the underdog, and supports the people so chosen in their national liberation struggle. The other, the class-utopian line, ignores nationalist or cultural consciousness, and attempts to bypass it, or transcend it, through raising the slogans of class unity. The Austrian social democratic Marxists were exceptional in not falling into either the nationalist or class-utopian traps, and in not accepting the doctrines of sovereignty associated with the rise of the capitalist nation-state, and indeed contemporary state-socialist regimes.[37] They argued that national identity must be recognised without necessarily accepting wholesale the central doctrine of nationalism: that each separate culture (*ethnos*) must have its own separate sovereign state. Conversely national identity should not be ignored in the pious belief that it will be dissolved by class unity or wither away in a prospective socialist paradise. Whilst the Northern Ireland conflict has both religious and nationalist dimensions, the Austrian socialist tradition is worth re-examination and adaptation.

A power-sharing settlement in the North with an Irish dimension, or co-operative devolution on the Kilbrandon lines, tackles head-on the central grievances of a considerable majority of Northern nationalists whilst not ending the British citizenship of Northern Protestants. It ends Unionist/Protestant supremacy, not their identity. (Those who believe that the Unionist/Protestant identity consists solely of triumphal supremacism are as blindly sectarian as those they condemn.) A power-sharing settlement recognises that the central cleavage is between nationalist and Unionist, but the evolution of power-sharing institutions need not preclude other cleavages developing, based on class, socialist or liberal ideology. The evidence of other states, such as Belgium or the Netherlands, which have experienced power-sharing coalitions across religious, cultural or ethnic divides, shows not only that they are feasible, but also, that they are frequently transitional – their success weakens the importance of the primary non-class based cleavage, and facilitates the complication of politics with a liberal/socialist cleavage. Accordingly, if the bulk of British Left can stifle its usual impatience and romanticism, and reflect upon its strange and 'unholy' partisanship for Catholic nationalism against Protestant Unionism, there is every reason why it should come to support the opportunities opened by power-sharing arrangements.

These abstract arguments may seem absurdly optimistic in the face of contemporary realities, but they have been sketched to suggest that there is no reason why socialists should not consider power-sharing and an Irish dimension sensible ways of eventually getting their politics on the agenda. The Left should stop analysing Northern Ireland as a set of traffic lights where the choices are green, red or orange. The task is to facilitate the reddening of green and orange in a co-operative fashion. Such a strategic perspective does not constitute naïvety, but rather a determined effort to defeat politically both ultra-loyalists and Sinn Fein. Contrary to Left mythology, Northern Ireland is not unreformable.[38] The major problem of social democratic reformism, in all parts of the British Isles, is that it has barely begun.

Policy Objectives

What realistic policies should a future Labour government pursue in Northern Ireland? Six main objectives should be paramount. In descending order of importance they should be: co-operation with the Irish Republic, the promotion of local power-sharing, the implementation of equal citizenship, the liberalisation of the legal and policing system, the promotion of secularism, and finally, the development of the Labour Party and movement within Northern Ireland.

1. Co-operation with the Irish Republic

A Labour government and an Irish government will have shared interests in cross-border security co-operation, security within Northern Ireland, promoting investment in the whole island of Ireland, and the functioning of joint agencies to deal with EEC-related expenditures and activities, especially agriculture. Bilateral co-operation in the areas of public transport, mass communications, and energy provision will be mutually beneficial for people on both sides of the border.

2. Local power-sharing

Local power-sharing has already been defended in this essay. How can Labour promote it? If Unionists refuse agreed devolution at the level of Northern Ireland as a unit, then as part of its broad commitment to de-centralisation, Labour should contemplate creating local governments with greater powers. Incentives for power-sharing at the local level can be built into the statutes establishing them. For example, it can be stipulated that councils can only make policy with the support of two-thirds of the members, and that committees have to represent parties in proportion to the numbers of members elected. In the absence of agreement, policy-making will return to the Northern Ireland Office, the Councils will not function, and politicians cannot draw expenses. The boundaries of local governments can be drawn to ensure that nowhere will there be a permanent extraordinary (over two-thirds) majority of Unionists or nationalists. Whilst these details are simply suggestions, the project should be to create the incentives, negative and positive, for power-sharing across the sectarian divide. In 1975, the Labour government, with Merlyn Rees in the NIO, made the mistake of holding a Convention which essentially relied on the parties to agree amongst themselves. A future government must intervene and offer selective incentives to induce power-sharing.

3. Equal citizenship measures

The economic constraints any government of Northern Ireland will face are well documented in the essays which follow. Labour's objective is simple to formulate, but difficult to implement: raising the aggregate welfare of the working class whilst rectifying the substantial material disadvantages of Catholics who are disproportionately concentrated amongst the unemployed and low-skilled. The difficulties in generating economic growth will make more arduous the redistributive policies required to rectify the legacies of discrimination against Catholics in both private and public sector employment. However, the experience of affirmative action and quotas in anti-discrimination policies pursued in the United States has shown, if proof were required, that racism and sexism in employment can be tackled substantively, if slowly, in capitalist America. Religious discrimination should prove no more obdurate in a social democratic Britain. Giving teeth to the Equal Opportunities Commission and the Fair Employment Agency – for instance, allowing them the right to inspect at random, fix quotas, fine discriminatory organisations and so on – should not be beyond the competence of a reform-minded Labour administration.

4. Genuine law and order

Reform cannot do its work with counter-productive repression. The Labour Party is already committed to the repeal of the Prevention of Terrorism Act and, less clearly, to the reform of Diplock courts. Labour can and must show that the defeat of terrorism does not require 'state terrorism'. Political mobilisation, the abolition of emergency legislation, and the re-establishment of due processes of law (with jury trials in Britain if necessary) will be more effective, and achieve more support, than emergency legislation and 'assembly-line' justice. The Standing Advisory Commission on Human Rights and the Police Complaints Boards can be given teeth with a Bill of Rights to sustain them, and power-sharing party members nominated to sit on them. A Labour government should also contemplate splitting Sinn Fein and the IRA by offering commuted sentences and partial amnesties to the IRA (and Loyalist paramilitaries) in return for surrender. Should the Provisionals refuse, as is likely, defeating them through legitimate policing will be easier as the government's generosity will have been repudiated. And provided that legitimate Catholic grievances, articulated in the Inter-Governmental Conference, or in the forums of agreed devolution, are being dealt with, the social base of the IRA will crumble. A major recruitment drive for Catholic applicants for a re-named police force could then be conceivable. The UDR should be abolished, or purged. Until the impact of these measures has worked itself through and is successful, British troops cannot be withdrawn, but they can be regulated by the law.[39]

5. Secularisation and community

Northern Ireland's population is comparatively more secularised than the Irish Republic's (with the exception of sections of the Dublin bourgeoisie). Whilst religious belief has not caused the conflict, it has exacerbated it, and Labour should self-consciously advance existing levels of secularisation, without making it the leitmotif of its policies. For example, whether or not education is devolved to power-sharing local governments, it can be stipulated that central grants will be progressively withdrawn from schools in which the religious imbalance amongst teachers and pupils cannot reasonably be explained. Whilst coercive educational intergration would be foolish, and no attempt should be made to close schools, the available selective incentives to concentrate minds should be manipulated. Steps can also be taken to encourage the integration of the teacher-training colleges. The right to restrict leisure-activities on Sundays should be removed from local councils and, similar secularisation steps taken across the Northern Ireland legal and social policy systems.

A far more difficult task will be to try to overturn the residential segregation which has increased since the 'troubles' erupted in the late 1960s. Frankly, I can see no simple and feasible policy prescriptions which might achieve residential integration rapidly.

6. Building a Labour foothold

Labour must abandon constitutional support for Irish nationalism, the 'unification by consent' policy, as unworkable folly, but not for the reasons advanced by Clare Short.[40] It is not folly simply because Unionist consent will not be forthcoming. It also would make Northern Ireland more ungovernable. Serious commitment to the policy would imply that a Labour government would spend its whole time exhorting Loyalists to negotiate unification with the Republic, encouraging power-sharing only as a means towards an eventual British departure, and so on. Such a strategy would amount to a more or less permanent incitement to riot, and remove the prospects of obtaining Unionist consent for the Anglo-Irish Accord and the reform of Northern Ireland. Labour should *retain*, for symbolic reasons, the clause in the Anglo-Irish Agreement which states that unification would be legislated for if desired by a majority of the population of Northern Ireland, but *abandon* the NEC resolution of 1981 which obliges Labour to work towards that end. Why should a democratic socialist party work towards persuading Northern Irish Protestants to accept cultural subordination in a polity which most feminists and socialists find more repugnant than Britain?

No better signal could be given to Unionists of Labour's intention to maintain the union, albeit with the Inter-Governmental Conference, and with power-sharing, than a commitment by the party to enter Northern Ireland politics itself. Normally this suggestion is made by wide-eyed members of Militant who possess an amazing faith in Labour's electoral capacity to win the votes of the Northern Ireland working class even though it has major difficulties obtaining a majority of the British working class. My support for the entry of Labour into Northern Irish politics does not derive from Militant. Rather, Labour's participation in Northern Ireland politics, as a reformist unionist, and trade-unionist, party in favour of power-sharing and an Irish dimension, will modestly assist the re-alignment of Northern Irish politics around issues which are not exclusively focused on territory, religion and atavistic hostilities.

Notes and Acknowledgements

This essay was completed at the end of July 1986. My thanks to those public officials who made themselves available for non-attributable interviews, and to Patrick Dunleavy, Nick Ellison, Michael Hebbert, Fred Halliday and Lorelei Watson for their helpful criticisms. The usual disclaimers apply.

[1] *Guardian*, 16 November 1986.

[2] *Irish Times*, 21 April 1986.

[3] The assumptions of these models are expounded by Graham Allison, 1971, *Essence of Decision*, Little, Brown and Company.

[4] Jim Allister, the DUP Chief Whip in the Northern Ireland Assembly, claims that the Accord has made Northern Ireland a 'shared colony' – *Irish Times*, 11 May 1986. Harold McCusker, Deputy Leader of the Official Unionist Party (OUP) asserts that the British have already conceded sovereignty over Northern Ireland to the Irish Republic – *Irish Times*, 24 February 1986.

[5] *New Ireland Forum*, Stationery Office, Dublin, May 1984. The Forum report was agreed by the four major constitutional nationalist parties in the Irish Republic and Northern Ireland (Fianna Fail, Fine Gael, the Irish Labour Party, and the Social Democratic and Labour Party). The Forum deliberated, received evidence and commissioned research for a year. In conclusion it offered three possible models of a new Ireland: a unitary state, a federal/confederal state, and joint authority. FF preferred the first model. FG, the ILP and the SDLP preferred the second, and especially the third models. To obtain an agreed report FF's preference was the nominally agreed first choice.

[6] Claire Palley, 'When an Iron Hand Can Beckon a Federal Union', *Guardian*, 20 January 1986. Palley's article is a perfect specimen of wishful thinking: she assumes into existence what she would like to occur. She starts with the premise that in 'about' 35 years the Protestant and Catholic populations will be about equal, and reasons that a majority will then be forthcoming for 'reunification'. She concludes that Protestant awareness of their demographic destiny should lead them to negotiate the best deal possible in an Irish federal union. Both her demography and psephology are dubious. Paul Compton, 'The Demographic Background', in D. Watt (ed.), *The Constitution of Northern Ireland*, London 1981, shows that most assumptions of an inevitable Catholic majority are ill-founded. There are also considerably more Catholic Unionists than Protestant Irish nationalists, so even a future hypothetical Catholic majority will not be sufficient for a nationalist majority – see Edward Moxon-Browne, 1983, *Nation, Class and Creed in Northern Ireland*, Aldershot, 1983. Breeding for victory, or negotiating federalism because of the other side's fertility rates, are not sound political strategies ...

[7] The 26 counties of the Irish Free State (1922-37).

[8] 'In Northern Ireland now we have signed an agreement in which the Prime Minister of Ireland, notwithstanding the fact that he faces and has to live with a Constitution which has aspirations of sovereignty over Northern Ireland,

has in fact accepted that for all practical purposes and unto perpetuity, there will not be a united Ireland because he has accepted the principle of consent that the will of the majority in Northern Ireland must predominate and that Northern Ireland, which is our fervent wish, remains part of the United Kingdom.' *Irish Times*, 4 December 1986. King's message was substantially accurate, but had to be 'clarified' because the gloss 'in perpetuity' is incompatible with the Irish Constitution. King's message, designed to placate Unionists, caused uproar amongst Nationalists.

[9] The Assembly (1982-6) was the ill-starred child of Jim Prior's rolling devolution scheme. It foundered upon a nationalist boycott by both SF and the SDLP. Since late 1985 it had become simply an agitation-forum against the Accord, prompting the moderate Unionists in the Alliance Party (APNI) to withdraw. King was forced to dissolve the Assembly as he did not want the elections due in the autumn of 1986 to occur amidst the current levels of polarisation.

[10] In this respect the Accord conforms, intentionally or otherwise, with the prescriptions of the Capotorti Report, 1979, prepared for the United Nations Subcommission on the Prevention of Discrimination and the Protection of Minorities; see also Kevin Boyle and Tom Hadden, *Ireland: A Positive Proposal*, Harmondsworth 1985, p.47.

[11] Direct rule has only been interrupted by the brief power-sharing Executive in the first five months of 1974.

[12] *Irish Times*, 29 May 1986.

[13] Ibid., 8 May 1986.

[14] The Kilbrandon Committee, an unofficial all-party body established in 1984 to give a more considered response to the New Ireland Forum than Thatcher's simplistic 'Out! Out! Out!', favoured a form of joint authority which they called co-operative devolution. A five member ministerial executive composed of one Irish Minister, one British Minister and three Northern Ireland representatives elected by proportional representation (i.e. two Unionists and one Nationalist) would make up the Government of Northern Ireland. The idea was to produce two alternating majorities (a British-Unionist majority, or an Irish-British-Northern Ireland Nationalist majority) depending on the line-up of the participants.

[15] *The Equal Citizen*, No.3, 22 December 1986.

[16] For a good example, see John Martin, 'Marxist Interpretations of Northern Ireland', *Capital and Class*, No.18, 1982, and for a bad example the caucus-group journal *Labour and Ireland*.

[17] See, *inter alia* A. Morgan, 'Socialism in Ireland – Red, Green and Orange' in A. Morgan and B. Purdie (eds), *Ireland: Divided Nation, Divided Class*, London 1980 and P. Bew and N. Patterson, *The British State and the Ulster Crisis*, London 1985.

[18] The scale of the British subvention for public expenditure on non-security related items, even during the high-tide of monetarism, shows that Northern Ireland has enjoyed more than the full-share of benefits of membership of the British welfare state. Fergus Pyle cites the Coopers and Lybrand study which showed that Northern Ireland citizens benefit over 40 per cent more per capita than other citizens of the UK from (non-security) public expenditure –

Irish Times, 14-16 April 1986. See the essays by Rowthorn and Canning *et al* in this volume.

[19] Enoch Powell, 'Dirty Tricks That Link Dublin and Westland', *Guardian*, 20 April 1986.

[20] A Lijphart, 'Typologies of Democratic Systems', *Comparative Political Studies*, No.1, 1968, pp. 3-44.

[21] NOP Market Research Ltd, *Political Opinion in Northern Ireland*, London 1974, p.16.

[22] E. Nordlinger, *Conflict Regulation in Divided Societies*, Occasional Papers in International Affairs, No.29, Harvard University, 1972, plausibly argues that both élite motivation and autonomy are essential for successful conflict-regulation in open regimes.

[23] *Belfast Telegraph*, 17 December 1985.

[24] Interview with NIO official.

[25] Evelyn Glenholmes, a suspected IRA terrorist, walked free from a Dublin court in March 1986 because British officials bungled extradition procedures and compelled the Irish court to quash the British application.

[26] The Stalker affair, which is the most threatening episode in the evolution of the Accord, and which is unfolding as of writing, centres on whether the RUC, MI5, the Home Office, or others, have conspired to obtain the suspension from duty on unknown charges of the Deputy Constable of Manchester Police who had been given the task of investigating whether or not the RUC had a shoot-to-kill policy in Armagh during 1982.

[27] *Irish Times*, 18 June 1986.

[28] *Guardian*, 23 June 1986.

[29] Harry West, the former leader of the OUP 1974-79, Austin Ardill and David McNarry, are the first group within the OUP to have offered power-sharing to the SDLP. Hume dismissed their informal talks with SDLP leaders because the Unionists wanted the suspension of the IGC, and because the West group are no longer influential within the OUP – *Irish Times*, 6 March 1986.

[30] Paul Arthur, 'Anglo-Irish relations and the Northern Ireland Problem', *Irish Studies in International Affairs*, 1985 No.2, has cogently argued that British policy-making has been characterised by two features: quarantining the Irish issue from mainstream politics, and maintaining international respectability. These features exemplify the NIO's internal and external tracks respectively.

[31] Bew and Patterson, op.cit. pp. 39-131.

[32] Talk of Thatcher as the British equivalent of de Gaulle is wildly exaggerated. There are few appropriate parallels between the Irish government and the Algerian national liberation movement, still less in terms of legitimacy between the Provisionals and the FLN (unless one makes Islam and Catholicism the basis of comparison as the ultra-left is reluctant to do). The impact of Northern Ireland on Britain in the 1970s and 80s, with the exception of attempted assassinations of key political figures, has not been anything as dramatic as that of Algeria on French politics in the 1950s. There is also no evidence that Thatcher or the British state are preparing to withdraw – such speculation misreads both the effective administrative

integration of Northern Ireland into the UK since 1972 and underestimates the *realpolitik* of successive Irish governments.

[33] Liam O'Dowd, Bill Rolston and Mike Tomlinson, *Northern Ireland Between Civil Rights and Civil War*, London 1980.

[34] Bew and Patterson, op.cit.

[35] J. Elster, 'Marxism, Functionalism and Game Theory', *Theory and Society*, 1982, No.11, 453-82.

[36] G. Bell, *The British in Ireland: A Suitable Case for Withdrawal*, London 1984, articulates the emotions of most Labour constituency activists.

[37] See T. Bottomore and P. Goode, *Austro-Marxism*, Oxford 1978.

[38] M. Farrell, *Northern Ireland: The Orange State*, London 1976.

[39] Calls for UN troops to go into Northern Ireland are naive. UN intervention is nowadays an admission of a terminal conflict, and a recipe for ethnic partitioning.

[40] Clare Short, in *Marxism Today*, January 1986, in effect advocates unification by coercion: self-determination for Catholics but not Protestants ... The hazards of being an MP in Birmingham Ladywood must explain this strange partiality.

Paul Bew and Henry Patterson

The New Stalemate: Unionism and the Anglo-Irish Agreement

At the time of writing, nine months since the Anglo-Irish Agreement was signed at Hillsborough on 15 November 1985, Northern Ireland is in the middle of a period of vicious sectarian confrontation and violence. This had its initial focus on the Orange marches on 12 July but has subsequently intensified into one of the most ominous developments in the recent period: the first enforced population movements of any size since the early 1970s (in the Oldpark area of North Belfast). In the arena of high politics, the RUC's decision to allow an Orange march through a predominantly Catholic area in Portadown has produced a major public row between the Joint Chairmen of the Anglo-Irish Inter-Governmental Council. Even inveterate Agreement supporters like the *Irish Times* columnist Mary Holland was forced to reflect on the increasingly pathetic nature of the claims being made by Irish and British officials and ministers that the summer would see a major confrontation with the Unionists and, after they had been 'faced down', the beginning of a solution to the Northern problem.[1]

The decisive rejection of even an extremely restricted legislation of divorce by the Republic's electorate in the referendum in June 1986, was a major shock to the pro-Agreement forces in the British state and media where support for the Agreement was usually in inverse proportion to any grasp of the political and ideological realities in either of the Irish states.

The major defeat for Garret FitzGerald's Coalition government came just three years after his vaunted 'Constitutional Crusade', launched in 1981 to create the pluralist Ireland which would hopefully attract Protestants, had collapsed miserably when FitzGerald had capitulated to right-wing Catholic pressure and agreed to hold a referendum on the question of whether abortion – already illegal in the Republic – should also be banned in the constitution. The moral credibility of the rather shop-soiled liberalism of that government was even more undermined by the fact that Peter Barry, the Irish joint chairman of the Inter-Governmental Council, had given an extremely lacklustre performance in his role as head of the government's campaign organisation during the divorce referendum. It is thus becoming easier to raise certain fundamental criticisms of the Agreement as the massive hype in Britain and Ireland subsides. In particular it is clear that both the intensification of sectarian animosities in Northern Ireland and the public inter-governmental rowing that has occurred since Hillsborough were entirely predictable. These are not, as apologists of the Agreement would have it, part of a short-term and inevitable period of uncertainty and instability to be got over before the Agreement receives widespread support. They are, rather, manifestations of a situation which will continue as long as British policy remains unchanged.

The problem with the Agreement is not, as its nationalist critics from Fianna Fáil to Sinn Fein allege, that it copper-fastens partition.[2] This claim is based on Section A, Article I of the accord in which the two governments:

(a) affirm that any change in the status of Northern Ireland would only come about with the consent of a majority of the people of Northern Ireland

(b) recognise that the present wish of a majority of the people of Northern Ireland is for no change in the status of Northern Ireland.

In fact the Republic's recognition of Northern Ireland was deliberately ambiguous. It refers to acceptance of the 'current status' of Northern Ireland but this current status is nowhere defined. This is simply to ensure that the Agreement does not conflict with the Republic's juridical claim to sovereignty over Northern Ireland as defined in its constitution. (A similar 'recognition' by a previous Coalition government in the Sunningdale agreement of 1973 produced an explosive court case in the Republic where the constitutionality of the government's actions was questioned.) Hence the document nowhere refers to Northern Ireland as an integral part of the United Kingdom, and claims by the Northern Irish Secretary, Tom King, that it gave a new recognition to the rights of Unionists broke down when even pro-Agreement legal experts pointed out that it did not.

In fact such a 'copper-fastening' of partition would have reflected neither the long-term interest of the British ruling class, which is certainly not in the maintenance of the status quo, nor of the central party which the Agreement was designed to shore up, the SDLP. In the negotiations which led to Hillsborough, the Irish government was well aware that the SDLP would not be able to accept any agreement which did not provide for some form of institutional recognition of its diagnosis of the Northern problem – that it could only be dealt with within a framework that transcended the Northern Ireland state.

What the Thatcher government faced between the Provisionals' first major eruption into politics with their victories in the 1982 Assembly elections and Hillsborough was not simply a major perceived threat to constitutionalist nationalism (i.e. the SDLP).[3] For John Hume, the SDLP's leader, was well aware how British and Irish government fears of a rampant mass Provisionalism could be used to his party's advantage (not to mention the concerns and leverage of the US State Department). As early as 1979 Hume was using the developing Second Cold War to his party's advantage by writing in the journal *Foreign Affairs* about how instability in Ulster threatened Western strategic interests, with Northern Ireland 'a strategically placed area in the Atlantic approaches to north-west Europe, potentially ripe for subversion if political neglect continues'.[14] As a result, Hume was very successful in ensuring that his own definition of the problem was to a large degree influential in the framing of the Agreement. That this was so, despite the many problems inherent in its facile simplicities, reflected, in part at least, a long-standing distaste for Unionism in the British ruling class. This has intensified as the new generation of British political leaders has largely forgotten the Republic's neutrality in the war against fascism. Unionism's obduracy was seen as having prevented the emergence of a medium-term objective – a restabilisation and reinsulation of Northern Ireland through the creation of a set of devolved governmental institutions based on some form of 'partnership', preferably power-sharing government, including representatives of constitutionalist Catholic politics. In the longer term it was hoped that such an experience of shared government would prepare the Unionists for their devoutly desired final exit from the United Kingdom.

This distaste for the Unionists was compounded by the marginality of Northern Ireland for the British ruling class – save in its darker fantasies about it being a backdoor through which some slouching monster of Sinn Fein/Bolshevism would infect the 'mainland'. This has meant that each new 'crisis' is met by the same degree of largely uninformed alarm. In the circumstances after the Assembly elections this produced a desperate willingness to believe in the stature and modernising zeal of both FitzGerald and Hume. This became most evident in the largely uncritical acceptance of the New Ireland Forum Report as a significant and self-critical departure for Irish nationalism. But as we have argued at greater length elsewhere,[5] this document is singularly banal and traditional on the central question of Ulster Unionism. A similar analysis of Unionism was incorporated into the strategic calculations behind the Agreement. It is this view of Unionism which represents the Agreement's central and irredeemable flaw.

The full dimensions of this analysis of Unionism are best appreciated by considering it as articulated most volubly and repetitively in the writings and speeches of John Hume. At one level, Hume depicts Unionists as almost uniformly reactionary: 'They are one of the most right-wing forces in Europe – nobody else would stand for them, anywhere.'[6] However, at another level he recognises that there are more moderate elements with whom dialogue may be possible under certain conditions. It is here that the role of the British state is seen as crucial by Hume. For him it has been the historic failure of the British state to face up to Unionist intransigence in crucial conjunctures – 1912, 1920 and 1974 – which has allowed the 'extremists' to dominate Unionist politics. There is no acknowledgement, however, in anything that Hume has written or said that the politics and ideology, not to mention military activities, of Irish nationalists could in fact have played a much more significant role than the British state in ensuring the dominance of intransigent currents in Unionist politics. In labelling Unionist politics as reactionary, Hume lumps together two aspects of the Northern Ireland conflict which must in fact be strictly separated if any progress is to be possible – the democratic question and the national question.

The first concerns all those issues which relate to those historic and current practices which discriminate against Catholics. In so far as Unionist politics has been or is involved in the defence and justification of such practices then clearly all Hume's strictures are valid. However, there are also various traditions within the Protestant community which would not defend such practices, but which are still militantly opposed to any change in the constitutional status quo: 'moderate' or 'liberal' Unionists, not to mention that hybrid tradition of 'socialist Unionists'. It is precisely because as a traditional Irish nationalist Hume cannot accept that there can be a democratic basis to partition that his analysis of Unionist divisions is inevitably hopelessly confused. For although the history of Protestant politics and ideology is replete with divisions on democratic and class issues, on the national question, even in its supposedly more humane and liberalised post-Forum form, there is no significant intra-Unionist division – the liberals and the neanderthals make common cause.

Here Hume's analysis of the British state's last failure to confront Unionism – the UWC strike of 1974 which destroyed the power-sharing executive of which he was a member – is of significance.

> The main Unionist political group at that time, and particularly its leader, the late Brian Faulkner, showed courage and political agility, and the response of most Unionists to the experiment was by and large benign. The pusillanimity of the Labour government in London, in failing to resist the predictable destructiveness of the demagogues and paramilitaries on the extremes of Unionism set back the situation almost irremediably ...[7]

What is completely missing from this account is any reference to the fact that whilst the power-sharing part of the Sunningdale agreement was at least acceptable to a majority of Unionists the other part of the agreement – the Council of Ireland which some members of the SDLP were representing as a transition mechanism to a United Ireland – was to produce massive Unionist disquiet.[8] Once again we have a failure to appreciate that it is the 'over-determination' of democratic and reformist objectives by nationalist objectives that undermines liberal and accommodationist currents within Unionism, and not some supposed lack of nerve on the part of the British state.

These points are of more than historical interest because it is clear that Hume's essentially flawed analysis has contributed centrally to the current calculations in both Dublin and London. In particular it is hoped in both capitals that a show of firmness on the part of the British government will produce a climate in which Unionist moderates will be prepared to deal with the SDLP within the over-arching framework laid out at Hillsborough. There has been something faintly nauseating in reading and listening to the editorialists and representatives of what is supposed to be modernising nationalism as they exult in the fact that the Unionists are now up against the scourge of the Argentinians and the miners. Hume, in an interview in April was typical:

> I always expected a furious Unionist reaction to the Agreement, but the Protestant boil had to be lanced. Mrs Thatcher is the right person in the right place at the right time and they are recognising that she will not be broken.[9]

In the same interview Hume predicted that the Ulster crisis would be resolved by the end of the summer of 1986, once the Unionists had learned painfully that the Agreement would be kept in place and that they could only obviate its more obnoxious feature – the role of the Inter-Governmental Conference – by agreeing to talks with the SDLP to create a devolved government. The crude manipulative logic behind this prediction was described by a southern civil servant (in a conversation with one of the authors) as the 'shoehorn effect'. Apart from the fact that even if devolution were to come about, the conference would still, under the terms of the Agreement, continue to exist, the assumptions behind such reasoning are all vitiated by a basic misunderstanding about the nature of

Unionist divisions. For although there are clearly divisions over how to respond to the Agreement and clear evidence of mass reluctance to be led into any active confrontation with the British state over it, there is very little evidence that any significant current of Unionist opinion would negotiate with the SDLP as long as the Agreement is in place.

Hume finished his interview by claiming that the choices for Unionists were narrowly limited: 'They can either accept the sovereignty of the British Parliament, talk to Dublin or go for independence.' The argument about sovereignty of the British parliament is totally spurious for two reasons. First, as any 'O' level student of British politics would know, at least since the last quarter of the nineteenth century, the emergence of a mass electorate, mass parties and effective party discipline in the House of Commons has relegated that legislative body to a place of clear subordination to Cabinet and Prime Minister. As another critic of the agreement has put it,

> It can be safely said that the vast majority of the 473 MPs who voted in support of the Agreement neither knew what they were voting for, nor cared. None of them have any Northern Ireland constituents to worry about, after all.[10]

Secondly, if the text of the Agreement is taken seriously, then at least as far as Northern Ireland is concerned the British government is itself prepared to regard the sovereignty of Westminster as something much less than absolute. Section B, Article 2 says that the Inter-Governmental Conference will deal with on a regular basis '(i) political matters, (ii) security and related matters, (iii) legal matters, including the administration of justice, (iv) the promotion of cross-border co-operation.' What constitutes 'political matters' is nowhere defined and it is clearly possible for the Republic's government to interpret it as covering an extremely wide range of issues and areas in Northern Ireland. At the same time, the British government is committed – by Article 2, Section (b) – to make 'determined efforts' to resolve any differences that arise within the Conference with the Irish government. As far as the FitzGerald government and the media in the Republic were concerned, this amounted to something which was more than consultation, though less than joint authority – the Forum option thought most moderate by constitutional nationalists. As John Cooney (the *Irish Times* political correspondent) put it on the day after Hillsborough, it was ' ... a formal and binding agreement ... giving the Republic a foothold in decisions governing Northern Ireland'.[11]

In such a context admonitions from Hume about the need for Unionists to respect the sovereignty of Westminster will be treated with a mixture of incredulity and contempt. Of the other two options, talks with Dublin are clearly inconceivable in the foreseeable future and the clear evidence of opinion polls is that there is not significant support for independence amongst the Protestant population. None of the three options is likely to be chosen. But Hume omitted another possible course of action, which, as we shall see when developments in Protestant politics are considered in more detail, seems to be a more likely possibility. This would be that, eschewing the more confrontational tactics being urged by the DUP, the Unionists refuse to be drawn into negotiations with the SDLP and maintain an effective boycott of negotiations as long as the Agreement is in place. The calculation here would be that in these circumstances there would be a strong possibility of the Agreement self-destructing.

It is certainly the case that if the 'shoehorn effect' does not work, and there are no signs of any significant current of Unionist opinion being prepared to consider talks with the SDLP to bring about devolution, then a central component of the Hillsborough strategy would have collapsed. Both governments would dearly love to have a buffer of locally elected politicians between them and the situation in Northern Ireland. This is particularly the case for the Southern Irish government, for without devolution it must bear the burden of a whole range of complicated issues and potentially explosive demands from Northern Ireland's Catholics. In short, therefore, our argument is that as the reasoning behind the Agreement about Protestant politics was fundamentally flawed, the chances of devolution are slim. Let us now consider in more detail the actual development of Unionist and nationalist politics since Hillsborough in this light.

The Protestant Community

The initial reaction of almost the entire Protestant community to the Anglo-Irish Agreement was one of shock and dismay, which was registered in the large Unionist vote in the January 1986 by-elections. The significant drop in Protestant support for the Alliance Party should be noted here. In the early part of 1985 the Unionists, both OUP and DUP, were apparently running scared. The Protestant political leadership had felt the chill wind of British disapproval and for the first time was somewhat uncertain; it dropped its demand for the scrapping of the Anglo-Irish Agreement and called instead for its 'suspension'. If a suspension took place, it promised to negotiate in good faith with the SDLP on power-sharing and devolution. At this point, the British and Irish governments probably overplayed their hand; had the Agreement been suspended the Unionist leadership would have been under significant pressure within its own community to resolve the crisis – and Ulster's apparently exposed position within the Union – by dealing generously with the constitutionalist leaders of the Catholic Nationalist community. The possibility that the Agreement might lead to power-sharing – always a long shot – receded and is now off the political agenda for the foreseeable future. (The fact that the removal of Articles 2 and 3 cannot, given the divorce referendum result, be part of any devolution deal, also tells against its likelihood.) In recent months the Unionists have got used to the shock of living on the 'window ledge' of the Union and there now seems to be little pressure on the leadership to reach any deal with the British government or the SDLP. There is a widespread assumption that a period of protracted political struggle lies ahead.

Much attention has been paid to the emergence of Peter Robinson, the hard-line Democratic Unionist MP for East Belfast, in particular, following the mass Loyalist strike or 'day of action' in March, in which he was well to the fore. The DUP, heavily influenced by Paisley's small town and rural evangelicals, found it difficult to get a foothold in Protestant working-class Belfast in the 1970s. Robinson made the key breakthrough when he won East Belfast in 1979 and has consistently pushed up his vote since then, turning East Belfast into a safe seat in a way which Gerry Adams has yet to do in

West Belfast. Grammar school educated, Robinson is a tough and shrewd politician who has changed the DUP style in certain respects. Though himself a sabbatarian, he is, for example, prepared to allow a ratepayers' vote on the matter of Sunday opening of an ice rink in his Castlereagh bailliwick, something which more traditional Paisleyites would baulk at. Robinson seems to have good relations with forces such as Alan Wright's Ulster Clubs movement and the UDA, which are at the sharp end of Unionist resistance to the Anglo-Irish deal.

In significant degree, Robinson's eminence merely reflects a bout of unusual hesitancy on the part of the Revd Ian Paisley, the DUP leader. Paisley, who has aged visibly, has hardly seemed to be the apparently awesome force he once was. He was caught off guard by the signing of the Agreement and for some months he appeared to be bemused and politically out of sorts. His responses lacked their usual sureness, notably when he appeared for a brief moment in February 1986 to have accepted Mrs Thatcher's terms for a compromise. The closure of the Northern Ireland Assembly in June was a particular blow to Paisley's prestige as he, more than any other Loyalist, had invested a great deal in this summarily dismissed elected forum. But the mass nocturnal occupation of Hillsborough in July by a disciplined body of men – with Robinson again a local figure – has restored much of the DUP's traditional momentum. Robinson was merely building on this by his participation in the occupation of Clontibret, a village two miles inside the Irish Republic. There is no sign as yet, however, that the DUP can challenge the 'Official Unionists' for the role of dominant political force in Protestant politics.

The Official Unionists are more respectable, less willing to countenance a massive confrontation with the British state. They were shocked by the wave of Protestant attacks on the RUC in March 1986 and have now disowned the use of the strike weapon. Their leader, Jim Molyneaux, is a relatively colourless politician who quietly nurtures 'integrationist' rather than devolutionist views. Yet the Official Unionists have been significantly influenced by the most surprising and unexpected political development of recent months: the emergence of the 'Campaign for Equal Citizenship' under the leadership of Robert McCartney QC. Essentially, the Campaign for Equal

Citizenship argues that the refusal of the main British parties to organise in Northern Ireland condemns the province to the endless repetition of a politics based on sterile sectarian issues. McCartney's argument has had a major impact on Official Unionist opinion – especially the Young Unionists – and the devolutionist lobby in that party is very much on the retreat. In Jim Prior's day, the Northern Ireland Office used to speak of the five realities which governed Northern Ireland politics. It may just be that we should add a sixth: there will be no settlement based *primarily* on devolution because the Official Unionists are not interested enough and the Democratic Unionists – who would dearly love to have Stormont back – will never offer satisfactory terms to the SDLP

The Catholic Community

On the Catholic side, political developments have been more predictable. One of the British government's key objectives in signing the Agreement was to reduce Sinn Fein's electoral support prior to the isolation of the IRA. The results of the January mini referendum appeared to suggest that the Agreement had done just that. But two council by-election results in Magherafelt and Fermanagh in March 1986 saw Sinn Fein's vote return to pre-Agreement levels and it is also doubtful if they will suffer as a result of the increased communal aggravation of the summer. Once again they claim to stand as the protectors of the Catholic community. The party of constitutionalist nationalism led by John Hume was intended to be the principal beneficiary of the Agreement, and most of its members still support the Anglo-Irish process. The recent largely cosmetic reform package (flags and emblems change, measures to aid the Irish language and a new police complaints procedure) as announced by junior Northern Ireland minister, Nick Scott, is an attempt to sustain, or, perhaps, more accurately, to regenerate the momentum for this group which has lost some credibility recently because of the Agreement's failure to deliver concrete benefits to the Catholic community in general, and – to take a particular case – because of the RUC's decision to allow an Orange march down the Catholic Garvahy Road district in Portadown on the 12 July.

The Agreement itself was very much the achievement of John Hume, the leader of the SDLP. Hume has argued repeatedly that when the British government finally stood up to the Loyalists, a more compliant leadership would emerge on that side. The current period is providing an interesting harsh test for that proposition. Hume continues to insist that 'bully-boy' tactics having failed to break Thatcher – 'reasonable' Unionists will soon emerge to negotiate with him. Few can be found to accept this scenario. Even Nick Scott, whose views often seem to be a faded and nihilistic reprise of Hume's – without Hume's relatively attractive Parnellian theme of eventual reconciliation – talks of a five-year haul; it is not an enticing prospect. Meanwhile, Hume's main ally, Garret FitzGerald, is now out of office. FitzGerald's sub-Thatcherite remedies were associated with a decline in the fortunes of the Irish economy. The scourge of emigration is once again a major talking point. When they voted in the 1987 general election electors thanked FitzGerald for his 'historic achievement' in negotiating the Agreement but rejected him nonetheless, because of his economic record. (For a generation, at least, the economy and not the 'national question' has been the main issue in the Republic's elections.)

FitzGerald, who has enjoyed a hugely uncritical media acclaim in the UK, had anyway run out of impetus. Always well to the right of centre on economic matters, FitzGerald gained a certain progressive image in 1981 on account of his 'constitutional crusade' to remove the Catholic sectarian elements from the Republic's constitution. Five years later, the Republic's constitution is *more* sectarian with the inclusion of new prohibition on abortion, and the massive defeat of the divorce proposals probably signals the end of any further hopes of liberalisation for some years. Equally, FitzGerald's one other individual contribution to political debate – a commitment not to negotiate with the British over the heads of Unionists – has been casually abandoned on the spurious and inaccurate grounds that 1982-85 saw an irresistible electoral surge in favour of Sinn Fein. FitzGerald repeated Redmond's error: in the 1890s Redmond insisted on the need for an internal accommodation with the Unionists and opposed those who said the thing to do was to get the British to intervene against them; by 1910 he had moved to a more conventional, less generous nationalism with ultimately disastrous results. History in this case has repeated itself, and Garret FitzGerald has gone down the identical path with so far identical results.[12]

The British Conundrum

Here is the conundrum for the British government. It has carefully designed an Agreement which probably cannot be broken by Unionist resistance. There is no sign that the Unionists can deliver a knockout blow. The Agreement has even survived severe internal disagreements. So far, so good, but the fact remains that the wider purposes which the Agreement was designed to achieve are more unattainable than ever. That section of the Tory leadership (Hurd, Howe and Chris Patten) which thought in terms of gradually detaching Northern Ireland from the UK has received a rude shock from the outcome of the Republic's divorce referendum – which is widely perceived as a vote for partition. It is now clear that removing the province from the UK, if dependent to any degree on internal liberalisation in the South, is doomed; it is only by openly applying force following an imposed 'act of unity', such as is apparently contemplated by Labour's Clive Soley, that unification can be achieved. Even here it is clear that the Irish state cannot begin to bear the financial burden of Northern Ireland. Those who sought primarily an 'internal' 'Unionist' solution (King, Thatcher and Tebbit) are, however, equally discomforted. In the early months, King could point to the electoral reverses suffered by Sinn Fein in the January mini referendum and the emergence of the Progressive Democrats (PD) in the Republic as an apparently major force, with a leader, Desmond O'Malley, who favoured the abandonment of the irredentist Articles 2 and 3 of the Irish constitution which express a territorial claim over Northern Ireland.

Sinn Fein seems to have recovered its position in the North and the activities of the IRA (which seems to have little to fear from the new cross-border security arrangements) have intensified. Meanwhile, as the results of the 1987 Irish general election have shown, the PDs have done most damage to Garret FitzGerald's Fine Gael. King, who liked to lecture the Unionists on their attachment to the shibboleths of the past, as opposed to the relatively enlightened attitudes in the South, now finds to his chagrin that both parts of Ireland are equally wedded in traditionalism. His immediate reaction, now apparently passed, was to give an interview to the *Belfast Telegraph* apparently downgrading the Agreement which provoked no fewer than eighteen points of protest from Dublin. Otherwise, King operating with a policy he inherited from Hurd, seems to have little clue as to what to do often leaving the running to the fatuous Scott. Yet unless the British government seriously reviews its strategy the current gradual deterioration of the Ulster environment will continue; this is especially so, if future developments significantly touch the RUC ('Stalkergate') or the judiciary.

Shortly before the Agreement was signed, Tom King seemed happy to envisage Charles Haughey working it. Since then matters have become more complex. In Brussels, King spoke of the Agreement as guaranteeing 'partition in perpetuity'; in July he responded to the *Belfast Telegraph*'s query about a possible suspension of the Agreement by saying that he could not accept a suspension of Article 1 in which the Dublin government acknowledged partition. The difficulty is that with Haughey as Irish leader, King will, in effect, have accepted a unilateral Irish suspension of Article 1. For everything that Haughey has said in criticism of the Agreement amounts to one thing; he does not accept the right of the Northern majority to self-determination, and any statements by him in the past which apparently bear this meaning (for example, the Downing Street communiqué of 1980) are misunderstood. It will be a difficult matter for the British government to blur over – but since the Agreement was signed equal, if not greater, difficulties have been slurred over. The overwhelming likelihood is that the British will accommodate Haughey but there will be a price to pay; firstly, the loss of that small but influential section of the Protestant community (mainly in the professional classes) which defended the Agreement largely on the grounds that Haughey opposed it and that FitzGerald could be trusted, and secondly, the intensification of the resistance of the great majority of the Protestant community.

Given this impasse, is there any benign way out? One measure the British government might consider is the reintroduction of periodic border polls; this would reassure Unionists and perhaps those foreign businessmen who – in the recently expressed view of Sir Charles Carter, chairman of the Northern Ireland Economic Council – are now doubly reluctant to invest in Northern Ireland because they see the Hillsborough Agreement as the first step to a British withdrawal.[13] It would also deepen the logic of consent apparently contained in Article 1(a) in which 'the two governments affirm that any change in the status of Northern Ireland would only come about with the consent of the majority of the people in Northern Ireland'. It may even help to preserve the beleaguered centre – at the moment a strong pressure exists for even liberal Protestants who might otherwise be attracted to the Alliance Party, to vote for the two main Unionist parties as the only sure means of indicating their views on partition. (The argument that border polls should be avoided because they would reveal the unpalatable reality of significant support for independence amongst Protestants has little to recommend it.)

The British government could also consider appointing Northern Ireland Office ministers from either or both communities; these would have to be authentic political representatives and not 'castle Catholics' or the newer breed of 'castle Protestant' in the Brian Mawhinney mould. Such a move would, at least, help to dispel the secrecy – broken only by Scott's leaks to the nationalist press – which surrounds the working of the Conference and the Maryfield secretariat. Finally, the British government might consider responding to the new integrationist mood within Official Unionism; and this means more than tinkering with Grand Committees and the Order in Council process at the heart of the Direct Rule system. The Campaign for Equal Citizenship may make a ridiculously exaggerated claim when it suggests that full access to the British party system will lead to the modernisation of Ulster politics; many of the stubborn sectarian realities will remain. It is the Achilles heel of this campaign that it has so little to offer nationalists, but nevertheless, it *is* a civil right to be able to join the parties which form the government of the state in which one lives. The huge ideological obstacles ('Northern Ireland is a dump', 'should be kept at arm's length', and so on) towards taking this step which exist in British parties should not obscure that fact. As it stands, the Agreement discusses only one long-term end: a united Ireland. In the interim it proposes only two alternatives: the Inter-governmental Conference or power-sharing devolution with a strong Irish dimension.

The prognosis is one of an expanded symbolic recognition within Northern Ireland of the nationalist identity while expressions of the British or Unionist tradition tend to be increasingly curbed or circumscribed. (It does not help that the very powerlessness of Protestants to affect the working of the Agreement increases the pressure for manifestations of an Orange sort in the areas which they do control, for example, Shorts aircraft factory.) This is a recipe for sectarian confrontation. It seems foolish, at least, not to allow for a greater expression of the relatively secular and modernising aspects of the Unionist tradition. The Agreement itself speaks of 'respecting the identities of the two communities' and of 'the right of each to pursue its aspirations by peaceful and constitutional means', and the Forum Report's only conceivable claim to originality was its recognition of the British tradition in Ulster. It is surely compatible with both these themes to permit greater access to mainstream British politics for those who desire it.

In 1977, when Conor Cruise O'Brien gave his Ewart Biggs lecture *Neighbours*, it was entirely right to support direct rule, as he did, against integration as such a move would upset the precarious equilibrium and be perceived, as he put it, as a Unionist 'goal'. But the Anglo-Irish Agreement has now upset that equilibrium anyway and there seems to be a case for looking at a new 'twin track' development: full participation in British politics for those who want that and Irish representation at the highest level of government within Northern Ireland for those who want that. It renders devolution – and a historic compromise based primarily on that – impossible, but devolution and the historic compromise at the political level is probably impossible anyway; it is simply asking too much of a community which is likely to be bedevilled by terrorism for the foreseeable future. It is perhaps enough that they can live together.

These proposals do not involve the destruction of the Anglo-Irish Agreement though they do imply a path of development which is different from those outlined in the Agreement. (It is not necessary to believe that Sinn Fein's electoral surge in the 1982-85 period was irresistible – it had in fact probably peaked in 1983 – to acknowledge that Sinn Fein would stand to benefit somewhat from the open collapse of the Agreement.) The proposals will, however, almost certainly not be applied because of the understandable distaste of the major British parties for the Ulster scene. The alternative however is grim: a steady increase in unemployment which in itself will do much to render nugatory the new recognition of the Irish identity; the intensification of sectarianism and the gradual deterioration of the environment, with Britain even more reluctantly footing the increasing social services bills. Already we have had the absurd scenario of a severe cut in the government's housing budget – which affords significant employment to Catholics, who are hardest hit by the province's 22 per cent unemployment rate – in order to finance the increase in the security budget necessitated by the Agreement. The 'healing process', to borrow Hume's phrase, has not begun and is not likely to begin in these circumstances. It is surely time for a serious reappraisal of the working of the Accord.

Notes

[1] *Irish Times*, 16 July 1986.
[2] For a clear and useful summary of the nationalist position, see Anthony Coughlan, *Fooled Again*, Cork and Dublin 1986.
[3] See Paul Bew and Henry Patterson, *The British State and the Ulster Crisis*, London 1985, p.123.
[4] 'The Irish Question: a British Problem', *Foreign Affairs*, Vol.58, 1979/80.
[5] Bew and Patterson, *op.cit.*, pp.127-35.
[6] Interview with S. Deane and B. Fitzpatrick, *The Crane Bag*, Vol.4, No.2, 1980, p.40.
[7] *Foreign Affairs*, Vol.58, 1979/81, p.305.
[8] See Bew and Patterson, op.cit., pp.52-68.
[9] *The Observer*, 27 April 1986.
[10] Hugh Roberts, *Northern Ireland and the Algerian Analogy*, Belfast 1986, p.12.
[11] *Irish Times*, 16 November 1985.
[12] Paul Bew, *Conflict and Conciliation in Irish Nationalism 1890-1960*, Oxford 1987.
[13] *The Times*, 20 August 1986.

Bill Rolston

Alienation or Political Awareness?
The Battle for the Hearts
and Minds of Northern Nationalists

> As a result of this Agreement, Northern nationalists can now hold
> their heads high.
>
> Garret FitzGerald

> We have signed an Agreement in which the Prime Minister of the
> Republic of Ireland ... has in fact accepted for all practical
> purposes and into perpetuity that there will never be a united
> Ireland.
>
> Tom King

Introduction: Interpreting the Anglo-Irish Agreement

There have been many contradictory claims made about the
'Anglo-Irish' Agreement,[1] signed by British Prime Minister
Thatcher and the Taoiseach of the Republic of Ireland,
FitzGerald, in November 1985. At times these contradictions
could be 'explained' publicly in terms of misinterpretation. For
example, less than a month after the signing, Secretary of State
for Northern Ireland King stated that FitzGerald now accepted
the impossibility of a united Ireland. He later apologised for
presuming to speak for FitzGerald, but not, interestingly, for his
own sentiments about the eternal nature of partition. Whether
this was a misinterpretation or not, it is a strange agreement
which allows the British to parade it as a bulwark to a united
Ireland, despite the clearly expressed aspiration of a sizeable
number of Northern nationalists for such a political solution,
while at the same time enabling FitzGerald to present it as a
defence of the nationalist aspirations of the Northern minority.

One explanation for such diversity could be that each of the political forces with a stake in the outcome of the Agreement, whether as signatories or otherwise, must play to different audiences and must therefore emphasise different aspects of the deal, even to the point of exaggeration and misinterpretation. But a closer look at the details of the Agreement reveals that there is little substance involved and that it is in fact sufficiently vague to allow for any number of interpretations. In effect, the Agreement provides a shopping list of matters which are open for discussion between the British and Southern Irish governments. In the modern world such matters are frequently discussed between sovereign states in numerous arenas, such as the EEC. The presentation of this list therefore is no more than a possible agenda for ongoing inter-state discussion; it is certainly not a list of demands or obligations.

There are, it is stressed, two principles at the base of the Agreement.[2] The first is that – for the first time in such a public manner – the Southern state acknowledged that there should be no constitutional change in the North without the consent of the (Unionist) majority there. The second is that Northern nationalists should have a right to aspire to a united Ireland. *Of themselves*, these are little more than ideals. Moreover, there is nothing *inherently* contradictory in accepting both ideals simultaneously.

With so little substance the deal is, like the proverbial abstract painting, open to various interpretations; to Unionists it is the beginning of the sell-out of Ulster, to the Northern Ireland Office it is Southern acquiescence in the continuing partition of Ireland, and to the Southern government it is a step towards a peaceful settlement between Northern nationalists and Unionists. In a real sense, none of these interpretations is wrong.

But, because the Agreement is so imprecise, its success or failure rests on how it is sold to each of its target audiences.[3] Of all those audiences, one was seen, by the Southern government in particular, as crucial; in fact, it could be said that it was for this audience primarily that the Agreement was thought up in the first place. So, in this essay the focus will be on that one audience, Northern nationalists, and on the manner in which the Agreement fits into the battle between militant Republicanism and constitutionalist nationalism, between Sinn Fein and the Social Democratic and Labour Party (SDLP).

The SDLP and Alienation

At the core of SDLP policy is a commitment to power-sharing in the North. For the party, devolved government without power-sharing can only be Unionist domination of nationalists. Yet it must be said that the desired flowering of democracy through power-sharing has encountered a very unfavourable climate. A brief power-sharing executive in 1974 was brought down by the Ulster Workers' Council strike, and it was clear in the decade afterwards that the British were hesitant to repeat the experiment. The Constitutional Convention of 1975, reflecting its majority Unionist make-up, came out against power-sharing. Atkins' 'Round Table Talks' of 1979 were merely that, talks without any British commitment to backing SDLP demands. Later Prior's Rolling Devolution never gained the slightest hint of momentum. In effect, if not also intention, British policy for ten years had either backed or failed to challenge the Unionist veto on SDLP scenarios for political progress. The SDLP was left out in the cold.

As a party, the SDLP had changed in some ways in that decade. Created from the top down by the coming together of a number of candidates elected in 1970 on a civil rights platform it had always represented an amalgamation of interests — nationalist, social democratic and socialist, the last of a rather general, populist nature.[4] The departure of the socialist wing (Gerry Fitt and Paddy Devlin) in the late 1970s meant not only a change of leadership but also a shift in the party's centre of gravity. The SDLP now had two camps, a social democratic wing, led by party leader John Hume, a rational, articulate and business-like urban politician, and a more nationalist wing, led by Hume's deputy Seamus Mallon, who drew behind him much of the party's rural membership.

The problem facing Hume was complex. He had to bring his party in from the cold. In essence there was a deep sense of alienation within the SDLP. With no devolved government in the North, an SDLP boycott of the Assembly, the irrelevance and Unionist domination of most local council matters, and only one Westminster MP, there was not much scope for a party supposedly pledged to bring about a united Ireland by constitutionalist means. Moreover, there was the very real danger that alienation would drive the nationalist wing in an ever more militant direction; certainly the party's calls for the disbandment of the Ulster Defence Regiment and its continued reluctance to give blanket support to the Royal Ulster Constabulary (RUC) have derived from Mallon rather than Hume.

Hume's skill was to search for a solution to the problem by changing strategy and widening the arena of debate. Instead of negotiating with the Northern Ireland Office or pleading with the British for a commitment to power-sharing, he sought to mobilise support from political parties in the South. The outcome of this was the New Ireland Forum of 1984. Three Southern parties – Fine Gael, the Labour Party and Fianna Fáil – and the SDLP met in Dublin for some months, taking evidence from various groups and individuals. The final report of these deliberations was to be a kind of blueprint for political progress. In reality it was less than that. Major differences, for example between Charles Haughey of Fianna Fáil, committed to a united Ireland as the preferred option, and FitzGerald (strongly influenced by arguments from two academic lawyers, Boyle and Hadden[5]), committed to a joint authority solution. In the end the Report presented three possible options for political progress – a united Ireland, joint authority and a federal solution – but did not in fact choose any one of them.[6] Despite the absence of unanimity, Hume had scored a major point. He had persuaded the government parties and opposition in the South jointly and publicly to declare as central to the North's problems 'the alienation of nationalists from political and civil institutions', to condemn the British for having no policy in relation to the North except 'crisis management, that is, the effort to contain violence through emergency measures', and to call on the British to show the will to pull the SDLP in from the cold, even if that meant challenging the Unionists. The four parties quickly added that their intentions towards the Unionists were entirely honourable and that they were not attempting to force them into a united Ireland.

The Forum Report represented a coup by Hume. At one stroke, he had broken out of the sterile confines of political debate in the North, had persuaded the main political parties in another state to condemn Britain for not heeding SDLP pleas, and had increased his party's legitimacy by showing himself capable of statesman-like manoeuvring. He had also, despite the Report's comforting assurances to Unionists, managed to impress on them that the SDLP intended to have its way with or without Unionist acquiescences.

Yet, there was one nagging question which remained despite all the SDLP elation over the Forum. Why did it take ten years of alienation before this move occurred? The absence of a leader of Hume's calibre is only part of the answer. Of much more importance in determining the urgency to bring the SDLP in from the cold was the spectre of Sinn Fein.

The Rise of Sinn Fein

In the 1970s Sinn Fein was not a major influence in nationalist politics in the North. It was often seen by many – including those in the IRA itself – as a mere adjunct to the IRA, the 'poor cousin' of the Republican movement. This was despite the fact that it was technically a separate and self-sufficient branch of the movement. Even the legalisation of the party in 1975 by Merlyn Rees did not lead to any major developments. Rees sought to woo a part of the Republican movement to the electoral process, to abandon the bullet for the ballot. But the Republican movement was not for wooing. Sinn Fein boycotted elections up to and including local government elections in the midst of the hunger strike of 1981. There were numerous Sinn Fein cumainn (branches) in the North, but their work was more or less confined to activities campaigning against repression.

The hunger strike was to change that. In April 1981, a matter of weeks before he died on hunger strike, Bobby Sands, a serving Republican prisoner, was elected MP for Fermanagh and South Tyrone. Although an important event, it was not unique. Prisoner candidates had been returned in elections in Ireland many times before. Like Sands, they had been elected on an abstentionist ticket, usually on a wave of emotional support. Their success was thus usually short lived. After Sands' death the Republican movement regarded it as important to contest the Fermanagh and South Tyrone constituency again, successfully as it turned out. But Republicans did not take part, even on an abstentionist basis, in the local government elections in the North in May 1981. This was later acknowledged as a mistake.

> The lack of direct involvement by the Republican movement in the elections is now recognised as a serious miscalculation. It is now clear that an opportunity has been lost by Republicans to make some permanent gains from the hunger strike and to further erode the sway the collaborationist SDLP holds over the nationalist people.[7]

This acknowledgement reached the status of party policy when Danny Morrison received support from the delegates at the 1981 Sinn Fein Ard Fheis (party conference) when he asked them: 'Will anyone here object if, with a ballot paper in one hand and the Armalite in the other, we take power in Ireland?'[8]

Following this shift towards electoral politics, Sinn Fein took five seats in the election to the Northern Ireland Assembly in 1982. In a proportional representation contest the party polled 9.3 per cent of the first preference votes, compared to the SDLP's 18.8 per cent, which amounted to 35 per cent of the nationalist vote. More impressively, its vote was 17 per cent of the poll in the seven constituencies where it actually put up candidates. In June 1983, the trend continued with the General Election. Sinn Fein polled 13.4 per cent of the vote, 43 per cent of the nationalist vote, even though only one candidate was successfully returned, Gerry Adams for West Belfast. And in May 1985 59 Sinn Fein councillors were returned in local government elections.

These electoral successes were worrying to a number of political groups, not least the SDLP. Their initial response was to dismiss the rise of Sinn Fein as merely an emotional response to the hunger strike. By June 1983 this argument was beginning to sound very thin. Hume's claim that Adams had only borrowed the West Belfast seat from the SDLP and his party's assertion with each successive election that Sinn Fein had peaked did little to lessen the impact of one important message. Sinn Fein did not have to become *the* nationalist party at the polls; all it had to do was to make sure that the SDLP could no longer present itself as *the* nationalist party. Even without Sinn Fein becoming the dominant party on the nationalist side, one of the very few bases of legitimacy for the constitutionalist nationalists – a near monopoly on nationalist electoral support – had been removed.

But the problem for the SDLP was even deeper. It had previously been a canon of Republican politics that elections in a partitioned Ireland were fought on an abstentionist basis. But the Sinn Fein councillors elected in the North took their seats. Many of them have been capable and hard working. In addition, they have a strong party machine behind them. In this sense Sinn Fein differs significantly from the SDLP. The latter party took over the mantle of the old Nationalist Party no more clearly than in its relationship to grass-roots support. Begun as a party with only a leadership, the SDLP never saw an urgency in building up constituency groups or a middle level. It was a party of individual elected representatives, whose relationship to the nationalist people was often no more than to call on them to vote SDLP at each election. Sinn Fein, on the other hand, had had a decade or more of some grass-roots work in nationalist areas, admittedly narrowly confined to issues of repression. But after the hunger strike the new-found legitimacy of Sinn Fein led it into work on various other issues, such as housing, social security and debt in local areas. The most visible sign of this was a network of Sinn Fein advice centres.

The main SDLP response was to dismiss these activities as opportunist. Hume stated that Sinn Fein's only contribution to the community had been that they had filled graves, filled jails with young people and lengthened dole queues.[9] Another SDLP response was suddenly to see the need to appear more relevant to the nationalist people *between elections*. A youth branch of the SDLP was started, for example, and some attempt was made to produce literature. Despite this, comparisons with Sinn Fein still frequently bordered on the embarrassing. The SDLP had few advice centres, and at the level of mass communication, the SDLP's infrequent *SDLP News* (first issue, December 1985) bears no comparison with Sinn Fein's *An Phoblacht/Republican News*; the former is poorly typeset, badly produced and incredibly parochial, dealing only with the SDLP, whereas the latter not only justly deserves the self-awarded title 'Ireland's largest selling political weekly', but also has a great deal of news and analysis not merely confined to Ireland.[10]

Given the SDLP's lack of day-to-day links with the nationalist grass-roots, it is in fact the SDLP which can be suspected of opportunism by a sizeable proportion of nationalists. For many working-class nationalists in particular, the SDLP is the voice of the nationalist middle class. Sinn Fein, on the other hand, speaks the language of many in the nationalist working class. Sinn Fein may be a novice in the game of agitation for social and economic improvement, but is seen by many as committed and sincere. Its solid base in nationalist working-class communities is an important source of electoral support. And, although that support may ebb and flow depending on what the other branch of the Republican movement, the IRA, is doing at any one time, there is no denying that this base in the community ensures Sinn Fein of a potential vote in excess of the militant Republican section of Northern nationalism.[11] In short, some nationalists vote for Sinn Fein *because* of its links with the IRA, while others can continue to vote Sinn Fein *despite* these links.[12]

It is this development of the immediate post-hunger strike period which was most threatening to the SDLP and which pushed it in a direction other than building up community legitimacy – that is, it plugged into the already existing 'Anglo-Irish' framework.

'Anglo-Irish' Relations

Before the hunger strike, an Anglo-Irish process had begun between the then Taoiseach Haughey and Thatcher. Haughey had stressed the need for such a process as a forum for discussion of 'the totality of relationships in these islands'. More fundamentally, it is likely that Haughey believed that such a process might lead to a break in the log-jam of the North and that he could go down in history as the man who began the process which led eventually to the unification of Ireland. For her part, Thatcher had little to lose by agreeing to a continuing discussion. On the contrary, if such deliberations could lead to increased cross-border co-operation in security, including easier extradition of suspected Republican offenders from the South to the North, she had much to gain.

The process never really developed, however. For a start,

Thatcher was not enamoured by Haughey's style or his 'republican' aspirations. Moreover, Thatcher, true to form, expected inter-state co-operation to be, if not unilaterally, then at least disproportionately to her benefit, and was sorely miffed by Haughey's refusal to back her Falklands/Malvinas 'crusade' at the United Nations. In short, although there was an 'Anglo-Irish' process afoot into which the New Ireland Forum could foreseeably fit, that process had not developed far and was not at the top of the list of British government concerns. Thus it was perhaps not surprising that Thatcher rejected the Forum Report. What was astonishing was that she gave such short shrift to each of the three possible political options put forward in the Report: 'Out, out, out,' she replied to each in turn. The cursory nature of her rejection perhaps needs further explanation.

Firstly, the deliberations which led to the Forum Report were conducted without Thatcher. That alone was enough to have her interpret the Report as an attempt to dictate to her, a conclusion surely enhanced by the Report's criticisms of British policy in the North. Secondly, before the General Election of 1983 Thatcher had said that Sinn Fein gains would worry her.[13] Despite that admission, she seemed remarkably unmoved by the rise of Sinn Fein. Certainly she had not introduced any new initiatives or made any moves to come to the SDLP's rescue. Yet the Forum's purpose was to coerce, embarrass or persuade her into doing just that. As the Argentinians, various EEC partners and Britain's miners had discovered, Thatcher was not one to do under duress what she had not herself found it necessary to do previously. Thirdly, the Forum Report was published on 14 November 1984. One month before, on 12 October, Thatcher had narrowly missed death when the IRA had blown up the Grand Hotel in Brighton during the Conservative Party Conference. Thatcher was in no mood to have anything to do with Irish nationalism, even its constitutional variant.

The finality of her rejection of the Report seemed to thwart in one stroke Hume's strategy of using the South to bring pressure on Britain to make some space for constitutional nationalism in the North. The SDLP was affronted, as Chairman Sean Farren made abundantly clear.

We in the SDLP always had less than whole-hearted confidence in
the intellectual ability of Mrs Thatcher personally to appreciate the
intricacies and complexity of the Northern situation. It now
appears that she has decided to focus the full venom of her
anti-Irishness on the SDLP ... We in the SDLP are not
down-hearted that Mrs Thatcher feels so venomous towards us that
she will seek to destroy us. That same hatred which she has
directed towards the miners and is rending the social fabric of
Britain will eventually consume her and all that she stands for.[14]

The Forum Report seemed to be the last hope for the SDLP,
and its ignominious fate at the hands of Thatcher seemed to be
cause for despair.

Yet exactly one year later Thatcher sat down with FitzGerald
in Hillsborough Castle and signed an Agreement which, it was
claimed by Fine Gael and sections of the SDLP, was joint
authority (one of the rejected Forum options) in all but name.
But any suspicion that the Iron Maiden had executed an
uncharacteristic U-turn is dispelled by a number of
considerations. To begin with, Fine Gael and the SDLP
notwithstanding, Thatcher did not interpret the Agreement as
joint authority. Rather, as later pronouncements made by King
and herself made clear, the British view was that what was
entailed was merely an agreement between two sovereign states
to talk about a matter of common concern, the North. The
British did not surrender their sovereignty over the North.
Although discussions could foreseeably cover a wide range of
matters, it became clear that the British intended to allow the
South less direct say in actual policy making and administration
in the North than, say, the EEC currently has. Moreover, there
was the potential for the Agreement to become the sort of
inter-state arrangement which Thatcher likes, namely, one in
which she concedes little or nothing in return for concessions
from the other side. From the British side, the promise to
recognise the aspirations of Northern nationalists for a united
Ireland as legitimate was not spelt out in any way whatsoever; in
fact, as we shall see, the negotiations, sometimes heated, since
November 1985 have involved the Southern government
(directly) and the SDLP (indirectly) in pressuring the British into
adding some flesh to the bare bones of this promise.

For the South, the concessions were much greater. The

South's constitution states that the six counties in the North are a rightful part of the Southern state's territory. Although Southern governments have usually done little to realise that claim, preferring for the most part strategically timed rhetoric, FitzGerald, in signing the Agreement, had given his government's name to an historic compromise – that Ireland would remain divided as long as Northern Unionists desired it to be. In the Dáil debate following, Haughey attacked FitzGerald:

> This Agreement is manifestly contrary to the Constitution ... The whole basis of this document is an acceptance of British sovereignty over Northern Ireland ... For the first time the legitimacy of partition has been recognised by the Republic ...[15]

FitzGerald's concession must have cost him some votes in the 1987 election; the notion of a united Ireland may be little more than a mystical one in the minds of many Southern voters but 1987 was not the first time that the issue became a central one in a Southern election.

More specifically, the South also conceded in regards to an equally touchy subject in traditional Southern politics. The Constitution allows a person wanted by the Northern or British police to avoid extradition on the grounds that the alleged offence was politically motivated. This practice has come under sustained criticism from the British in recent years, resulting in a number of successful extraditions to Britain and the North.[16] But in signing the Agreement, FitzGerald agreed that his government would finally become a signatory to the European Convention on the Suppression of Terrorism. The resulting ease with which extradition could take place would be one more gain for Thatcher.

Losing so little and potentially gaining so much, Thatcher had no problem in entering into negotiations with the South. And this is one further way in which the Agreement differed from the Forum Report; the former involved Thatcher from the beginning, the latter did not. The Agreement could not, therefore, be read in any way as a case of anyone dictating to Thatcher. In addition, she may well have been advised that pique, even under provocation such as that at Brighton, was no way to handle Anglo-Irish relations, and that a deal with

FitzGerald now (especially a favourable one) was a much preferable alternative to negotiating with the dreaded Haughey later.

In short, the Agreement had Thatcher's blessing because of its potential value to Britain. Given that, it surely came as a great surprise to her the extent to which the Unionists rejected, and continue to reject the deal – to the point of resignations and by-elections, council and parliamentary boycotts, attacks, physical and otherwise, on Northern Ireland Office ministers, cross-border invasions, paramilitary posturing and a revived assassination campaign against nationalists. The focus of this essay rules out an in-depth consideration of Unionist logic in this respect but it needs to be said that the basis of Unionist rejection of the Agreement was twofold. Firstly – and Thatcher should well understand this – they were insulted at being left out of the process whereby the deal emerged. The British response that the negotiations were between sovereign governments is little consolation when it is *their* state, Northern Ireland, which is at the centre of the negotiations. Furthermore, their anger is increased by the knowledge that the Northern minority now have a direct line of communication in relation to ongoing Anglo-Irish discussion via the Southern government, while the majority in the North must rely on leaks from sympathetic policemen and civil servants.

Secondly, the Unionists read the 'Anglo-Irish' arrangements as Southern interference in Northern affairs, the thin end of the wedge of moves towards a united Ireland. The British can retort that FitzGerald has conceded the Unionist veto on political progress, but that does little to reassure Unionists. Moreover, the possibility of long-term gains for the North from the minor British concession – recognition of Northern nationalist aspirations – is no consolation in a situation in which the British are seen to be treating the Unionists like children, acting *for* them rather than (by resurrecting a majority-rule devolved government) allowing them to act themselves. Little surprise, then, that the Unionists should respond like spoiled children, screaming 'No' at every opportunity.

The in-built contradiction of the Anglo Irish Agreement is that British utterances about the lack of substance in the deal and its potential gains for Unionists were made simultaneously with Fine Gael and SDLP claims about the real gains it held for nationalists. John Hume's statement, on the day of the signing, that much more than consultation was involved, that the new inter-governmental arrangements would allow both the British and Southern governments to deal with all the issues previously under the control of the old Unionist government at Stormont and that 'the British have stated in this Agreement that there is no British interest, strategic or otherwise, in being in Ireland', were as good as a green flag to the Unionist bull.[17]

From the point of view of the SDLP the inherent contradiction of the Agreement led to a dilemma. Was the party to sing the praises of the deal, thus angering Unionists, or were they to placate the Unionists, assuring them that what was involved was relatively insubstantial, and thus lose out on any chance of increased legitimacy in the eyes of nationalists? The dilemma was easily solved; as with the Forum Report, but even more emphatically, the SDLP decided that Unionist feelings were not the priority. As the party's chairman, Alban Maginness, put it:

> ... if Unionist politicians had cared to look seriously at what was going on here year after sterile year for the past decade, they would have irresistibly been drawn to the conclusion that negotiating a power-sharing deal with the SDLP was their best alternative ... Therefore, they are very much the authors of their own much-lamented misfortune.[18]

As far as the SDLP was concerned, what Northern nationalists thought of the Agreement was much more important.

After the Agreement: Justice and the End of Alienation?

The deal was said, by both British and Southern signatories, to assure Northern nationalists a legitimate and rightful place in Northern society. But, before that could happen, a number of ways in which they are currently excluded had to be tackled. The problem was that the Agreement did not specify how this desired end would be achieved. So there was a great deal of speculation, by media pundits and others, about what specific reforms to benefit nationalists would actually result. Front candidates in this speculation were: a tighter control over the Ulster Defence Regiment (UDR), a revamped police complaints procedure, reforms in the Diplock court system, restrictions on annual Loyalist parades and the repeal of the Flags and Emblems Act. But one year after the signing of the Agreement, it is clear that the predictions were for the most part wide of the mark.

Ulster Defence Regiment

Little has been done to control or reform the UDR. In December 1985 greater professionalisation of the regiment was announced, including the lengthening of basic training for part-time soldiers from nine to fourteen days. Such moves were supposed to lead to a more professional and therefore more disciplined force, one less prone to 'excessive behaviour' towards nationalists. But such a connection would seem at best dubious. This section of the so-called security forces has, to quote Seamus Mallon, 'a ratio of serious crime ... twice that of the ratio within the general community, and we have a violent community'.[19] It is a regiment over 97 per cent Protestant in membership,[20] whose relationship with the nationalist community in areas such as Armagh is reduced to one of straightforward harassment and murder. In fact, prior to the Anglo-Irish Agreement both Mallon and FitzGerald called for the disbandment of the regiment altogether. Such calls have not been made since. Is it to be presumed that FitzGerald and the SDLP are satisfied that greater professionalisation will solve the problem of the UDR? If so, it is certain that many working-class nationalists will not be so easily satisfied. Nor would they have been pleased had another proposed reform been actualised – namely, that the UDR be accompanied on patrols by the Royal Ulster Constabulary (RUC). For many nationalists this would be seen as at worst double trouble, or at best a more sophisticated form of repression.

Police complaints procedure

Changes in the police complaints procedure were to be a major element in making the RUC more acceptable to nationalists. Ultimately, as Peter Barry, Foreign Minister in the South, put it,

The acid test of the Anglo-Irish Agreement will be that young Catholics and nationalists will be able to join the RUC without feeling any less nationalist in their own eyes or those of their family and friends.[21]

It might be expected that such a process could well begin with a reform of the police complaints procedures. But, although such a reform is being implemented through the new, more 'independent' Police Complaints Authority, it is hard to see what specific benefits there are for nationalists. In fact, it is difficult to see how the minor changes involved in the new procedures will control the 'excessive behaviour' towards nationalists of the supposedly few 'bad apples' in the RUC any better than the previous complaints arrangements. After all, if Assistant Chief Constable Stalker could not persuade the police to incriminate themselves during investigations, what hope has an investigating officer of a much lower rank, even if he has the backing of the new Police Complaints Authority? The problem of policing the police is revealed in the Annual Report of the current Police Complaints Board for 1985; of the 232 cases of 'alleged irregular conduct' by RUC men at holding centres against people detained under the Prevention of Terrorism Act, 'more than half were incapable of investigation because of lack of cooperation with the investigating officer'.[22] The new complaints procedure has no answer to such conspiracies of silence.

Diplock courts

'Dublin Pressure Ends Diplock Courts', announced the *Irish News* on 22 July 1986, rather prematurely as it turned out. Although it is clear that the substitution of three judges for one in the no-jury courts hearing 'terrorist' cases in the North is one of the strongest demands on the British from FitzGerald and Barry, and would bring about a common situation as regards 'special' courts North and South, the British have not yet agreed to that demand. Moreover, it seems unlikely that they will do so. Only one week after the *Irish News* scoop, Lord Hailsham announced he would be appointing more judges in Britain to handle the increasing number of criminal trials. However, he specifically ruled out more judges for Northern Ireland on the grounds that there were not enough experienced senior barristers available for such a promotion.[23] Southern attempts to have the British end the supergrass system – which allows people to be sentenced solely on the uncorroborated evidence of alleged former accomplices – have been equally unsuccessful.[24]

Loyalist parades

Loyalist parades occur each summer in the months of July and August. Often, as in Portadown, they pass through totally or predominantly nationalist areas, where Unionist triumphalism is displayed at close quarters. Police and army 'protection' for nationalists in such situations means in effect that local communities are kept under street, if not house, arrest while a path is cleared for Loyalists from outside the area to march. In 1985 Portadown became one of a number of flashpoints, leading Barry to demand from the British that in 1986 such parades be banned and the ban enforced by the RUC. The very hint of banning, and at the behest of a Southern politician into the bargain, was grist to the mill for Unionist fury. But coming close to the event, King made it clear in a lengthy newspaper interview that the South could have no say in RUC operational decisions. As if to rub salt in the wounds, the RUC 'solved' the Portadown problem by diverting the 12 July march from its traditional route through one nationalist area to an alternative route through another nationalist area.

The Flags and Emblems Act

From the very first days of the Agreement, it was stated by numerous commentators that the North's Flags and Emblems Act would be repealed. Although not directly forbidding the flying of the tricolour, it allows great scope to the RUC to interpret when its display might provoke a breach of the peace. Under the legislation, flying the Union Jack cannot in any circumstances be judged provocative. The Act will probably be repealed, but there is likely to be little change in either popular or police behaviour. Nationalists have flown the tricolour at funerals, parades and so on before this, even if they were breaking the law, and the repeal of the law is not likely to lead to very many prosecutions of Unionists for flying what is after all their national flag, the Union Jack.

In summary, as a supposed exercise in give-and-take, the Anglo-Irish Agreement has involved the South in a lot of giving and the British in a lot of taking. The South might have found this acceptable if substantial changes occurred in the North. However the changes have been few, and those which have occurred have been presented by the British as having been planned prior to and/or independently of the Anglo-Irish process. Thus, Brigadier Preston of the UDR denied that changes in training for the regiment, announced shortly after the signing of the Agreement, resulted from the Agreement.[25] More recent moves to make it possible to withhold government grants from firms not affording equality of opportunity to Catholics were said by King to have been on the cards from before the Agreement.[26] The obvious reticence of the British to embark on a full-scale attack on ending the alienation of nationalists in the North led to a deep frustration on the part of the Southern government. Barry announced on 4 June in the Dáil that he was 'quite dissatisfied' with the rate of progress from the British side. But such was the need to protect the image of the deal as being one of substance that, little more than a month later, he was predicting a package of British reforms in the autumn. The media, and in particular Irish newspapers sympathetic to constitutional nationalism, took this to mean reforms in the Diplock courts and the repeal of the Flags and Emblems Act, as well as legislation to allow nationalists to erect street signs in Irish (something they already do in the absence of any such legislation). Whether such a package materialises or not is open to question,[27] but, even if it does, it is clear that it does not begin to tackle the more substantial problems of repression of nationalists. How, for example, does one go about reforming the UDR?

It is significant that in the speculation about reforms resulting from the Agreement, the broad philosophical notion of justice for nationalists has been reduced to a concern to reform the criminal justice system in a few ways – policing, courts, laws, etc. That focus may derive in part from a belief that reforms in this area are possible, whereas reforms in all the other areas of the 'shopping list' laid out in the Agreement are much more difficult; reforming the criminal justice system is easier than guaranteeing overall social justice. At a time when the Northern economy teeters on the brink of total collapse, it is difficult to see how even two governments with all the will in the world could produce a substantial number of jobs and then distribute them in such a way as to lessen the current imbalance whereby nationalists are two-and-a-half times as likely to be unemployed as Unionists. But, the suspicion must be that the criminal justice system has been targeted for reform for other, more ideological, reasons.

In his initial statement on the Agreement, Hume argued that 'a great deal would depend on the implementation of the Agreement, particularly in the field of justice'.[28] The first issue of *SDLP News* repeated this connection between justice and success. When Mallon made his maiden speech in Westminster, his central argument was that 'if we want peace, we must base it on justice'.[29] Thus, for the SDLP the strategy is clear; as alienation stems from injustice, so justice will lead to a lessening of alienation. Such logic is not unique to the SDLP, but has been voiced by others in the nationalist middle class, including some dignitaries in the Catholic church. Bishop Cathal Daly of Belfast has frequently stated that the Sinn Fein vote is a protest vote, that it represents a plea for better social and legal conditions rather than an actual support for militant Republicanism. In similar vein Father Denis Faul, a veteran campaigner against state repression in the North, makes it clear that his motivation does not derive from Republican aspirations, and then assigns a similar lack of Republicanism to the nationalist people as a whole.

> ... an instant pull-out by Britain and a forced unity make no sense to the Catholic people. First there must be a just and equal society created here; reconciliation must exist between all Irishmen. Justice is a prerequisite.[30]

Although there are some in the Catholic hierarchy who would not share the simplistic generalisations of Daly and Faul,[31] it is clear that sections of the Catholic clergy and hierarchy, the SDLP and the Southern government share the same ideological space in seeing the road to a united Ireland as being a very long one involving a number of stages: justice in the North, followed by a dialogue between nationalists and Unionists, and finally a negotiated unity. The SDLP twist to this stages theory is that the measure of justice and equality will be that they achieve power-sharing in the North. And to that end, justice is the key. With justice, the nationalist people can be won over from supporting Sinn Fein. As Brid Rodgers of the SDLP stated:

> The plain truth is that the Hillsborough Agreement threatens the very basis of their support – the inequality, the alienation, the sense of grievance of nationalists. The Agreement can deal with these matters. The Agreement is already dealing with these matters. The Provisionals fear its potential.[32]

As has been pointed out above, there is little evidence to support Rodgers' conclusion that the Agreement is working. In fact, the SDLP's propensity to claim everything, from new police complaints procedures, to the decision, after many years of struggle by residents, to pull down the controversial Divis Flats complex in Belfast, as deriving from the Agreement is easily seen by many nationalists as a case of 'hyping it up'. In this sense, Sinn Fein is correct to state, even before the Agreement was signed, that

> Ordinary nationalists will judge the outcome of these talks not by the rhetoric of its supporters or opponents, but by the real substance, its effects on their lives and to the struggle of the Irish people for self determination.[33]

Similarly, despite some establishment claims to the contrary, the IRA has not responded with a massive military offensive against the Agreement; as even many Unionists will acknowledge, the IRA does not need the Agreement as a reason for its campaign.

These attitudes may seem to reveal a certain complacency on the part of the Republican movement: judging the Agreement to be doomed to failure, it appears satisfied to sit and wait for that failure to occur. Thus, responding to a challenge from Hume to give an alternative to the Hillsborough Agreement, an editorial in *An Phoblacht* was content to reiterate the age-old position that 'the only alternative is the demand of the majority of the Irish people for a free and united Ireland'.[34] Similarly, Danny Morrison's analysis of the origins and substance of the Agreement ends without providing the detailed blueprint which

Hume demands.[35] The Republican position has been to deny the legitimacy of the SDLP question, which is based on the assumption of arguing for alternative strategies *within* the Northern Ireland state.

But, while convinced that the deal will not work, Republicans also realise that there may well be major consequences for nationalists. To begin with, they await the arrival of increased repression of Republicans, whether the deal works or not. Secondly, as Adams put it in an interview with the party newspaper, Loyalist reaction to the Agreement, including their 'confrontation with the establishment', is not to be under-estimated: 'While a short-term diversion for nationalists, it may well prove to be one of the most far-reaching political developments of recent history'.[36] When any initial delight nationalists may have had over seeing the RUC 'getting the boot into' Loyalists had faded, it became clear that a campaign of assassination of ordinary nationalists was imminent; in the longer term, the increased possibility of British exasperation with Unionism or Unionist rejection of Britain could not but have major repercussions for all nationalists.

Conclusion

The Anglo-Irish Agreement is all about images. Hume is no sociologist, but he knows that what is real in the mind is real in its consequences. He and his party are involved in a life-and-death battle for the minds and hearts of the nationalist people, and it is that which is at the core of the Agreement. Since the rise of Sinn Fein, it has become clear to the SDLP (and the Southern government) that the rise of the one party is dependent on the decline of the other.

Thus, the priority in the strategy behind the Agreement is the suppression of Republicanism. Hume and FitzGerald are astute enough to realise that that cannot be achieved merely through repression, through simplistic British 'crisis management'. The banning of Sinn Fein, or the suppression of *An Phoblacht* is not sufficient when the Republican movement has such a degree of popular support. A more subtle approach was required, one which would drive a wedge between constitutionalist nationalism and Republicanism.

In this regard, the concept of alienation is central. To judge Sinn Fein support as resulting merely from a protest against injustice or unemployment is to reduce such nationalist voting behaviour to an atomised and mindless level. The Republican position as a coherent world view is denied any cogency, any legitimacy. Thus, the whole matter is a game of balances – the legitimacy of the nationalist position, supposedly enshrined in the Anglo-Irish Agreement, is posited on the total illegitimacy of the Republican position. Despite certain pseudo-Republican stances of the SDLP in the past, the struggle is now presented in stark terms: nationalists are seen as being of two sorts, acceptable and unacceptable, SDLP and Sinn Fein. Two weeks before the Agreement was signed, Sinn Fein President Adams, in his address to the Sinn Fein Ard Fheis, stated that the Thatcher-Fitzgerald talks were about 'creating a political climate in which this party can be isolated'.[37] Two months later FitzGerald confirmed this, stating on a radio phone-in that:

> We are determined to defeat the IRA, remove any possible basis they may have of support, North or South ... It's towards that end that the Agreement has been signed.[38]

The heavy artillery of this ideological battle is the reform of the criminal justice system. If the SDLP can deliver 'justice' to nationalists, then their legitimacy will be increased in nationalist eyes and the stage will be set for further and probably more directly repressive moves against Republicans. But justice is also the SDLP's Achilles' heel. Rodgers may say the Agreement is already working and Barry may claim that it will begin to work soon, but the main problem is what Thatcher will do. She has not delivered major reforms in the criminal justice system in the North yet, and she may not do so. She may decide, for example, not to push the Unionists any more, and therein is the weakness of the SDLP's position, even in the midst of apparent success. The Agreement is all that stands between the SDLP's rise and its decline. But, if there are no reforms, or not enough of them, or if they do not occur quickly enough, or if they do not change things substantially, then we may see an even greater alienation of nationalists from the SDLP.

Notes

[1] As in many aspects of Irish politics, terminology is all-important. Republicans do not refer to the Anglo-Irish Agreement, as it was a document signed by the Prime Minister of Britain on the one hand and the Taoiseach of only twenty-six of the thirty-two counties of Ireland on the other; they prefer to call it by the name of the town in which the Agreement was signed, Hillsborough. Given the historic significance of Hillsborough – the seat of the British Governor of Northern Ireland until that post was abolished – Unionists also refer to the Hillsborough Agreement, thereby underlining the treachery involved in Thatcher's actions. Thus, the term used throughout this essay, the Anglo-Irish Agreement, is not neutral, and should not be read as such.

[2] The text of the Anglo-Irish Agreement appeared in full in a number of Irish newspapers the next day; see, for example, *Irish Times* and *Belfast Telegraph*, both 16 November 1985.

[3] The role of the media in 'hyping up' the significance of the Agreement is worth referring to. The *Irish Times*, for example, appeared to have every one of its correspondents, except those for sport and farming, at the press conference held by Thatcher and FitzGerald at Hillsborough. The metres of newsprint produced by them afterwards was a major element in the selling of the Agreement.

[4] On the SDLP in general, see I. McAllister, *The Northern Ireland Social and Democratic Labour Party*, London 1977. For a 'lives of the saints' type approach to the Party's current leader, see B. White, *John Hume: Statesman of the Troubles*, Belfast, 1984.

[5] K. Boyle and T. Hadden, *Ireland: A Positive Proposal*, Harmondsworth 1985.

[6] *New Ireland Forum Report*, Dublin, Stationery Office, May 1984.

[7] 'Hunger Strike Opens up Election Front', *Iris* 1(2), 1981.

[8] *An Phoblacht/Republican News*, 5 November 1981.

[9] *Belfast Telegraph*, 25 May 1983.

[10] Sales of *An Phoblacht/Republican News* amount to 44,000 weekly. Sinn Fein claims that as many as 100,000 people actually read each week's edition.

[11] The IRA's campaign in the summer of 1986 of killing people who engage in any commercial business with the RUC or British Army could thus have an electoral spin-off in terms of a reduced vote for Sinn Fein if there were an election occurring soon afterwards. Some nationalists would regard the IRA as acting excessively in this instance.

[12] Although the concentration of this chapter is on nationalists, it must be remembered that how other protagonists in the situation act influences the actions of nationalists. Thus, the level of support, electoral and otherwise, for Sinn Fein derives from a complex mix of factors, which includes not merely what the IRA is doing at any one time, but also the level of state repression, the rise and fall of Loyalist assassination campaigns, etc.

[13] Sinn Fein responded with an election poster which said: 'Give Thatcher a headache – Vote Sinn Fein'.

[14] *Belfast Telegraph*, 30 November 1984.

[15] *Irish Times*, 20 November 1985.

[16] M. Farrell, *Sheltering the Fugitive?*, Dublin Press, 1985.

[17] *Belfast Telegraph*, 16 November 1985.

[18] Ibid., 13 January 1986.

[19] *Hansard*, 20 February 1986.

[20] *Belfast Telegraph*, 13 March 1986.

[21] Quoted in *An Phoblacht*, 5 December 1985.

[22] *Irish News*, 5 June 1986.

[23] *Belfast Telegraph*, 24 July 1986. [24] See 'Supergrasses', *Belfast Bulletin*, No.11, 1984.

[25] *Belfast Telegraph*, 4 December 1985.

[26] Ibid., 17 September 1986.

[27] In this regard the Northern Ireland Office is playing a clever game, strategically allowing anonymous leaks of an autumn package, while publicly denying any such package. For example, see King's strenuous denial, *Belfast Telegraph*, 17 September 1986.

[28] Ibid., 16 November 1985.

[29] Hansard, 20 February 1986.

[30] Letter to the editor, *Irish News*, 18 July 1986.

[31] For example, Cardinal O'Fiaich is aware that electoral support for Sinn Fein derives from state repression, the sound constituency and advice work of Sinn Fein, the legacy of the hunger strike deaths and from a clear republican ideology; 'they vote for Sinn Fein because that is the clearest way they have to indicate that they want to see the end of British colonialism in Ireland' (*Irish News*, 20 July 1985).

[32] *Irish Times*, 25 August 1986.

[33] Gerry Adams, presidential address to Sinn Fein Ard Fheis, quoted in *An Phoblacht*, 7 November 1985.

[34] Ibid., 1 July 1986.

[35] D. Morrison, *The Hillsborough Agreement*, Dublin/Belfast 1986.

[36] *An Phoblacht*, 12 December 1985.

[37] Ibid., 7 November 1986.

[38] Quoted in ibid., 13 January 1987.

Peter Mair

Breaking the Nationalist Mould: The Irish Republic and the Anglo-Irish Agreement

One of the most surprising features of contemporary discussions of the Northern Ireland problem is their tendency to take the prevailing attitude in the Irish Republic as read.* According to the conventional wisdom, the main political parties in the Republic, as well as the vast majority of voters, favour Irish unity and consider that a lasting solution to the Northern Ireland problem will be achieved only with the territorial unification of the island as a whole. The only obstacle to such a solution lies in the uncompromising attitudes of Ulster Unionists, and hence any effort to achieve unity must focus primarily on weakening or even breaking Unionist obduracy. Little needs to be done in the Republic itself, where the commitment to unity is seen to be one of the very few consistent characteristics of what is otherwise a rather diffuse and amorphous ideological consensus.

The purpose of this essay is to attempt to qualify some of these simplistic assumptions by tracing the attitudes of the parties and the public in the Republic of Ireland to nationalist issues and to Northern Ireland in particular. Its intention is to distinguish between different types of nationalism, to outline the apparent shift from traditional nationalism to a more recent and arguably more vigorous 26-county nationalism, and to discuss the impact of this shift on attitudes towards Northern Ireland at both elite and popular levels. The final section focuses on the debate concerning the recent Anglo-Irish Agreement, locating in that debate the essential contradictions and ambiguities which have derived from the shifting nationalist perspective.

The Dominance of Nationalism in Irish Politics

Regardless of their variety and outward sophistication, contemporary interpretations of politics in the Irish Republic almost invariably sustain one overriding conclusion: Irish politics is about nationalism – the appeal for an end to partition and the bringing together of North and South into a united 32-county Republic. The two major parties, Fianna Fáil and Fine Gael, differ in their inherited and seemingly immutable stances *vis-à-vis* this 'national question', and the contemporary variation in their commitment to nationalist demands still largely determines their respective electoral popularity. Fianna Fáil is the most successful party since, in the constitutional arena at any rate, it is also the most militantly nationalist party. Fine Gael has never managed to win sufficient votes to govern on its own because its commitment to traditional nationalism is not so pronounced. Nor is the third party, Labour, seen to be immune from this congealed political environment. Its persistent failure to break through to majority party status is regularly explained by reference to the evident difficulties of mobilising a politics of class in a context where the crucial collectivity is that of nation. The reluctance of the Labour leadership to advocate a distinct class-based politics is not seen to be pertinent in this case: Labour loses because of a hostile ideological environment, and the unwillingness of the party itself to challenge that environment is simply seen as a commendable recognition of political realities.

But despite these inter-party variations, it is also recognised that there exists an underlying consensus. Thus in the politics of the Irish Republic it is not a question of nationalism versus non-nationalism, or of unity versus continued partition, but rather a question of more versus less nationalism. For example, while Fine Gael may be seen to be lukewarm on the national question, the party nevertheless still favours unity. The party's full title is Fine Gael – the United Ireland Party, and even when Garret FitzGerald recently delivered a speech which prioritised peace before unity he was later careful to add a reference to 'our nationalist hopes and aspirations ... which I reasserted and which everyone in Ireland knows I am totally committed to, as part of my personal heritage'.[1] Even Labour stresses a commitment to unity, and the statement of principles and objects in its Constitution asserts that 'The Labour Party affirms that the national territory consists of the whole island of Ireland, its islands and territorial seas.' The emphasis on unity is also enshrined in the national constitution: Article 2 states that 'The national territory consists of the whole of Ireland, its islands and the territorial seas,' while, in recognition of the reality of partition, Article 3 concedes that:

> Pending the re-integration of the national territory, and without prejudice to the right of the Parliament and Government established by this Constitution to exercise jurisdiction over the whole of the territory, the laws enacted by that Parliament shall have the like area and extent of application as the laws of Saorstát Eireann [the Irish Free State] and the like extra-territorial effect.

The absence of any suitable alternative explanations also reinforces the conclusion that the national question lies at the heart of Irish politics. Thus, for example, Irish politics is clearly not about class: were that to be the case, Labour would not have remained on the ideological periphery. Nor is it about religion *per se*: were that to be the case, the politics of church versus state would have encroached on the party political arena long before it became important in the late 1970s. Nor does the internal urban-rural or east-west division account for a great deal, despite its importance in the initial period of party system formation.[2] Thus Irish politics *must* be about nationalism; otherwise it is about nothing at all.

In short, the conventional interpretation of Irish politics is that it is about nationalism now, in much the same way as it was about nationalism in the 1920s when Fianna Fáil and Fine Gael fought the Treaty issue. And while proponents of this view also recognise that in practice little is done to promote nationalist issues, they are quick to discount this as unimportant. That nobody actually does anything practical about removing partition is seen to be beside the point; at least the commitment is there. Padraig Flynn of Fianna Fáil expressed the ethos quite succinctly during the Dáil debate on the recent Anglo-Irish Agreement when he defended the Constitutional claim to Northern Ireland:

Does anybody really believe that the Irish people would reject Articles 2 and 3 of the Constitution if they were asked to do so? Whether Articles 2 and 3 are actively pursued or not from one generation to another is irrelevant to the argument today ... the real point is that the Irish people never lost their interest and thankfully their interest is enshrined in our Constitution.[3]

My intention is not to argue that nationalism is irrelevant. On the contrary, there is a sense in which it genuinely is the bottom line in politics. At the same time, however, as will be argued below, the commitment to unity appears to play a much more questionable role in the mobilisation of electoral support. Nationalism may be important; Irish unity is not, at least as far as the mass electorate is concerned. And the fact that Irish nationalism can be taken to mean something other than simple anti-partitionism was nowhere more manifest than during the lead-up to and the debate around the signing of the Anglo-Irish Agreement at Hillsborough.

Mass Politics and the National Collectivity of the Republic

The mobilisation of mass politics is organised around the appeal to collectivities, and the character of mass politics will vary across both space and time as the collectivities themselves vary. In one instance, the collectivity is defined by social class, in another by religious adherence, in yet another by national identity, and so on. The shifting balance of political power, and the displacement of one political bloc by another, can therefore be seen as a process in which incompatible and conflicting collectivities struggle for dominance on the political stage. One collectivity is politicised only to be challenged by another. The appeal to citizens on the basis of their common national identity and regardless of differing class positions, for instance, is challenged by an appeal based on class collectivities and which mobilises one group against another regardless of a shared national identity. The struggle for socialism, for example, can be seen as an enduring attempt to politicise a class collectivity in opposition to alternative collectivities based on nation, religion, or whatever. In the Irish case, of course, the history of mass politics is the history of appeals to a national collectivity. The non-emergence of a major socialist alternative is a consequence of the incapacity to mobilise an alternative and necessarily divisive collectivity of class. But even to concede the dominance of a national collectivity is still to beg the questions: how has this national collectivity been defined, how has the dominance of this collectivity been sustained, and what are the implications of its politicisation?

A recent survey of the German case by M. Rainer Lepsius offers some potential answers. For Lepsius, the nation is 'a conceived order, a culturally defined idea which determines a collectivity of people as a union'.[4] Where the criteria which define that collectivity vary, so also will the nature of the union which develops. Thus he suggests an initial differentiation between ethnic, cultural and legal criteria which lead, he argues, to the emergence of different types of nations with differing implications for their citizenries. The differentiation itself suggests that 'there is no sense in which the nation is an unequivocal order of social life that develops naturally. It is changeable over time, and it is capable of adapting to real power constellations of historical development.' In effect, and in precisely the same way in which there are differing notions of class and socialism, the conceived order which is the nation, as well as nationalism itself, 'is historically mutable and politically-culturally manipulable'.[5]

No less than the German case – and since the post-war division of Germany the parallels are fascinating – the Irish Republic offers a clear and undeniable example of alternative conceptions of the national collectivity. In brief, the Irish case has experienced a shift from an ethnically and culturally defined nation which involved an emphasis on the territorial unity of all 32 Irish counties, to a more state-derived 26-county nation, the ideological cohesion of which could be maintained almost without reference to irredentist demands. Contemporary Irish nationalism is a 26-county nationalism where, as O'Malley suggests, the issue of sovereignty has taken precedence over the issue of unity.[6] To be sure, the pronounced Catholic ethos of the 26-county state has ensured that a strong cultural component has persisted within this more recent state-derived nationalism. The Irish Republic is an essentially homogeneous Catholic state, and the nationalism which it sustains can afford to be substantially more Catholic and majoritarian than that which seemed to inform the nation-builders in the early part of the century. Nonetheless, the emergence of a new nationalism which derives its legitimacy from the 26-county state itself has necessarily eroded the ideological relevance of strictly irredentist nationalism, and although mainstream political rhetoric still pays obeisance to anti-partitionism, the demand for and commitment to Irish unity has lost much of its political relevance. Moreover, there is now evidence to suggest that even the rhetoric can be safely challenged.

The Decline of Territorial Nationalism

The drift from an emphasis on simple territorial nationalism can be dated back to at least the 1950s, when earlier hopes for a bright and benevolent future clashed with the reality of an impoverished present. The Constitution of the 26-county Republic had been signed, sealed and delivered in 1949. The Mansion House anti-partition committee had flourished momentarily, only to fade from view by 1951. The IRA border campaign, initiated in 1956, reached a high point with the election of four abstentionist Sinn Fein TDs (MPs) in 1957. But all were to lose their seats again in 1961, and the campaign itself was called off in 1962 primarily because of 'the attitude of the general public whose minds have been deliberately distracted from the supreme issue facing the Irish people – the unity and freedom of Ireland'.[7] By then, as even the most militant anti-partitionists realised, the issue was not Irish unity but simple economic survival.

In 1959, ten years after the formal declaration of the 26-county Republic, Sean Lemass succeeded Eamon de Valera as Taoiseach (Prime Minister) and leader of Fianna Fáil. The first decade of the newly declared 26-county Republic had been one of the bleakest since independence was first achieved in 1921. Total employment in industry had fallen by almost 9 per cent, and that in agriculture by almost 24 per cent;[8] Gross Domestic Product had grown by an annual average of only just over 1 per cent;[9] net emigration had exceeded 400,000.[10] The dream of an independent and self-sufficient Ireland had been transformed into a tawdry and relentless nightmare.

Lemass was to sponsor an alternative programme in order to

transform this bleak social and economic environment. The components of this alternative programme have been well documented.[11] In terms of the economy, Fianna Fáil under Lemass sought to move away from the emphasis on protectionism and self-sufficiency and initiated a major drive to liberalise trade and to attract foreign capital. Socially, the party intended to use the increased economic resources to fund a major expansion of the welfare state. Politically, the combination of renewed prospects of industrial employment and an increased commitment to welfare would facilitate a strengthening of its traditional alliance with the working class. In general, the party would effectively reconstruct its political hegemony and, in the process, would lay the basis for a major ideological shift in the prevailing nationalist ethos.

From the late 1950s onwards, the concern of Fianna Fáil lay with furthering the interests of the 26-county state. There is a sense in which this was nothing new. De Valera's dream of a green and gaelic Ireland, the push towards self-sufficiency in the 1930s, and the undeviating commitment to neutrality during the war years can all be seen as the essential building blocks for a 26-county state and as paying scant regard to the winning of Irish unity. But the pro-unity rhetoric remained emphatic throughout these years, and the realisation of Irish nationalist aims was continually predicated on the eventual achievement of territorial unity. These terms of reference were to change under Lemass: the national aim was to be the achievement of social and economic self-respect in the 26-county state, rather than the achievement of territorial self-respect in a new 32-county state. The realisation of the national interest lay in economic prosperity rather than territorial unity. The appeal to the nation and to the national interest remained as crucial as ever, but the reference points of that nation were to change. Economic growth was now the key national goal.

In short, a new nationalism and a new nationalist consensus began to emerge in the late 1950s. Nationalist ideology proved as potent as ever, and Fianna Fáil remained the standard-bearer *par excellence*, but the emphasis on territorial unity *per se* no longer played a crucial role. One evident symptom of this change can be seen in the adoption of particular policies which, although anathema to the old nationalism, proved quite acceptable to the new consensus. The appeal to foreign capital is one example, the Anglo-Irish Free Trade Agreement of 1965 and the application for membership of the European Community are others. More specifically, there was the evidence of a more conciliatory approach to Northern Ireland itself – the Lemass-O'Neill meeting in Stormont in 1965, the 1967 Report of the Committee on the Constitution which recommended a modification of Articles 2 and 3, and the replacement of the territorial claim by a new Article simply expressing an aspiration to unity, and so on. To be sure, the commitment to unity remained part of the everyday political rhetoric, and a minority of voters and political activists would continue to accord it primacy, but in general the demand for unity was pushed to the margins of the new consensus, and the vision of a green, gaelic and/or united Ireland became a relic of the past.

The Impact of the Northern Ireland Conflict

The first civil rights marches and the emergence of violence in Northern Ireland in 1969 had little immediate effect on this new consensus. The authors of the various party programmes continued to rest content with a couple of standard phrases expressing the commitment to unity and devoted the bulk of their efforts to policy pledges which were designed to fill the pockets of Irish voters. Where events in the North did have their greatest immediate impact was in the arena of security policy, as the competing parties sought to convince voters of their relative capacity to ensure that violence would be kept north of the border and so prevent it encroaching on the peaceful preserves of the Republic. For many, the breakdown of the Northern Ireland state was seen to threaten economic well-being rather than to presage unity. If nothing else, the new Irish nationalism was pragmatic.

This pragmatism was evident throughout the 1970s. The British 'occupation' was occasionally condemned, but Westminster's constitutional initiatives did win the support of both the coalition and Fianna Fáil governments of the 1970s, in that a better deal for Catholics in Northern Ireland seemed more important than the prospect of incorporating them into the Republic. Bipartisanship proved the order of the day, not so much because of all-party agreement on what could or should be done but rather because of a general acceptance that actually very little could – or indeed should – be done. Yet it must be emphasised that this arm's length approach was continually accompanied by the traditional pro-unity rhetoric, and the contradictions were manifest.

In a sense, Irish parties in the 1970s were walking a tightrope. On the one hand, the commitment to unity was maintained. On the other, a 26-county ethos had become firmly established and, particularly with the onset of the post-1973 recession, few voters seemed willing to welcome the inevitable disruption which would follow the incorporation of the troubled six counties. Traditional rhetoric had run foul of a contemporary reality, and the Irish political class found difficulty in marrying the two. Thus, on one extreme, polemicists such as Conor Cruise O'Brien urged a modification of the rhetoric and the final abandonment of the commitment to unity as a recognition of the new reality. On the other extreme, dissident Fianna Fáil members such as Neil Blaney and Kevin Boland advocated a more militant policy on Northern Ireland, urging a transformation of rhetoric into reality and a substantiation of the traditional Republican ideals. In the middle, albeit with some difficulty, lay the Lemass-style new nationalism.

Popular Attitudes to Northern Ireland

Since the outbreak of violence in Northern Ireland in the late 1960s a number of surveys have attempted to probe popular attitudes to Northern Ireland in the Republic. These have already been reviewed at some length by Rose and his co-authors,[12] and more recently in an excellent assessment by Cox.[13] Three trends are immediately identifiable: first, there has been a noticeable increase in popular approval of Irish unity (or at least a noticeable decline in popular disapproval); second, there has been a noticeable increase in scepticism about the likelihood of unity; and third, there is a noticeable increase in the reluctance to do anything to achieve unity. In short, unity would be nice, but we don't think it's going to come about, and in any case we're not prepared to do anything to bring it about.

Evidence of attitudes approving or disapproving of unity is

easily adduced: in 1970, shortly after the outbreak of violence, the proportion of survey respondents approving of unity was 70 per cent; in 1974, in the wake of the collapse of the power-sharing executive, this had fallen to 61 per cent; in 1983, it had risen again to 76 per cent, and in 1984 had fallen slightly to 74 per cent – a relatively minor shift taking the period as a whole. However, over the same four surveys, disapproval of unity declined steadily, from 29 per cent in 1970, to 16 per cent in 1974, to 15 per cent in 1983 and to just 10 per cent in 1984.[14] What is perhaps more interesting is to review attitudes to unity in the context of proposed solutions to the Northern Ireland problem. Here the context is quite different, for while approval or disapproval ratings treat attitudes in a virtual vacuum, attitudes to unity as a solution in the context of a range of other constitutional options offer a much more appropriate guide to policy preferences. Here the pro-unity lobby is weaker, but is also undeniably increasing. Thus in 1973, 37 per cent of respondents indicated that a united Ireland was their preferred solution, as against 42 per cent in 1977, 54 per cent in 1978 and 56 per cent in 1980.[15] Since then, no comparable survey questions have been tested, but it is perhaps indicative that in 1984 as many as 50 per cent stated that the unitary state option was their preferred alternative of the three Forum solutions (the other options were a federal/confederal state (22 per cent preference) or joint authority (15 per cent preference) with only 13 per cent indicating a preference for no all-Ireland solution).[16]

Together with the increase in pro-unity sentiment has come an increase in the levels of sympathy shown for the IRA. In this case there are three comparable surveys, carried out in 1978, 1980 and 1984.[17] Those reporting themselves as having 'no time' for the IRA have remained fairly constant over this period, registering 51 per cent in 1978, 49 per cent in 1980 and 49 per cent again in 1984. Those reporting actual approval for the IRA and its aims and methods has also remained reasonably steady, if quite miniscule: 2 per cent in 1978, and 5 per cent in 1980 and 1984. Where there has been a substantial increase, however, has been in the proportion of respondents indicating an admiration for the motives or ideals of the IRA, albeit disapproving of its methods: from just 32 per cent in 1978 to 41 per cent in 1980 and 39 per cent in 1984.

Within this sea of territorial nationalist commitment, it is rather surprising to note the development of attitudes to the likelihood of unity. Again, the trend is unequivocal: when confronted with a straight dichotomous choice between believing the border 'will go' and believing it 'will remain', the proportion opting for the former has fallen from 67 per cent in 1968 to 58 per cent in 1978 and to just 48 per cent in 1984. Those believing the border will remain has risen from 22 per cent in 1968, to 27 per cent in 1978 and to 38 per cent in 1984.[18]

When we add to this the attitudes to 'unity at cost', then the evidence of territorial nationalist commitment seems even more dubious. Thus in 1978, 43 per cent of those surveyed indicated that they would be prepared to pay more taxes in order to achieve unity, while 51 per cent resisted the idea. By 1980, on the other hand, only 29 per cent found paying more taxes an acceptable price for unity, and 63 per cent found it unacceptable. Finally, in 1984, only 23 per cent 'very strongly' agreed that they would be prepared to pay more taxes for a united Ireland, with a further 6 per cent tending to agree with the idea, 51 per cent tending to disagree, and 10 per cent strongly disagreeing.[19]

Obviously it is not just a question of 'who wants a united Ireland?', but also one of 'how badly do they want it?'.[20] While there is undoubtedly a clear commitment to unity, the depth of that commitment is much less certain. Few might abandon the aspiration, but there are also few who wish to do anything to realise it. To recall Padraig Flynn's version of the nationalist ethos, 'whether Articles 2 and 3 are actively pursued or not from one generation to another is irrelevant to the argument today … the real point is that the Irish people never lost interest.'[21] That said, and *pace* the sensibilities of Flynn, it should also be pointed out that even the degree of interest in Articles 2 and 3 is itself questionable. In the wake of Garret FitzGerald's ill-fated Constitutional Crusade of 1981 (see below), for example, some 35 per cent of survey respondents favoured dropping the offending Articles, with 46 per cent disapproving their abandonment.[22] Support for changing (as opposed to dropping) the Articles in order to reflect simply an aspiration rather than an actual territorial claim to unity proved even more pronounced, with another 1981 survey recording 48 per cent approval for such a change, and just 30 per cent disapproval.[23] It should also be noted, on the other hand, that this does not imply a concession to the Northern Unionists: when asked if Articles 2 and 3 should be withdrawn specifically as a gesture to feeling in Northern Ireland, only 23 per cent in 1978 indicated approval, with 65 per cent dissenting, and only 19 per cent indicated approval in 1984, with 64 per cent dissenting.[24] As far as concessions to the North are concerned, Irish nationalism does not prove very accommodating.

What can be concluded from this brief review? Firstly, support for the aspiration to unity is quite pervasive. Secondly, there is little support for anything beyond this, in that few citizens would be willing to pay more taxes to achieve unity. Thirdly, actual opposition to unity in the Republic itself is very much a minority position. Fourthly, militant support for unity is also a minority position. Finally, on the basis of the results of the recent referendums on abortion and divorce, as well as the scant survey evidence on attitudes to Articles 2 and 3, there is a widespread unwillingness to make concessions which might placate Unionist opposition to unity.

The Response of the Parties

And where does this leave the parties? More specifically, what do these figures suggest about the potential electoral kudos – if any – to be gained from adopting a more militant nationalism? As might be expected, the answer varies according to the individual party concerned. On the spectrum of territorial nationalism Irish parties can be ranked according to their militancy from Sinn Fein at one extreme, through Fianna Fáil, Labour (essentially neutral) and Fine Gael, to the Workers' Party (which currently advocates a socialist transformation both North and South before unity can be achieved but which does not mobilise on this 'anti-nationalist' platform). Voters can also be ranked on this spectrum, ranging from the minority who advocate militant support for unity, through the vast majority who aspire to unity but who are unwilling to do anything about it, to the minority who are actually opposed to unity.

Thus, on the surface, it appears that none of the major parties has an interest in mobilising outright opposition to unity – to do so would be to risk the alienation of the large electoral block in the centre of the spectrum. On the other hand, none of the major parties might be expected to mobilise militant anti-partitionism, since this might also alienate the centre block, composed as it is of voters who aspire to unity but who also worry about the economic, social and political costs of realising this aspiration. The risk of losing any significant support is always uppermost in the minds of party managers, for the electoral system of proportional representation in the Republic would ensure that this was automatically translated into a fall in the numbers of seats held by the party in the Dáil. On the face of it, therefore, one would expect an all-party consensus aimed at promoting the idea of unity while at the same time being careful to do nothing to achieve it. This certainly was the case throughout the 1960s and also, apart from a few grumblings within Fianna Fáil, for much of the 1970s. It is not the case in the 1980s.

One of the most important factors in disturbing this soft nationalist consensus in the Republic in the 1980s has been the emergence of Sinn Fein as an electoral force, both North and South.[25] The emergence of Sinn Fein in the North prompted the establishment of the New Ireland Forum in an attempt to restore the electoral fortunes of the SDLP and, in the process, forced the parties of the Republic into a much more conscious statement of their nationalist beliefs than had ever occurred before. This inevitably led to an exposure of the fundamental fracture in the nationalist consensus. Sinn Fein has also begun to pressure for space on the political stage of the Republic, however, and it is this intervention which is perhaps most crucial, for it acts as an extremist threat to Fianna Fáil on the nationalist political spectrum, and forces the latter – at least temporarily – to abjure the type of centre-seeking strategy promoted by Lemass and Lynch.

The Sinn Fein threat in absolute terms should not be exaggerated. The anti-H Block candidates managed to win only 2.5 per cent of the poll in 1981, and Sinn Fein itself won just 1 per cent in the February 1982 elections. But each vote which accrues to Sinn Fein, and each seat which it may win (two abstentionist anti-H Block candidates were elected in 1981) can be considered, with reasonable certainty, as a vote or a seat which would otherwise have gone to Fianna Fáil. Hence, however insignificant the Sinn Fein challenge might seem to be, it nevertheless is a challenge which threatens only Fianna Fáil. The other two main parties are relatively immune, as neither is in a position to compete for the militant nationalist vote. More importantly, however, the increased profile of Sinn Fein, both North and South, inevitably stimulates a more militant position among those voters who would welcome unity almost regardless of cost. And again, history and tradition suggest that these are more likely to be inclined towards Fiana Fáil. Thus Fianna Fáil is threatened in two senses: it is obliged to head off the direct challenge of Sinn Fein, and it must confront a growing anti-partitionist militancy within its own ranks. In neither instance can we anticipate equivalent problems for Fine Gael or Labour.

Thus while Fine Gael and Labour can more or less throw caution to the winds and compete for the broad block of voters in the centre of the nationalist political spectrum, Fianna Fáil must compete on two fronts. The party must attempt to appease more militant anti-partitionist sentiment while at the same time take care not to alienate those who simply aspire to unity. The Green Card is both asset and liability, and the party finds itself squeezed from both sides. This is not an enviable position.

What makes the Fianna Fáil position doubly difficult is the fact that those voters in the broad centre who simply aspire to unity can take the Fine Gael and Labour position as read. The *aspiration* to unity is now so ingrained in popular perceptions that those parties which reflect it need not even emphasise it. Conversely, any attempt to appease more militant anti-partitionist sentiment must be articulated. Thus Fine Gael and Labour can happily go to the country solely on social and economic issues and will not, in the process, alienate mainstream nationalist opinion, which can take their commitment to unity as a given. If, on the other hand, Fianna Fáil goes to the country solely on social and economic issues, its platform will be judged inadequate by those who wish to press the anti-partition demand. And while this was not a problem in 1977, when Fianna Fáil did devote its election programme almost entirely to social and economic policy, it is likely to pose a problem in the 1980s, in the wake of the mobilisation of Sinn Fein. Finally, if Fianna Fáil goes to the country on social and economic issues and a more militant anti-partitionism, it will reinforce its support among the more militant minority, but it will also risk alienating those who simply aspire to unity and otherwise might have welcomed the remainder of the Fianna Fáil platform. Again, it must be emphasised that the dilemma belongs largely to Fianna Fáil alone. More vocal anti-partitionist sentiment does not impact across the entire nationalist spectrum. It must also be emphasised that these considerations apply only to election campaigning itself, when votes are being sought. Once in the Dáil, alternative considerations may play a larger role, and certainly all three major parties devote a substantially greater time to Northern Ireland in the Dáil than they do when on the hustings.

Mention should also be made of the different party approaches to economic and social matters. In broad terms, Fine Gael adopts a neo-liberal stance on such issues, although its brand of monetarism is not as extreme as the Thatcherite version. In the last coalition government the emphasis was placed on reducing public expenditure and the new Progressive Democrats have a similar line on the economy promoting the new entrepreneurial economy. Fianna Fáil's economic policies, which owe more to the party's Republican past and its clientilist approach to politics than to any sophisticated economic theory, are of a soft Keynesian variety. In government the party normally increases public expenditure and establishes some type of corporatist arrangement with the employers and trade unions. It was not coincidental that one of Haughey's first actions as Taoiseach after the 1987 election was to bring together the 'social partners' for talks to establish a common strategy for economic recovery. As Irish voters begin to pay less attention to traditional nationalism, these differing approaches to economic and social issues will become the most important factor in deciding which party governs.

From Consensus to Conflict

The soft nationalist consensus of the 1960s and 70s had placed unity on the back burner. The focus of concern was the 26-county state. But while the recrudescence of violence in Northern Ireland had not forced a fundamental shift from this position, it nevertheless did oblige the parties at least to address the question of unity. Indeed, given the extent of nationalist mobilisation in Northern Ireland, it was inevitable that the precise nature of the aspiration to unity would require reassessment. The problem was, how could this be done without involving the Republic in a new, and probably unpopular, anti-partitionist drive? On the one hand, few of the political leaders were willing to follow the line advocated by Blaney or Boland and make a united Ireland a major political priority – to do so would be to risk electoral suicide. On the other hand, few wished to follow the apparently 'anti-national' stance of Conor Cruise O'Brien – that would also be to risk electoral suicide. In short, the problem was one of trying to cope with the Northern Ireland problem without either abandoning the aspiration to unity and at the same time not doing anything about it.

A new departure was required, and the key element in this new departure was to be the recognition that opposition to unity did not exist only in Westminster, but was also a feature of opinion within Northern Ireland itself. If unity were to be achieved, then it involved more than simply a British commitment to withdrawal; it also necessitated a willingness on the part of a majority in Northern Ireland to unite with the Republic, and this in turn necessitated an emphasis on effecting a major reconstruction of prevailing practices in the Republic itself. In other words, a focus on the domestic politics of the 26-county state could at the same time be seen to be doing something about territorial unity. On the face of it, this seemed an ideal solution to the problem: nationalist credentials would not be impugned, while the 26-county focus could remain intact.

At the risk of over-generalisation, much of the constitutional policy of the Republic since the late 1960s can be read as an enduring attempt to facilitate unity through the promotion of a more pluralist or accommodationist politics in the Republic itself. The 26-county focus remained, but the aspiration to unity was to be accommodated nonetheless. This process began with the 1967 Committee on the Constitution, the main three recommendations of which were to modify the prohibition on divorce, to remove the Article which accorded a special position to the Catholic church, and to modify Articles 2 and 3 in order to reflect an aspiration rather than a territorial claim to unity.

No action was then taken on these recommendations, but a referendum in 1972 did delete the reference to the special position to the Catholic church. The next step in this direction came in 1973 when, as part of the Sunningdale Agreement, the then (Fine Gael-Labour) government of the Republic 'solemnly declared that there would be no change in the status of Northern Ireland until a majority of the people of Northern Ireland desired a change in that status'.[26] That same government attempted – without success – a liberalisation of the anti-contraception legislation, which was eventually realised (by Fianna Fáil) in 1979, and further extended (by Fine Gael and Labour) in 1985. Most recently, however, accommodationist politics has received a significant battering in the passage of an anti-abortion Constitutional amendment in 1983 and in the hugely unsuccessful attempt to secure the passage of a referendum permitting divorce in 1986.[27]

The high point of this accommodationist drive can be dated in 1981, and to the 'Constitutional Crusade' pledged by FitzGerald shortly after his election as Taoiseach. The crusade was to be a conscious attempt to reconstitute political culture in the Republic along pluralist lines, a harking back to the more conciliatory and diversified ethos which had characterised Irish Republicanism in the late eighteenth and early nineteenth centuries. In essence, the intention was to move away from an intolerant and majoritarian Catholic nationalism. 'I believe that this part of the country has slipped into a partitionist attitude', stated FitzGerald when announcing his new crusade.

> We have created here something which the Northern Protestants find unacceptable ... What I want to do is to lead a crusade – a Republican crusade – to make this a genuine Republic on the principles of Tone and Davis ... I believe we could have the basis then on which many Protestants in Northern Ireland would be willing to consider a relationship with us, who at present have no reason to do so ... Our laws, constitution and our practices are not acceptable to the Protestants of Northern Ireland.[28]

By 1981, however, the accommodationist drive no longer enjoyed bipartisan endorsement. In so far as it had fitted into the ethos of the new, Lemass-style nationalism, accommodationism had earlier proved a welcome strategy to both Fianna Fáil and the coalition parties. Lemass himself had been a key figure in the 1967 Committee on the Constitution, and the Sunningdale package – negotiated while the coalition held office – had been welcomed by Fianna Fáil. The referendum to delete the Constitutional recognition of the special position of the Catholic church had been sponsored by a Fianna Fáil government, as had the first liberalisation of the ban on contraception. The election of Charles Haughey as leader of Fianna Fáil, however, signalled the end of this cross-party co-operation.

One could speculate endlessly on the reasons for this change. Haughey's personal commitment to a more militant Republicanism is clearly a major factor in the equation, but it is much more difficult to determine whether his election to the leadership of Fianna Fáil was a cause of the shifting attitudes or simply a consequence. As noted already, the heightened political profile of Sinn Fein was also important, in that it obliged Fianna Fáil to defend its Republican flank while at the same time it undoubtedly stimulated a resurgence of Republican feeling in the grass roots of the party. Again, one need only recall the opinion poll evidence recording a growing sympathy for the motives – if not the strategy – of the IRA. Finally, one can suggest that the severe crisis of Fianna Fáil's economic strategy in the late 1970s induced a return to traditional nationalist politics as a last-ditch attempt to salvage some political respectability: the appeal to economic expansionism no longer seemed credible, and Fianna Fáil was thus obliged to revert to a more traditional method of cementing its broad political coalition.

For whatever reason, the beginning of the 1980s witnessed the breakdown of the soft nationalist consensus, one of the immediate consequences of which was to be the collapse of the policy of accommodation – a collapse exemplified in the outcome of the abortion and divorce referendums. Haughey's accession to the Fianna Fáil leadership had followed months of intra-party dissent, one of the key components of which had been a sustained attack on Lynch's leadership for failing to reflect the traditional nationalist emphasis of the party. In September 1979, for example, Sile De Valera, the grand-daughter of Eamon and then a back-bench Fianna Fail TD, had delivered a highly-publicised speech accusing Lynch of abandoning the ideals of her grandfather. In the first year of Haughey's leadership, great emphasis was placed on the need to effect agreement between Dublin and Westminster as a precondition for unity: improved relations within Northern Ireland itself, and the furthering of a rapprochement between North and South were of secondary importance, since Northern Ireland was, in the famous Haughey phrase, 'a failed political entity'. If the soft nationalist consensus of the late 1960s and 1970s had recognised the relevance of Unionist opposition to unity, the new Haughey line was to re-emphasise the relevance of the British position. Thus, by May 1980, in the first of three articles in the *Irish Times* on Dublin's view of the Northern problem, Dennis Kennedy could assert that 'the ending of the British guarantee, and a British declaration of interest in encouraging the unity of Ireland seem the bare bones of Mr Haughey's Northern policy'.[29] Later in the series he was to ask: 'has unity by consent been abandoned?'[30]

In sum, the 1980s have witnessed the emergence of significant inter-party divisions on the Northern Ireland issue. While each of the main parties endorses the aspiration to unity, there is no longer a consensus on the means necessary to achieve it. For FitzGerald and the mainstream of both Fine Gael and Labour, the emphasis is on unity by consent. The strategy involves emphasising policies designed to bring an end to the conflict in Northern Ireland – the priority on peace and stability – to be accompanied by an emphasis on liberalising the laws and practices in the Republic itself. Then, and only then, can one speak of the possibility of unity. The emphasis is on a politics of accommodation (in both North and South) and on the unity of peoples rather than simply of territory. For Fianna Fáil, on the other hand, the emphasis is on territorial unity as a means of achieving peace and stability, and policy is oriented towards effecting a British declaration of intent to withdraw from Northern Ireland. If reform in the Republic should be necessary, then this can wait until the moment of unification, when a more liberal Constitution can be negotiated on an all-Ireland basis. Alan Shatter of Fine Gael caught the difference quite succinctly during the Dáil debate on the Anglo-Irish Agreement when he said:

Personally I would accord much greater importance ... to the achievement of unity and reconciliation between peoples than to the achievement of territorial unity. To Fianna Fáil it appears that the territorial imperative comes first.[31]

The Anglo-Irish Agreement

These inter-party tensions were brought to a head when FitzGerald signed the Anglo-Irish Agreement in late 1985. The key source of tension is the formalisation of the notion of unity by consent in the Agreement, that is a formal acceptance that the eventual unity of Ireland was predicated on the consent of a majority in the island as a whole. In other words, it is a formalisation of the accommodationist stance favoured by FitzGerald and rejected by Haughey. To be sure, as noted above, the practical necessity of achieving consent has been accepted by Fianna Fáil, but this was far removed from an acceptance in principle. 'Does that mean', asked an incredulous Haughey during the Dáil debate on the Agreement, 'that if the British government decide to leave Ireland or to legislate for Irish unity, Irish nationalists could not accept it unless the Unionists consented?'[32]

In essence, Fianna Fáil view the majority consent clause in the Agreement as a principled recognition of the right of the majority in Northern Ireland to refuse to join a united Ireland, and it was this which was to prove unacceptable. The Agreement itself was to be formally registered with the United Nations and, as Haughey pointed out, this made it 'different in character from anything stated in a communiqué. No Fianna Fáil government has ever concluded a formal agreement, involving recognition of Northern Ireland as a *de jure* part of the United Kingdom.'[33] As a result of this Agreement, he argued, 'we have, in fact, renounced our claim to unity.'[34]

This is not just a question of semantics. Traditional Irish nationalism sees the island of Ireland as an historically defined and indivisible nation, its destiny the prerogative of a majority of its people. No minority has a right to opt out of that nation, even if that minority constitutes a majority in one section of the national territory. In this sense, while partition is a reality which must be addressed, it has no moral or cultural legitimacy. Partition was imposed by Britain and is sustained by Britain and, as such, runs counter to the right of the Irish people to their own national territory, a right enshrined in Articles 2 and 3 of the Constitution. It is important to reiterate that these Articles do not reflect simply an aspiration to unity. Rather, the right to unity is asserted and sovereignty is claimed over the island as a whole.

For Garret FitzGerald and Fine Gael in 1985, on the other hand, the new accommodationist politics had elevated majority consent to the status of a principle. As FitzGerald emphasised when introducing the Dáil motion in favour of the Agreement, the 'aspiration to the political unity of this island is, as a matter of political and moral principle, conditional on the consent of a majority of the people of Northern Ireland' and, as might have been expected, such a position was seen to contravene the essential tenets of traditional Irish nationalism.[35] The Fianna Fáil response was therefore wholly predictable. While stating that 'we recognise fully the need to improve the situation of the nationalist community in the North of Ireland and we approve and support any effective measure taken on their behalf,' Haughey emphasised that 'we cannot accept ... the abandonment of our claim to Irish unity or the recognition of British sovereignty over the North of Ireland which is involved in this agreement.'[36] 'No government', he added later, 'no temporary majority has the right to sign away the rights of the Irish people.'[37]

Such inter-party conflict on the Agreement seems to open the possibility that Fianna Fáil may gain the monopoly of the available nationalist credentials. The electoral advantages of such a shift would seem undeniable: as Conor Cruise O'Brien has noted, 'In Ireland there is one condition that is decidedly more frowned upon than being a bad Catholic, and that is the condition of being *anti-national*.'[38] That Fianna Fáil stood alone in defence of traditional nationalism was certainly apparent to Haughey. Concluding his Dáil response to the Agreement he asserted that 'We will stand for our nationalist ideals, ideals that up until recently we believed were shared by all parties. We are not going to abandon the basic reason for our foundation as a political movement.'[39] Brian Lenihan, another senior figure in the party, put it more graphically: 'We now find ourselves as a lone party with the nationalist forces.'[40] The claim was disputed by Peter Barry, deputy leader of Fine Gael: 'we should all admit that no party on the nationalist side has a monopoly on Republicanism. No party is the only true guardian of the precious heritage of nationalism.'[41] However, the message was clear: in a contest of nationalist prowess, Fianna Fáil would be the inevitable victor. Fine Gael and Labour had been seen to renege on the nationalist heritage, and a massive popular rejection of their position would follow. Thus when Lenihan posited Fianna Fáil as the lone bastion of traditional nationalism he went on to add, 'We are very proud of that because the Irish people will support us and this will be reflected in the results of the next general election.'[42]

But was this simply bravado? How much genuine electoral kudos would accrue to a party claiming a monopoly of traditional nationalist credentials? As noted above, the vast bulk of the electorate would seem unwilling to go beyond simply the aspiration to unity, and would certainly be reluctant to suffer the potential economic, social and political costs involved. Opinion poll evidence also consistently shows that at election times voters are primarily concerned with issues such as unemployment, inflation, government expenditure, security and the like, while Northern Ireland ranks as a priority for only a tiny minority. While the recent referenda have shown that voters are reluctant to endorse an accommodationist stance in the Republic, it also seems evident that they are equally unlikely to endorse a militant anti-partitionist politics.

Haughey himself thus proved much more cautious than Lenihan in assessing the potential electoral consequences of the Fianna Fáil position: in the immediate wake of Hillsborough, for instance, he told the *Irish Times* that despite their criticisms, Fianna Fáil would not make the Agreement a major campaign issue; rather, they would be 'going to the country on economic issues'.[43] His caution was justified. Shortly after the Dáil debate the *Irish Times* published the first opinion poll on the issue, which showed that the Agreement enjoyed majority popular endorsement (59 per cent) despite the widespread belief that it was not going to advance the cause of unity, and, perhaps more importantly, it showed that an almost equally large majority (56 per cent) opposed the critical stance adopted by Fianna Fáil.[4]

Thus however important traditional nationalism may be to

the inter-party differences as evidenced in the Dáil, it is unlikely
to play a significant role in the competition for electoral support.
When votes are at stake, the issue of Irish unity is marginalised.
Both party behaviour and popular opinion reflect the
pragmatism of the new nationalism, however fractured the
consensus may be at the elite level.

Conclusion

What is the state of nationalist politics in the Republic in the
wake of the Anglo-Irish Agreement? First of all, there can be
little doubt that the conciliatory approach of Garret FitzGerald
and the coalition government is endorsed by mainstream
popular opinion. However pervasive the aspiration to unity,
there is a general consensus against going out on a limb to
achieve it. Irish voters will choose their parties on the basis of
their domestic social and economic policies; they will not allow
attitudes to unity to divert them from more mundane material
interests. That said, there are two caveats which must be
underlined. First, this does not imply that a party which rejects
the aspiration to unity could hope to win majority support,
however popular its domestic policies might otherwise be. Even
if Irish voters do not endorse militant anti-partitionism, they
nevertheless do want their parties to reiterate the anti-
partitionist aspiration. As far as the main parties are
concerned, therefore, the best strategy is to pledge themselves in
favour of unity and then to do nothing about it, but instead
concentrate on domestic promises and favours – in short, to do
exactly as they have been doing throughout the 1960s and 70s.
The second caveat is also important. In so far as Irish voters are
concerned about the material well-being and stability of the
Republic, they are unlikely to endorse a Northern Ireland policy
which might threaten this. Thus they will be wary of any policy
which might lead to a seepage of violence south of the border, or
any policy which might involve the Republic directly with
Northern Ireland Unionists.

The second major conclusion which can be drawn relates to
these points: any party which might emphasise or prioritise Irish
unity is unlikely to command a majority of electoral support.
This is fine as far as Fine Gael and Labour are concerned, since

their policies involve promoting reconciliation within the North and the South. The coalition priority is peace, not unity. For Fianna Fáil, however, the answer is not so simple. Faced with the sniping of Sinn Fein on its Republican flank, and confronting a more vocal anti-partitionism within its own ranks, Fianna Fáil is almost obliged to prioritise unity. To do otherwise is to risk a drift from its own ranks to Sinn Fein. 'We are the moral barrier against a violent and abhorrent form of nationalism,' claimed Haughey during the Dáil debate. 'It would be grossly irresponsible of us to abandon the cause of Irish nationalism, the ideal of a united Ireland and to hand it over as the exclusive property of those prepared to pursue it by violent means.'[45] At the same time, however, the party is aware that to prioritise unity is to risk the alienation of the large majority of voters in the centre of the nationalist political spectrum: thus, concluding his Dáil speech, Haughey insisted that 'Regardless of whether it costs us votes or popularity, we are not prepared to surrender by desertion the constitutional nationalist position.'[46] So how does the party escape the dilemma? The answer already seems implicit in Haughey's remarks immediately after the Hillsborough Agreement: the party would fly the unity banner in the Dáil, in party meetings and in party conferences, but would not make it a major campaign issue in a general election. Haughey would clearly establish his nationalist credentials, but would avoid seeking votes on that basis. Then, if Fianna Fáil managed to win the next election on 'economic issues', its victory could be magically read as a mandate for Irish unity. It is a reasonably clever strategy, and could well be successful – Fianna Fáil strategy generally is. In this case, however, there is already evidence of difficulty, in that the more militant line adopted by the party has prompted the departure of Desmond O'Malley and Mary Harney and their formation of the new Progressive Democrats party. The new party endorses the FitzGerald line on the Agreement, and in so doing harks back to the nationalist consensus of the 1960s and 70s. Moreover, it also managed to win the support of two other dissident Fianna Fáil TDs, as well as that of a dissident Fine Gael TD, and eventually won 12 per cent of the popular vote and fourteen Dáil seats in the 1987 election.

The third major conclusion concerns accommodationist politics. For whatever reasons, in the recent referenda Irish voters have clearly shown a reluctance to see the state advancing in a more liberal or pluralist direction. The Agreement may have won popular endorsement; accommodationist politics have not. Thus any steps towards unity from this particular direction also seem doomed to failure. A policy of transforming the Republic into a state fit for a large Protestant minority seems as unlikely to achieve popular support as does a policy of militant anti-partitionism. A policy of prioritising pluralism seems as likely to lose votes as does a policy of prioritising unity.

In the end, the most important finding is also the most prosaic. In the MORI survey of 1984, some 54 per cent of respondents were of the belief that unity would leave the Republic worse off financially, and this is perhaps the most crucial variable of all. Those concerned with British policy towards Northern Ireland would do well to take note of this, for while a demand for British withdrawal might win support in Britain itself, there is good reason to believe that it would be greeted with something close to horror in the Republic. Moreover, the failure of accommodationist politics suggests that even the much vaunted 'harmonisation policy', currently under consideration by the British Labour Party, would be unlikely to generate a favourable response in the Republic. Irish voters are content with a status quo in which the aspiration is loudly proclaimed, while no further action is contemplated.

The overall conclusion is then inescapable. The vast bulk of Irish voters are not interested in Northern Ireland, and are not interested in pursuing Irish unity – regardless of the means being advocated. There are no votes in 32-county nationalism. Thus any real move to press for Irish unity, be it from within the Republic itself, from Northern Ireland, or from Britain, is unlikely to be welcomed by the average citizen in the Republic. Unity would be nice. But if it's going to cost money, or result in violence, or disrupt the moral and social equilibrium, then it's not worth it. Certainly, politics in the Republic is about nationalism, but for much of the post-war epoch the vision of that nationalism has extended only to the 26 counties.

Postscript

As had been anticipated, the general election campaign in February 1987 was almost wholly dominated by economic issues, which, in this case, proved sufficiently crucial to force a new polarisation between the left (Labour and the Workers' Party) and the right (Fine Gael and the Progressive Democrats), while Fianna Fáil endeavoured to hold the centre ground.[47]

Sinn Fein contested 24 of the 41 constituencies, having abandoned its abstentionist strategy for the first time ever, and polled only 1.9 per cent of the popular vote. Both Fine Gael, with 27.1 per cent of the total vote, and Labour, whose coalition alliance had broken down in January following Labour's withdrawal from government, suffered a major erosion of their electoral support. Labour polled 6.4 per cent of first preference votes, a drop of nearly a third from the previous General Election and the party's worse performance since 1933. Several of its candidates, including its leader Dick Spring, scraped through by a handful of votes, and Labour's long-term prospects are far from bright. The Workers' Party, which unashamedly gives priority to economic issues in the South rather than 'the national question', stood in selected constituencies and received 3.8 per cent of the total vote, doubling its representation in the Dáil to four TDs. In the Dublin area the Workers' Party outvoted the Labour Party, which has always been a leading ally of the SDLP in its constitutionalist search for a united Ireland, and the party's success only serves to underline the extent to which economic rather than traditional Republican issues are the prime concern of the Republic's working class. Fianna Fáil also polled relatively badly, winning 44.1 per cent of first preference votes, its lowest vote since 1961. Although disillusionment with government in a context of severe economic recession might have been expected to benefit Fianna Fáil as the major alternative, the new Progressive Democrats acted as a crucial buffer in deflecting the swing. Indeed, the majority of the PDs' 12 per cent of the poll appears to have been drawn from the middle-class constituency of Fine Gael. When the Dáil reassembled on 11 March, Charles Haughey was elected Taoiseach with the help of the casting vote of the Ceann Comhairle (Speaker), and Fianna Fáil has now formed a minority government. The following day, Garret

FitzGerald resigned the leadership of Fine Gael.

The 1987 election and its aftermath offer an interesting perspective on Northern Ireland as a contemporary issue in the domestic politics of the Republic. As has been the pattern in recent years, the party programmes paid Northern Ireland scant attention. Labour allocated the problem just four lines in a 22-page programme, pledging the pursuit of 'peace and stability' in that section of its policy headed 'Ireland and Our Neighbours', and did not even mention the desirability of unity. Fine Gael also failed to emphasise unity, although it did devote almost three pages of its 72-page programme to heralding the achievements of the Anglo-Irish Agreement, and also claimed that the pledge by Britain to legislate for unity in the event that a majority of the people of Northern Ireland so desired it, had 'effectively removed the British question from Irish politics'. The Progressive Democrats pledged themselves in favour 'peace and reconciliation', endorsed the Anglo-Irish Agreement, and, in a separate policy document on the administration of justice, called for a 're-phrasing [of] Articles 2 and 3 in order to make clear that we favour unity by consent'. Nobody was going out on a nationalist limb.

Except perhaps Fianna Fáil. In the event, however, even Fianna Fáil was cautious. Thus while its Northern Ireland policy (one page in a 71-page programme) began by reasserting the belief 'that a united Ireland brought about by democratic means forms the best and most durable basis for peace and stability in Ireland', and while it also reiterated that Fianna Fáil 'cannot accept the constitutional aspects of the Anglo-Irish Agreement', such nationalist pledges were wrapped around with qualifications. Thus the commitment to unity was explicitly linked to the conclusions of the *all*-party Forum Report, while opposition to the Agreement was accompanied by a commitment to 'support any worthwhile reforms or improvement in the position of the Nationalist community that could be brought about through the [Anglo-Irish] Conference'.

The ambiguity of the Fianna Fáil attitude eventually emerged with some significance in the final days of the four-week election campaign. During the television debate between the party leaders, for example, FitzGerald accused Haughey of wishing to renegotiate the accord, and while Haughey insisted that 'we

cannot accept – Fianna Fáil and I personally – affording as a
matter of principle any recognition of sovereignty over any part
of this country to Great Britain,' he also expressed his regret
that Northern Ireland had emerged as an election issue, and
stated that his party would follow precedent and accept as
binding any formal treaty made between the outgoing
government and another sovereign power.[48]

This ambiguity persisted through to polling day and after, and
has been only partially resolved since the formation of the
Fianna Fáil minority government. Fianna Fail remains unhappy
with the 'constitutional implications' of the Agreement, but
nonetheless is committed to make it work. During the American
celebrations of St Patrick's Day, for example, Haughey was
willing to witness Ronald Reagan's signature of the certificate
authorising the transfer of $50 million as part of the US
administration's support for the Agreement, and which was
dependent on the new government's commitment to work within
and develop the accord. Brian Lenihan, the new Minister for
Foreign Affairs and now co-chairman of the Conference, proved
equally supportive of the Agreement, despite his own earlier and
quite virulent opposition mentioned above; speaking at a dinner
in Washington, for example, Lenihan was quite unequivocal in
insisting that; 'We will use the conference to improve the
position of nationalists in Northern Ireland.'[49]

Thus it now seems very unlikely that the new Fianna Fáil
government will attempt to effect a renegotiation – at least in the
short term. To be sure, the party may be unwilling to pursue the
accord with any enthusiasm, but a commitment to renegotiation
would demand placing the question of unity in a very prominent
place on the political agenda, and few voters would be willing to
countenance such a shift. Moreover, the Agreement itself
represents one of the very few issues which might effect a
combination of left and right in the Dáil against Fianna Fáil in
the centre. As a minority government, Fianna Fáil can survive
through to a full term only in so far as its opposition remains
divided within itself along left-right lines; and as long as the
issues relate to the economy and the welfare state, such a
division is more or less guaranteed. Were Fianna Fáil to
challenge the Agreement, on the other hand, it could well unite
Labour, the Workers' Party, Fine Gael and the Progressive

Democrats, and such a voting block could spell an end to this vulnerable Haughey administration.

That said, the issue of the Agreement will inevitably come onto the agenda in November 1988, when it is due for its first triennial review. Whether Fianna Fáil will then attempt to renegotiate the terms must remain a matter of speculation, but whether Fianna Fáil is still in government in November 1988 must also remain a matter of speculation. What is certain, however, is that Irish voters will be primarily concerned about their pocketbooks for the foreseeable future, while Northern Ireland will remain a foreign country.

Notes

* I would like to thank Leigh Hancher, Robert Millar and Paul Teague for their valuable comments on an earlier draft of this essay.
[1] *Irish Times*, 11 November 1985.
[2] See Tom Garvin, *The Evolution of Irish Nationalist Politics*, Dublin 1981.
[3] *Dáil Debates*, 361:2883-4, 20 November 1985.
[4] M. Rainer Lepsius, 'The Nation and Nationalism in Germany', *Social Research*, Vol.52, No1.1 (1985), p. 43.
[5] Ibid., p. 44.
[6] Padraig O'Malley, *The Uncivil Wars: Ireland Today*, Belfast 1983, p. 62.
[7] IRA statement quoted in J. Bowyer Bell, *The Secret Army: The IRA 1916-1979*, Dublin 1979, p. 334.
[8] David B. Rottman and Philip J. O'Connell, 'The Changing Social Structure' in Frank Litton (ed), *Unequal Achievement: The Irish Experience 1957-1982*, Dublin 1982, p. 67.
[9] Maria Maguire, *The Development of the Welfare State in Ireland in the Post-war Period*, Florence 1985, p. 295.
[10] John Blackwell, 'Government, Economy and Society', in Litton (ed.) op. cit., p. 43.
[11] In, for example, Paul Bew and Henry Patterson, *Sean Lemass and the Making of Modern Ireland, 1945-66*, Dublin 1982.
[12] Richard Rose, Ian McAllister and Peter Mair, *Is There a Concurring Majority About Northern Ireland?*, Glasgow 1978.
[13] W. Harvey Cox, 'Who Wants a United Ireland?', *Government and Opposition*, Vol.4 No.1, 1985.
[14] The polls were conducted by IMS (1970), MRBI (1974 and 1983), and MORI (1984).
[15] The polls were conducted by IMS (1973, 1977 and 1980), and IMS/Gallup (1978).
[16] MRBI poll.

[17] The polls were conducted by IMS/Gallup (1978), IMS (1980) and MORI (1984).

[18] The polls were conducted by Gallup (1968), Gallup/IMS (1978) and MORI (1984).

[19] MORI poll.

[20] Cox, op. cit.

[21] *Dáil Debates* 361: 2883-84, 20 November 1985.

[22] IMS poll.

[23] Lansdown Market Research poll.

[24] MORI poll. This same poll recorded only 37 per cent in favour removing the Constitutional ban on divorce as a gesture to the North, a proportion almost identical to that voting in favour of the change in the 1986 referendum.

[25] Of course there are also other factors involved. It can be argued, for example, that the incapacity of Lemass-style nationalism to flourish in a period of economic and social recession has forced Fianna Fail to revert to a more traditional nationalism in order to maintain the cohesion of its cross-class electoral coalition. See Bew and Patterson, op. cit., and Peter Mair, *The Changing Irish Party System*, London, forthcoming.

[26] Quoted in Ian McAllister, *The Northern Ireland Social Democratic and Labour Party*, London, 1977, p. 131.

[27] Many of these recent church-state issues are discussed in John Cooney, *The Crozier and the Dáil*, Cork, 1986.

[28] Quoted in ibid., pp. 7-8.

[29] *Irish Times*, 19 May 1980.

[30] Ibid., 20 May 1980.

[31] *Dáil Debates*, 361: 2978-80, 21 November 1985.

[32] Ibid., 361: 2597, 19 November 1985.

[33] Ibid., 361: 2590. 19 November 1985.

[34] Ibid., 361: 2586. 19 November 1985, emphasis added.

[35] Ibid., 361: 2569, 19 November 1985.

[36] Ibid., 361: 2581, 19 November 1985.

[37] Ibid., 361: 2599, 19 November 1985.

[38] Conor Cruise O'Brien, *States of Ireland*, London 1972, p. 197.

[39] *Dáil Debates*, 361: 2600, 19 November 1985.

[40] Ibid., 361: 3122, 21 November 1985.

[41] Ibid., 361: 3133, 21 November 1985.

[42] Ibid., 361: 3122, 21 November 1985.

[43] *Irish Times*, 16 November 1985.

[44] MRBI poll, *Irish Times*, 23 November 1985.

[45] *Dáil Debates*, 361: 2599-600, 19 November 1985.

[46] Ibid., 361: 2600, 19 November 1985.

[47] See the discussion in Chapter 5 of Mair, op. cit.

[48] *Irish Times*, 13 February 1987.

[49] Ibid., 18 March 1987.

Bob Rowthorn

Northern Ireland: An Economy in Crisis

It is now almost twenty years since British troops were sent to Northern Ireland, and the conflict in the province continues with no end in sight. A great deal has been written about the economic and political background to this conflict, but relatively little about what has actually happened since it first began in 1969. This essay has been written in an attempt to fill this gap; for reasons of space and time it is highly selective, and a number of important questions are ignored or touched upon only in passing. In particular, explicit discussions of politics has been kept to a minimum, and the emphasis is mainly upon economic questions. The essay is divided into four parts. It begins with a detailed examination of the economic crisis which beset the province in the 1970s. The second part poses the question whether the crisis has reduced Northern Ireland to a workhouse economy: to answer this a detailed 'national' accounts balance sheet has been compiled for the first time. The next part contrasts the economic fortunes of Northern Ireland with those of the Republic of Ireland. It concludes with some general observations about future prospects and possibilities.

Crisis and Decay

Since the early 1970s the economy of Northern Ireland has experienced a dramatic reversal of fortunes. The province has been gripped by a prolonged industrial crisis, the rapid growth of the preceding decade has been reversed and industrial output is now well below the historic peak achieved in 1973. Industrial employment has fallen by around 40 per cent and some industries, like synthetic fibres, have virtually disappeared. In the initial years of the crisis, falling industrial employment was

111

offset by a rapid increase in service employment, especially in the public services, which experienced a spectacular expansion under the Tory administration of Health and the ensuing Labour administration of Wilson and Callaghan. As a result, total employment continued to rise during the 1970s despite the industrial crisis. The expansion of public services in Northern Ireland during this period was financed by the UK government using revenue derived mainly from taxes levied on people living on the British mainland. Since the Thatcher administration took office in 1979, however, government policy has altered radically. The Thatcher government is unwilling to finance further large-scale expansion of the public services in Northern Ireland, and employment in this sector of the economy is now virtually stable. Meanwhile, industrial employment continues to fall and, for the first time in post-war history, there has also been a significant fall in the number of people employed in private services. Under the Thatcher government, all major types of employment in Northern Ireland are either stagnant or in decline. This is reflected in a sharp increase in the unemployment rate, which is now well over 20 per cent.

The social impact of the economic crisis in Northern Ireland has been uneven. For many of those fortunate enough to keep their jobs, there has been a noticeable rise in living standards since the early 1970s. At the same time, the expansion of public service employment has meant the creation of many well paid professional jobs in health, education, the civil service, the police and the prison service. On the other hand, rising unemployment has led to a marked increase in the number of people living in poverty. This polarisation is visible in both religious communities. In both communities there has been a considerable rise in the number of public service professionals, and in both there has also been a sharp rise in the amount of unemployment and poverty, especially amongst manual workers. However, the situation is on average much worse for Catholics than for Protestants.

The above is a brief outline of the developments which have occurred in the economy of Northern Ireland since the early 1970s. Before going on to examine future prospects, let us first consider these developments in more detail.

The Industrial Crisis

In the early 1970s manufacturing industry continued to expand quite rapidly in Northern Ireland, and it was only the world slump of 1974 which brought this growth to a halt. Since then manufacturing industry has been in a state of more or less permanent crisis. Like Great Britain the province has experienced two major slumps, one in 1974 and the other in 1979-80. However, in Northern Ireland these slumps have been more severe than in Britain and recovery from them much weaker. Manufacturing employment has fallen almost continuously throughout the crisis, and by 1985 was over 40 per cent below its 1974 level. The decline has slowed down in the mid 1980s but has not stopped entirely, and the province is still losing manufacturing jobs at the rate of 1-2 per cent a year.

A striking feature of recent years has been the rapid growth in labour productivity. In the face of severe competition and tough market conditions firms have responded with a vigorous drive to reduce costs. Production methods have been rationalised and new labour-saving equipment installed, usually with generous financial aid from the British government. This response has helped many firms to survive which would otherwise have gone under. Even so, total manufacturing output has fallen. Between 1973 and 1985, Northern Ireland experienced a 17 per cent fall in manufacturing output, while at the same time there was a 41 per cent rise in output per worker. It is this combination of falling output and rising productivity which explains the spectacular fall in employment. Note that, despite the improvement in recent years, manufacturing productivity in Northern Ireland is still on average, about 15 per cent below the level in Great Britain.[1]

It is interesting to compare Northern Ireland's experience with that of the Irish Republic during the crisis. In both parts of Ireland, labour productivity has risen noticeably faster than in Great Britain. The increase has been greatest in the South, which has undergone a major structural shift from traditional to modern industries in recent years, but even so the productivity performance of the North has been impressive. The situation, however, is quite different when it comes to output. In the North, manufacturing output has fallen since the early 1970s by even more than in Great Britain. In the South, on the other hand, output has continued to rise strongly, albeit at an irregular pace. This increase in output has not been sufficient to prevent a fall in manufacturing employment in the South in recent years, but the fall has been less dramatic than in the North. The manufacturing sector of Southern Ireland may not be an unqualified success, but its performance is in all respects superior to that of Northern Ireland or, for that matter, Great Britain. The main reason for this difference is the South's continued ability to attract outside investment in modern, growth sectors of manufacturing industry. As we shall see below, this is an area where the North has conspicuously failed in recent years.

So far we have been discussing the manufacturing sector as a whole. As might be expected, the picture is more complex if we look at individual industries. A few industries have done well and managed to increase their output considerably despite the recession. Of these the most important are aircraft and motor vehicles and parts. Others – such as ship-building, clothing and chemicals – have so far weathered the storm and are showing signs of life in the mid-1980s. Finally, some industries have experienced a major fall in output, the most extreme example being the synthetic fibre industry which has gone from star performer to virtual collapse within the space of a few years.

Thus, on the output side, the picture is mixed and there are still some areas where Northern Ireland is doing quite well. On the employment side, however, the situation is more gloomy and the picture is one of widespread decline. There are, however, a few exceptions, like aircraft or motor vehicles and parts, where employment has increased. But the total number of jobs involved is fairly small and does not affect the general picture of an almost universal decline in manufacturing employment.

It is worth noting that even where firms have done well and managed to grow, or at least survive, under hostile market conditions, this has often been at considerable expense to the British government. Industrial subsidies in Northern Ireland are on average approximately twice as high as in other depressed areas of the United Kingdom.[2] In some cases the scale of these subsidies is truly remarkable; during the mid-1980s, for example, Harland and Wolff shipbuilders has received financial support averaging around £8,000 per job a year, which is almost sufficient to meet the entire wage and salary bill of the company.[3] Cumulatively, this company, which now employs less than 5,000 people, has received more than £500 million (at 1986 prices) in government aid.[4] Another example is Shorts, the aircraft manufacturer. This is often regarded as one of Northern Ireland's more successful companies because of its diversified product range and extensive sales in the USA and elsewhere. Even so, it has lost money almost every year since the mid-1970s, and after a profitable year in 1985 is once again in the red. These examples illustrate clearly the fragile nature of Northern Ireland's industrial base. The continued growth or even survival of many companies depends crucially on British government aid, without which they would be unviable in their present form. Indeed, despite massive government aid, both Harland and Wolff and Shorts are now in serious trouble and large-scale redundancies are imminent.

The industrial crisis in Northern Ireland is due to a combination of factors, of which the following are perhaps the most important: events in the world economy as a whole; the dependence of the Northern Ireland economy on exports to the UK; the industrial structure of Northern Ireland; the branch plant nature of the Northern Ireland economy and its dependence on outside firms; the armed conflict and political instability in the province.

Manufacturing industry in Northern Ireland is strongly export-oriented and therefore vulnerable to events in the outside world. The slow growth of the world economy since 1973 has undermined the export market for Northern Ireland's products in a variety of ways and has led to a more hostile competitive environment. The UK, which is Northern Ireland's main trading partner, has grown especially slowly during this period, thereby further reducing the demand for industrial exports. Moreover, at the start of the crisis in 1973 the economic structure of the province was unfavourable, with an above average share of problem industries like synthetic fibres and shipbuilding, both of which have suffered grievously throughout Western Europe.

The other factors listed above are of particular importance, not just in explaining the past, but because of their influence on future industrial prospects in Northern Ireland. Under the development strategy pursued before the crisis, the province became almost totally dependent on the goodwill of outside firms. Only 8.5 per cent of all industrial jobs promoted during the period 1946-67 were in companies indigenous to Northern Ireland.[5] As local firms disappeared they were replaced by the subsidiaries of large outside firms from the UK, the USA and elsewhere. These subsidiaries were typically 'branch plants' lacking both administrative autonomy and research and development facilities of their own. For their parent companies, the branch plants in Northern Ireland often functioned as marginal producers in providing valuable output in times of boom, but amongst the first to suffer cut-backs and closures in times of crisis. The transformation of Northern Ireland into a 'branch plant economy', dominated by producers of this type, made it extremely vulnerable to external shocks and when the world boom came to an end in 1974, it was inevitable that Northern Ireland would suffer disproportionality as giant firms rationalised their operations and closed down many of their marginal activities. Tobacco provides a good example. In response to falling demand for their products, the large tobacco firms have closed down many of their Northern Ireland facilities so as to concentrate production in core plants located elsewhere. The fate of tobacco and synthetic fibres illustrates vividly the vulnerability of a branch plant economy dominated by outside firms.

In the case of Northern Ireland, this vulnerability is of particular importance in view of the armed conflict now in progress. When deciding which plants to close down in the course of restructuring, a large firm will normally avoid risk and choose safe locations where the long-term security of operations is assured. In this respect, Northern Ireland is at a severe disadvantage when compared with more tranquil sites elsewhere in Europe. Although they are loath to admit it in public, the conflict is almost certainly a factor helping to explain why so many firms have closed their branch plants in the province over the past decade or so.

The conflict also helps to explain why so little new investment has been attracted to Northern Ireland during the past decade. Despite considerable financial inducements, few outside firms have been willing to undertake new investment in the province when other, more secure, sites are available in the South of

Ireland, Britain and elsewhere. A few exceptional firms have been attracted, but some of these, such as De Lorean and Lear Fan, have survived for only a fairly short time before closing down. The failure to attract new investment from outside is often ascribed in official publications to Northern Ireland's 'bad image' abroad. This suggests the problem is one of perception, that outsiders are mistaken in their fear of investing in Northern Ireland. The truth, however, is somewhat different. There is armed conflict in the province, sectarian strife is rife and the political situation is unstable, and until a lasting political settlement is achieved, it is unlikely that Northern Ireland will ever attract new private investment from outside on a significant scale.

Efforts have been made to foster local industry through such bodies as the Local Enterprise Development Unit (LEDU). However, success has been limited. At the last count, in February 1984, the total number of people employed on LEDU projects was 7,896. Although no precise figure is available, perhaps 6,100 of these are employed in manufacturing industry and the rest in services. Moreover, some of the enterprises fostered by LEDU act as subcontractors to outside firms operating in the province, and if the latter were to leave these LEDU enterprises could not survive.

Recent studies have revealed other weaknesses in the small firm sector of the Northern Ireland economy.[6] Compared to their counterparts elsewhere in the UK, small manufacturing firms in Northern Ireland suffer from poor management, are less innovative in product design and less aggressive in marketing, and their products are lower in quality and more expensive in price. This is a fairly comprehensive catalogue of failings, and it is clear that many of these firms would collapse without the generous financial assistance they now receive from the government. Thus, despite attempts to foster local enterprise, Northern Ireland still has only a minimal capacity to generate industrial growth in its own right.

A Workhouse Economy

One important by-product of the conflict and the continuing economic crisis in Northern Ireland has been an extraordinary dependence of the province on subsidies from Great Britain.

Without the British subvention – or some equivalent source of
external finance – living standards in Northern Ireland would
fall dramatically and the social and economic fabric of the
province might well disintegrate. The IRA campaign has not yet
driven Britain out of Northern Ireland, but it has certainly made
the province into a major financial burden on the British
government and destroyed any capacity the province might
have had to stand alone as a viable independent entity.

This section is concerned with the overall structure of
Northern Ireland's economy and its links with the outside world.
It shows how Northern Ireland has experienced a considerable
rise in real expenditure since 1970, so that average living
standards are now much higher than they were when the conflict
first broke out. This rise in expenditure has occurred despite a
virtual stagnation in the 'wealth-creating' sector of the economy;
it has been financed through a massive subsidy from outside the
province. Northern Ireland now resembles a vast workhouse in
which most of the inmates are engaged in servicing or
controlling each other. Like the typical workhouse, it imports a
great deal from the outside world whilst providing few exports in
return, moreover, as in the case of a workhouse or prison, the
gap between imports and exports is financed out of taxes levied
on the external population. This analogy with a workhouse or
similar institution is not meant to be insulting; it is, rather,
intended to illustrate the nature of Northern Ireland's
relationship with the outside world: the total dependence of the
province on external support and its inability to survive in its
present form without that support.

Output

Table 1 gives information on the output of goods and services in
Northern Ireland in 1984. Output is divided into three major
categories: transportable goods, other non-government output
and general government output. Transportable goods consist of
agricultural products, fuels and manufactures. As their name
suggests, these are goods which can, in principle, be exported
from the province. General government output consist of public
administration, the security services, health, education and the
like; also included under this heading are private and

Table 1: Gross Domestic Product in 1984: Northern Ireland and UK Compared

£ per head of population at current prices

At Factor Cost.[1]	Northern Ireland	UK	Northern Ireland as percentage of UK
1. Non-government output			
a. Transportable goods:			
Agriculture, forestry and fishing	189	106	179
Fuels	—	390	—
Manufacturing[2]	708	1244	59
Total transportable goods	897	1740	52
b. Other non-government output:			
Construction	207	280	74
Public utilities	117	136	86
Distribution, catering	420	656	64
Transport and communication	200	351	57
Finance and business services	352	655	54
Ownership of dwellings	185	296	63
Other services	272	322	84
Adjustment for financial services	−134	−267	50
Total other non-government output	1619	2429	67
2. Government output			
Public administration and defence (excluding HM forces)	370	255[3]	145
HM forces	151	79[3]	191
Education and health[4]	535	454	118
Total government output	1056	788	134
Gross Domestic Product	3572	4955	72

Notes
[1] i.e. net of taxes and subsidies.
[2] Includes mineral oil and processing, mining and quarrying.
[3] Estimate.
[4] Includes the private sector, together with church schools and the like.
Sources: NI Annual Abstract of Statistics, UK National Accounts.

semi-private health and education services (e.g. Catholic schools), many of which are government financed. The third heading, 'other non-government output', is merely a catch-all category which covers everything not elsewhere included. The bulk of items under this heading are produced in the private sector and are mainly destined for local consumption. Few of these items are exported directly, though some, like electricity are essential for the production of manufactured goods and thereby contribute indirectly to exports. (The same is, of course, true of certain government services, like education, which also contribute indirectly to exports.)

From this table we can see that GDP per head in Northern Ireland is 72 per cent of the UK average; if North Sea oil is excluded from the comparison, the ratio is 76 per cent. However, these overall figures are grossly misleading and conceal enormous intersectoral variations. In the realm of government services, for example, Northern Ireland 'produces' one third more per head than the UK average; this is mainly due to the large number of police and soldiers deployed in the province, though it also reflects the existence of a relatively large health and education sector in Northern Ireland. At the other end of the spectrum are transportable goods, where Northern Ireland produces only 52 per cent as much per head of population as the UK average. This low ratio is explained by the fact that the output of fuel in the province is negligible and the manufacturing sector is small. The situation with regard to fuel should improve in the future when the deposits of lignite (brown coal) around Lough Neagh are developed; these are estimated to be in the region of 1,000 million tonnes and their exploitation should greatly reduce Northern Ireland's present dependence on imported coal. With regard to manufacturing, however, the situation is likely to get worse and the gap between Northern Ireland and the rest of the UK will continue to widen as it has done since 1974. The one area in which Northern Ireland's economy is fairly strong is agriculture where output per head of population is almost 80 per cent above the UK average. However, the potential for further growth in agriculture is limited and this sector could be hit very hard when the EEC's Common Agricultural Policy is eventually reformed – as sooner or later it must be. Taking transportable goods as a whole,

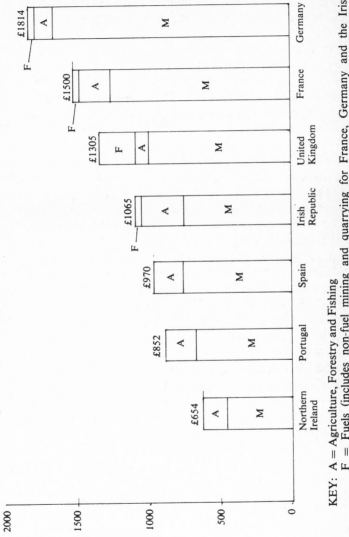

Figure 1: Output of Transportable Goods in 1984 (£ per capita at 1980 prices)

KEY: A = Agriculture, Forestry and Fishing
F = Fuels (includes non-fuel mining and quarrying for France, Germany and the Irish Republic).
M = Manufacturing (includes fuels for Portugal and Spain).

Northern Ireland is clearly very backward and, with the exception of lignite, its future prospects are poor.

Just how backward Northern Ireland is in the production of transportable goods can be gauged from Figure 1. In 1984 the total output of such goods in Northern Ireland was estimated £674 per head of population (at constant 1980 prices). This compares to £1,305 in the UK, £1,500 in France and £1,814 in West Germany. Moreover, it is well below the level observed in Spain and Portugal – two of Western Europe's poorest countries – where the output of transportable goods per head was £970 and £852 respectively. As far as such goods are concerned, Northern Ireland is now on a par with middle-range Latin American countries like Argentina or Chile. It is, in effect, an underdeveloped country kept afloat by subsidies from the UK.

A striking feature of Figure 1 is the relatively good performance of the Irish Republic. The output of transportable goods in the Republic was an estimated £1,065 per head in 1984, nearly 60 per cent above the level in Northern Ireland. A more telling comparison, perhaps, is between the Republic and the UK. If we exclude fuels from this comparison, the output per capita is almost the same in the two countries. It is only North Sea oil which gives the UK an edge, and without this oil the output of transportable goods per head of population would be only marginally greater than in the Republic. Despite its formidable economic problems – unemployment, a huge national debt, etc. – the Republic is no longer a desperately poor country. In terms of manufacturing output per head, the Republic overtook Northern Ireland in the late 1970s, and on present trends could overtake the UK by the end of the century.

The remaining major grouping in Table 1 consists of the items listed under the heading 'other non-government output'. Apart from construction and public utilities, these are all services. Here again Northern Ireland is backward and output per head of population is, in general, well below the UK average. Few of these items are exported and the bulk are destined for domestic use. In recent years, one of the main exports under the heading 'other non-government output' has been the revenue earned from day-trippers from the South, who come over the border on shopping expeditions to take advantage of lower prices in the North; this source of revenue, however, is both precarious and of marginal importance. The amount spent by these visitors is considerable – £114 million in 1984 – but much of this goes on items which are imported into Northern Ireland from elsewhere, so the net receipts are much smaller.[7] The province also gets some export earnings from more traditional kinds of tourism and from consultancy, finance and other services, but total receipts from service exports of all kinds are not very large; they are probably well below the amount spent by the residents of Northern Ireland on such imported services as external travel, air and sea transport, finance, business consultancy and the like. Although proper trade statistics are not available, it seems almost certain that Northern Ireland has a large deficit in traded services with the outside world.

Expenditure

Complete figures on expenditure in Northern Ireland are not available so we have been forced to estimate certain items of government and capital expenditure. The estimates are fairly rough, but they are good enough for our purposes and indicate the general orders of magnitude involved. Table 2 shows output and expenditure at current prices over the period 1970-84. Before considering the actual numbers shown in these tables, we shall first explain what the various items mean. Output is divided into the three major categories described above: transportable goods, other non-government and general government output. Expenditure is also divided into three major categories: consumers' expenditure, general government final consumption and gross domestic capital formation. Consumers' expenditure consists mainly of personal expenditures on goods and services by individuals resident in Northern Ireland, together with some expenditure by private non-profit making bodies. General government final consumption consists mainly of current expenditure on goods and services which can be identifiably attributed to Northern Ireland. Included under this heading are items such as health, education, local and provincial administration, the police and prison service, the Ulster Defence Regiment and certain other kinds of military expenditure. However, items of 'national' expenditure – such as Whitehall administration, the nuclear strike force or the British Army on

Table 2: Output and Expenditure in Northern Ireland, 1970-84

| | £ million at current prices | | | |
	1970	1973	1979	1984
At factor cost[1]				
Domestic output				
transportable goods	360	487	992	1391
other non-government	413	612	1647	2513
general government	137	225	890	1639
(A) Gross Domestic Product	910	1324	3529	5543
Domestic expenditure				
consumers' expenditure	616	932	2578	3818
general government final consumption	153	256	1041	1977
gross domestic capital formation	299	346	1121	1296
(B) Total Domestic Expenditure	1068	1534	4740	7091
(C) Balance of Trade (=A−B)	−158	−210	−1211	−1548
cf Official Subvention[2]	89	315	1059	1533

Notes
[1] i.e. net of taxes and subsidies.
[2] Combined subvention from GB and EEC.

the Rhine – are excluded and Northern Ireland's share in such expenditure does not appear in the tables. The final item of expenditure is gross domestic capital formation, which covers all forms of capital expenditure in the province. Both output and expenditure, it should be noted, are measured at factor cost, i.e. net of taxes and subsidies.

Total domestic output and total domestic expenditure satisfy the following relationship:

Output – expenditure = exports – imports
Exports – imports = trade balance in goods and services.

If domestic output and expenditure are exactly equal, exports equal imports and the trade balance is zero. However, this has not been the case in Northern Ireland for many years, and expenditure has consistently exceeded output. The table shows that expenditure on transportable goods – which account for the majority of consumers' expenditure and gross domestic capital formation – rose strongly up to 1979. Since then it has fallen somewhat but is still approximately 15-20 per cent above the level observed in 1970. Comprehensive statistics on expenditure on and output of transportable goods are not available. However, rough estimates suggest that total expenditure on transportable goods in Northern Ireland exceeds the output of such goods by around 70 per cent. To put it differently, the output of transportable goods is equivalent to only 60 per cent of expenditure on such goods. These figures provide a good indication of how far the province overspends its income. If forced to live within its means, Northern Ireland would experience a catastrophic fall in material living standards, which would fall to 60 per cent of the present level, or even less.

The combination of falling domestic output of transportable goods, together with rising expenditure on such goods, is the main factor behind the large increase in Northern Ireland's trade deficit with the outside world during the 1970s. This deficit increased from an estimated £880 million in 1970 (in 1980 prices) to £1,490 million in 1979. During the 1980s the deficit has declined somewhat, mainly because the fall in capital expenditure since 1979 has reduced the demand for imports. Even so, at £1,200 million (in 1980 prices), the deficit remains well above the level observed in 1970. Alongside the increase in Northern Ireland's trade deficit with the outside world, there has been a marked shift in the method of financing this deficit. In 1970, just after the outbreak of the conflict, Northern Ireland was still attracting a great deal of outside investment from private firms. These investment funds were used to finance the importing of goods and services from abroad, and in this way the province was able to cover much of its deficit with the outside world without recourse to government aid.

Since 1970, however, the situation has changed. Not only is Northern Ireland's trade deficit larger, but, for reasons explained elsewhere, the inflow of outside capital has virtually dried up. As a result there is now a large financial gap which is filled mainly by aid from the British government – which has increased dramatically – together with funds from the European Economic Community. During recent years, the combined annual subvention to Northern Ireland from these sources has averaged more than £1,200 million (at 1980 prices). In current prices, of course, the figure is even greater: in 1985, for example, the official subvention to the province was over £1,700 million at current prices, which is equivalent to approximately £1,100 per head of population.

To sum up: there are two reasons why the real value of government aid to the province has grown substantially over the past fifteen years: the province has a much larger deficit than it had in 1970, and capital flows into Northern Ireland which used to count for around 30-40 per cent of the deficit have now dried up, so that government aid must now finance virtually the entire trade deficit. The analogy made earlier between Northern Ireland and a workhouse is accurate. Like the typical workhouse, Northern Ireland is not a viable entity which can survive in its present form without external support. The province produces nothing like sufficient to meet its current requirements of goods and services, and if financial support were abruptly withdrawn, the province would suffer a massive fall in average living standards. The result would almost certainly be bitter sectarian conflict as rival communities sought to preserve their jobs and living standards. Large sectors of the population would be reduced to abject poverty, whilst many skilled personnel, able to obtain well paid jobs elsewhere, would leave the province and the economy would decline still further.

The Irish Republic

This essay would be incomplete without some discussion of the Irish Republic, a topic interesting not just in its own right, but also for the light it throws on Northern Ireland. As conventionally measured, total output (GDP) per capita is somewhat greater in the North than the South. However, this comparison is misleading in the present context for it conceals differences between one sector of the economy and another. It also suggests that the North has a stronger economy than the South, whereas in reality just the opposite is the case. To get a true picture of the relative strength of the two economies, we should look not at GDP as a whole but at the output of individual sectors. Of particular importance in any small, open economy, a type we are considering here, is the export sector. If the export sector is weak, the standard of living in such an economy will inevitably be low – unless, of course, it is fortunate enough to receive financial aid from the outside. Existing statistics do not permit an adequate comparison of the role of international services in the two Irelands, but it seems likely that the per capita output of these is considerably greater in the South than the North. For transportable goods, statistics are better and allow us to make a rough numerical comparison. In the case of agriculture, output per capita is around 100 per cent greater in the South than the North, whilst for manufacturing the disparity is around 25 per cent. Neither economy produces a substantial amount of fuel, though the South does have a modest output of commercial peat and natural gas. For transportable goods as a whole, output per capita in the South is about 40 per cent above the level achieved in the North.

This disparity in manufacturing output is of recent origin and is increasing rapidly. Whereas the North has failed to attract outside investment of any scale during the past decade, the South has proved a popular location for multinational companies wishing to serve the European and other markets. Much of this investment has gone into 'new' industries, like electronics and chemicals, which are dominated by outside firms. The result has been a spectacular growth in modern, export-oriented manufacturing industries in the South of Ireland. The peculiarities of the tax system in the South probably exaggerates this trend, but even so much of it is undoubtedly genuine.

Growth in the new industries has been accompanied by a prolonged crisis in traditional industries – textiles, clothing, footwear, food, drink and tobacco – where total output has stagnated and employment has fallen sharply in recent years. Since most of these traditional industries are dominated by indigenous Irish firms, the transformation in output structure from traditional to modern is leading to a shift in control from domestic to foreign capital. Thus, in terms of control, the Southern economy is becoming increasingly like that of the North, which is also dominated by outside firms. However, in terms of industrial performance there is a world of difference between them. Over the past decade, the South has been conspicuously more successful in achieving industrial growth, and official statistics indicate that its total manufacturing output is now three times that of the North. As already mentioned, the official statistics may be misleading and the fact that the South has a much larger population than the North must also be taken into account. However, even allowing for these factors, it is almost certain that the output of manufacturing per head of population in the South of Ireland is now greater than in the North.

Thus, as far as the export sector is concerned, the Northern economy is distinctly weaker than its Southern counterpart. Why then is Gross Domestic Product higher in the North? The answer lies, of course, in the other, non-export sectors of the economy. The North has an extremely large government sector. This government sector is financed mainly from Britain, yet its output is included in Northern Ireland's GDP.

The different financial situation of the two Ireland's is reflected in their balance of trade with the outside world. As pointed out earlier, exact figures are not available for Northern Ireland, but at a rough estimate exports of goods and services fell short of imports by approximately £1,000 per head of population in 1985. This deficit was financed by the official subvention from Britain and the EEC. The situation in the South could not be more different. Whereas the North has a large deficit with the outside world, the South now has a moderate trade surplus. In 1985 exports of goods and services from the South exceeded imports by approximately £100 sterling per head of population.

The existence of a trade surplus in Southern Ireland is a recent phenomenon. Following the second oil shock in 1979, the South experienced a sharp deterioration in its trade balance, and to cover the resulting deficit the Republic borrowed heavily from other countries. Because of this borrowing, the Irish government now has foreign debts of more than IR£8,000 million. In sterling, the debt amounts to approximately £7,000 million, which is equivalent to £2,000 per head of population. The interest payments on a debt of this magnitude are, of course, very large. In addition, there are also the profits of foreign multinationals to consider. Much of the Southern economy is now dominated by multinationals, and because of generous tax concessions the profit rates they earn are the highest in Europe.

For example, US companies earn 24 per cent a year on their investments in Southern Ireland as compared with an average return of 5.6 per cent in the EEC as a whole. The net cost to the South of interest payments and profit repatriation by foreign multinationals is now equivalent to one-eighth of Gross Domestic Product, and absorbs one-fifth of all export earnings. In financial terms, this amounts to approximately £500 sterling per head of population.

The South is now caught in a debt trap of Third World proportions. To service its gigantic debt and cover profit repatriation by foreign investors, the country requires a very large trade surplus. After years in deficit, the South finally has a trade surplus, but this is quite small and by no means sufficient to cover interest payments and the like, so the country at present finds itself still borrowing simply to meet the cost of servicing a debt whose origin lies in the past. The South is facing a typical Third World dilemma. Like many a Third World debtor, the South is no longer overspending its income and now has a trade surplus, but it is sinking ever deeper into debt simply because it is borrowing to meet the cost of servicing its existing debt. This is not a dilemma faced by Northern Ireland, which has been fortunate enough to have an external supporter – in the shape of Britain – willing to meet its deficit with the outside world. Whereas Northern Ireland has been able to overspend its income and, within fairly broad limits, expect Britain to foot the bill, this is not the case with South. Any major overspend by the South can only be financed by borrowing, and this explains why the South is now so much in debt, whilst the North is not.

Unfortunately, such borrowing cannot go on forever, and sooner or later the day of reckoning must come. This day has now arrived and the South is currently facing a severe debt crisis. It is approaching the limits of international borrowing and by some means or other it must bring the debt situation under control. Fresh borrowing must be halted and, if possible, a start must be made on repaying the existing debt. This objective can only be achieved through an austerity programme designed to alter the balance between national income and expenditure, so the country's expenditure no longer exceeds what can be financed without large scale borrowing. Indeed, such a programme has already been in operation for several years, as the Irish government has sought to reduce borrowing through a combination of higher non-corporate taxes (ie VAT and personal income tax) and public expenditure cuts.

According to the FitzGerald government, non-corporate tax rates are now extremely high and cannot be increased any further, so from now on the whole emphasis of the austerity programme must be on expenditure cuts. The claim that tax rates have reached their upper limit is open to question. There are still many well-off people in the South whose productive contribution is minimal and who could be taxed more heavily without harming the national economy. Moreover, it might also be feasible to claw back some of the lavish tax concessions now enjoyed by foreign multinationals operating in Ireland. Taking all of these factors into account, it is by no means clear that tax rates have reached their maximum and that public expenditure cuts must bear the full weight of an austerity programme. Having said this, however, it remains true that some kind of austerity programme is required. Southern Ireland cannot repudiate its national debt – it is far too vulnerable a situation for that – and some means must be found to reduce total national expenditure public and private combined to a level the country can afford.

What, then, will happen to the Southern economy, assuming that political conditions continue much as they are at present and the South remains a relatively stable country offering a secure environment to foreign multinationals? Under these conditions, the long-term economic prospects are mixed. With its low wages and generous tax concessions, the country will remain an attractive location for multinationals. Moreover, efforts are now being made to encourage the multinationals to locate more of their research and development and marketing facilities in Ireland, in addition to the basic production facilities. If successful, such a policy could give a real boost to the Southern economy. Finally, greater efforts are being made to stimulate indigenous producers, especially in industries which produce for the export market. Taking all of these factors into account, it seems likely that output in the modern sectors of the Southern economy will rise moderately fast over the longer term.

The present austerity programme for dealing with the debt

crisis may inhibit growth in the short-term and will be unpleasant for those who suffer its effects. But, over the longer term, its impact on economic growth is unlikely to be very serious. So far as economic growth is concerned, therefore, long-term prospects are moderately good. However, this does not mean that everything in the future will be fine. The South has a very high level of unemployment – around 18 per cent – and its labour force is increasing rapidly because of the country's high birth rate. With even moderately fast growth of the present high-productivity type, the number of jobs available will be far below the amount required. So, even under optimistic projections, unemployment will remain very high for a long time to come. One result of this will be increased emigration as unemployed Irish people seek work abroad, and indeed emigration from the South is now occurring on a fairly large scale.

Thus, whilst long-term economic prospects in the South are much better than in the North, they are by no means enviable. The South, like the North, will continue to suffer from high unemployment for many years to come and many of its people will remain poor, even though the country may enjoy a moderately fast rate of economic growth.

What should also be clear from the above account is that because of the deficit problem there is no way in which the Republic could take over the financing of the subsidy to Northern Ireland from Britain if the latter decided to withdraw from the province and start negotiations to reunite both parts of Ireland. In such a scenario, unless some alternative source of finance could be found, there would be a considerable reduction in living standards for the average person in a united Ireland. No matter what future political framework is constructed for Northern Ireland, it is clear that the British or some other body outside Ireland will have to finance the subsidy to the province so as to avoid major strains on the social and economic fabric of the province.

The Future

So far we have been concerned mainly with the present situation in Northern Ireland. This section will be concerned with the future. It will consider which factors are likely to be of most importance in influencing the economic future of Northern

Ireland, how these factors are likely to be affected by political events and, conversely, how political events may themselves be shaped by economic realities. Two factors will be of particular importance in determining the economic future of Northern Ireland: the amount of external aid the province receives in the coming years, and the extent of conflict and instability within the province.

The foregoing analysis makes it clear that any abrupt withdrawal, or drastic reduction in the amount, of external aid to Northern Ireland would have dire economic and social consequences. The standard of living would fall sharply, many thousands would be thrown out of work, social welfare benefits would be severely cut or abolished altogether and large numbers of people would be forced to leave the province. Managerial and skilled staff able to get work abroad would emigrate, and the economy would decline still further. The fragile economic and social fabric of Northern Ireland would probably break up, and the end result could be virtual civil war as the two communities battled for control of the limited resources and employment opportunities which remained. External aid from Britain (or some other source) must therefore continue if an economic disaster is to be avoided in the province.

The present conflict has done enormous damage to the industrial base of Northern Ireland, and is easily the most important single factor preventing a sustained economic recovery in the province. To end the conflict, and establish a stable peace, would not in itself guarantee economic recovery, but it would be a major step in this direction. Interestingly, Northern Ireland is a good location for multinational firms, and with a stable peace the province would be able to attract a significant amount of outside investment. This in turn would stimulate indigenous firms by providing a demand for locally produced goods and services. Peace would also stimulate local production in other ways. It would generate an atmosphere of optimism and hope, with the result that many creative and skilled people, who now leave the province in despair, would remain and contribute to longer-term development. It would also help the tourist industry which has been hampered by the conflict.

Thus there are many different ways in which peace would be

beneficial to the economy of Northern Ireland. On the other hand, peace might have some negative effects which should be taken into account. These all concern government expenditure. The most obvious item is, of course, security. If the conflict were to end, the security forces would be severely reduced in size and their members either dismissed or transferred out of the province: one consequence would be a considerable loss of income for the province. The brunt of any cuts would inevitably fall on Protestants, simply because the local security forces are now almost entirely Protestant, as are those who service them in their home communities.

The security forces might not be the only area to experience cuts if peace breaks out. For example, with peace some of the special privileges now enjoyed by manufacturing industry in Northern Ireland might be removed. Subsidies and investment incentives might be reduced to the same level as in other depressed regions of the UK, and government orders might no longer be assigned to Northern Ireland on preferential basis as they are to some extent today. Such changes would lead to some loss of jobs in manufacturing, and once again the main losers would be Protestants. Thus for Protestants peace would be a mixed blessing. Some would gain, but more would lose in the short term. Over the longer term, however, gains would outweigh the losses, and peace would be to their ultimate advantage.

For Catholics the situation would, of course, be different. Virtually none of them would lose their jobs following the establishment of peace and new employment opportunities would be created through the economic expansion resulting from peace. Moreover, some Catholics would also find employment in the security forces which would in time become an acceptable occupation for Catholics under peaceful conditions; in the short term, then, Catholics would be the main beneficiaries of peace.

The above remarks apply to peace within the UK framework. However, the same general points would apply under a different framework such as an independent Northern Ireland or a united Ireland. No matter what the constitutional framework, peace would facilitate economic recovery in the North, though in the short term some people might lose from it. The single most important factor for economic recovery is therefore the resolution of the present conflict.

Conclusions

The main points of this essay can be summarised as follows. Firstly, the economy of Northern Ireland is now in a desperate situation. Since the present armed conflict broke out, many of the existing multinationals have run down their operations or left the province altogether. Despite lavish financial incentives, it has proved impossible to attract a significant amount of new outside investment because of the risks involved. Efforts to stimulate local industry, to replace the gap left by departing multinationals, have met with limited success.

Secondly, despite the weakness of its economic base, *average* living standards in Northern Ireland have risen a great deal since the conflict began. This rise has been made possible by the gigantic amount of financial support the province receives from the outside, mainly from the British government. External aid to Northern Ireland currently amounts to well over £1,000 per head of population annually. This aid is used mainly to support the very large public sector in the province, which is now, directly or indirectly, the main source of incomes for the local population. It is also used to support firms in the private sector. If external aid were to be cut off abruptly, or drastically reduced, the economic and social consequences would be catastrophic.

Thirdly, as long as the present conflict continues the economic prospects for the province are bleak. While some measures are conceivable to promote economic growth in the short term, the outbreak of peace would make the single most major contribution to economic recovery. This, in my view, is beyond question. It is officially recognised in the Anglo-Irish (Hillsborough) Agreement, though whether this Agreement will actually achieve the desired objective is open to doubt.

Notes

[1] *Regional Trends 1986*, Table 10.1, p.126.
[2] In 1983-84 the amount of regional preferential assistance to industry per manufacturing employee was as follows: Northern Ireland, £1,065; Wales,

£536; Scotland, £508; North-East, £326; North-West, £160; see *Regional Trends 1985*.

[3] The exact figures are as follows: 1981-82: £7,947; 1983-84: £8,123; 1984-85: £7,972; 1985-86: £7,931.

[4] This figure includes redundancy payment aid.

[5] Northern Ireland Economic Council, *Economic Strategy and Historical Growth Performance*, Belfast 1983 p.5.

[6] D. Hitchens and P. O'Farrell, 'Inter-Regional Comparisons of Small Firm Performance: The Case of Northern Ireland and South-East England', Working Papers in Economics, Occasional Paper No.24, Queen's University of Belfast, December 1985.

[7] *Northern Ireland Annual Abstract of Statistics 1985*, p.159.

Frank Gafikin and Mike Morrissey

Poverty and Politics in Northern Ireland

Introduction

Northern Ireland's status as the most deprived region of the United Kingdom is well known.[1] Ever since its establishment as a separate state, the industries which had created the economic base for partition have been in decline. The consequence for Northern Ireland, given the failure of Unionist governments to take action, was an endemic state of poverty. As Parker and Driver comment:

> A survey of the Belfast working class in 1938-39 revealed that 36 per cent of those investigated were unable to afford sufficient food, clothing or fuel to maintain health or working capacity.[2]

In the field of housing policy in the inter-war period, Birrell and his co-authors indicate that despite a similar level of subsidy 'private builders provided 69 times fewer houses than private builders in England and Wales. At the same time local authorities built 127 times fewer houses.[3] In the areas of jobs and housing Northern Ireland stood out as a significant failure even within the heavily depressed UK economy.

In the post-war period the advent of the welfare state and policies designed to reindustrialise the regional economy brought relative prosperity. Nevertheless, Northern Ireland failed to achieve the high employment levels of other regions, and its housing stock retained substantially higher rates of unfitness than that in England and Wales. Ditch has described the welfare state in Northern Ireland as exceptional in that it developed in the absence of full employment and political consensus.[4] Any consideration of the problem of poverty in Northern Ireland therefore immediately encounters the paradox that while it is an area with acute and historic patterns of deprivation, which received inadequate attention from the Unionist administrations in the province and from British governments at Westminster, there has been little development of poverty-focused politics. The political preoccupation with either defending or destroying the state has overshadowed all else.

The purpose of this essay is to examine the relationship between poverty and politics in Northern Ireland, concentrating in particular on the conditions which might open up opportunities for political activity around issues of poverty. The focus is on three dimensions of the problem; firstly, there is a brief discussion of the relationship between poverty and politics in the light of contrasting interpretations of the nature of the Northern Ireland state; next there is a presentation of contemporary data on poverty in Northern Ireland indicating that it remains the most deprived region in the UK, despite the recent rapid decline of other regions; finally, there is a discussion of the impact of nearly twenty years of acute political crisis on poverty and poverty programmes, concluding with an evaluation of the situation after the Anglo-Irish Agreement. Of necessity this involves a switch in the chronology since the data on poverty employs the most recent information available and the political crisis began in the late 1960s. However since the latter forms the direct context for a consideration of the Anglo-Irish Agreement, it was considered appropriate to locate the two together.

Poverty and Politics in Northern Ireland

The debate about whether it is possible to campaign politically on issues of poverty in Northern Ireland depends on the position adopted about the nature of the state itself. One view holds that the central contradiction involves an imperialist conflict in which the main protagonists are the progressive forces centred around Republicanism and the repressive institutions of the British state.[5] From this point of view, partition was a device orchestrated by the British to frustrate a potential revolutionary politics in Ireland. As Greaves declares, 'Partition was aimed at stifling a revolution that was in progress in Ireland and raising an insurmountable barrier in the path of another.'[6]

An alternative position concentrates on the politics of Unionism, according it a greater autonomy than being a mere adjunct to imperialist design.[7] Probert goes a little further, locating this analysis within a global perspective in which the emergence of multinational capital and the related decline of local capital in both parts of Ireland created different kinds of dependency than those of the traditional imperialist model.[8]

Views on how a politics of poverty can be mobilised therefore depend on the overall analysis of the situation. The traditional imperialist model, for example, identifies a coincidence in Ireland between socialism and nationalism. The former cannot be effectively constructed without a victory for the latter. From this perspective, attempts to organise united working-class action around socio-economic issues are doomed to frustration since the sectarian distribution of employment and income does not create the material conditions for such unity. Opponents of this position claim that this understates the relative autonomy of Unionism by assuming partition to be the outcome of a positive choice by Britain in its search for the most effective means to secure its capitalist interest in Ireland. Specifically, it is claimed that the imperialist model fails to appreciate the extent to which successive British governments came under pressure not only from the Unionist ruling elite, but also from the Unionist working class, both judging their economic interests to be better secured by the maintenance of the Union with Britain. Working-class Unionists should not, therefore, be seen as the dupes of their Orange masters, as they have often been characterised by their Republican opponents: their support for the British link may have had a rational core which is not readily amenable to nationalist enlightenment. Recognising this, the best hope for a progressive politics is to end persistent nationalist claims which drive Unionist workers into a beleaguered reactionary response, and attempt to realise their radical potential in struggles around poverty, employment and indeed democracy.

The direct intervention of the British state in Northern Ireland in the 1970s is also subject to different interpretations. At one level this development was seen as introducing a rational administration, at another as unleashing an imperialist war machine, and at yet another as reproducing previous sectarian structures. According to the last two interpretations, reforms which might be secured by political pressure are not primarily about alleviating poverty but are about managing in non-coercive ways the political/military challenge to the state.

It is not our purpose to evaluate these contrasting interpretations, but merely to point out that one's view of the efficacy of campaigning around issues of poverty is inevitably conditioned by whatever position is adopted. The exception to this thesis is the newly emerged strategy in which poverty is seen as a means of helping sustain support for other political objectives. The best example of this is the recent political mobilisation by Sinn Fein which began around reaction to the hunger strike, but was developed through the establishment of numerous advice centres which carried out welfare rights campaigning with an unprecedented *élan*. Sinn Fein members, committed to Britain's withdrawal from Ireland, fight vigorously for the claimant rights awarded by the British state. This strategy does not have the character of 'transitional' or unmeetable demands, and Sinn Fein likes to boast of its successful record in this field.

All of this suggests that the relationship between poverty and politics in Northern Ireland is complex. In a state in which the maintenance of a particular political order was based on the capacity of the Unionist Party to constantly reproduce a Loyalist social and political bloc, concessions were occasionally necessary to retain the integrity of the bloc. As Patterson has argued, the coherence of the bloc could never be taken as given, was subject to frequent fissures and inter-class antagonisms, and had to be continually renewed.[9] Further, Byrne has contended that the Protestant section of the working class made demands that went beyond the limits of sectarian self-interest.[10] His example was the demand for a full introduction of the provisions of the British welfare state which, with the exception of housing and jobs in welfare agencies, was of considerable material benefit to Catholics. Thus the tensions inherent in reproducing the Loyalist bloc coupled with the genuinely workerist demands occasionally raised by Loyalist workers created the necessary pressures for concessions. The best examples of this process were seen in the politics of Unionism during and immediately after the Second World War, when the government was forced to move to a programme of reconstruction and, despite some ministerial opposition, willing embrace the development of welfarism.

It is also important to distinguish between the formal and informal political arenas in considering poverty and politics in Northern Ireland. Given the traumatic circumstances surrounding the establishment of the state, the protracted disaffection it encountered from its nationalist opponents and the perceived threat from the Southern state which claimed it as part of its territory, it is unsurprising that at the level of formal politics, the issues of Northern Ireland's existence and its defence were predominant. At the informal level, there was frequently a greater flexibility and opportunity to develop a critique of government policy on a socio-economic front. This was manifest historically in the Outdoor Relief Strike, in the campaign against homelessness after the Second World War, in the election of Communist councillors in Belfast in the late 1940s, in the Belfast Corporation rent strikes of the 1960s and, most of all, in the persistent efforts by a weak trade union movement to develop an economic challenge to Unionism. It would, however, be a mistake to overestimate the significance of such developments; many were short-term and subject to fracture along sectarian lines, but their very existence demonstrates the possibility of some form of political mobilisation around the issues of poverty.

The development of the civil rights campaign is a powerful example of the complexity of the problem. While the campaign had its origins in the discriminatory allocation of housing, many of the demands were for economic and social rights, a response to the pervasiveness and uneven distribution of poverty. The response of the O'Neill government was ambivalent. In the end a mixture of coercion and reform policies was adopted. The attitude of the Protestant section of the population was equally uncertain, some endorsing the demands as part of a rational modernised political order, many confronting civil rights demonstrators with rabidly sectarian violence. Two interpretations are possible; either that the demands for reform in themselves provoked violent opposition because of the centrality of sectarianism in ideology and politics, or that the demands were designed to destabilise politics as part of the transition to a united Ireland. Both focus on real elements of the situation but neither is able to encompass it.

The civil rights campaign was able to transform the nature of political discourse precisely because it could not be characterised as a simple Republican challenge. The notions of 'normal' political rights and social justice were powerful metaphors in an informal political mobilisation that produced significant effects. Within a year the Northern Ireland government was forced to concede significant reforms. However the continuing use of coercion, the irresponsible deployment of the non-professional coercive apparatus (the B Specials) and the spread of sectarian violence convinced many that reforms were impossible and that the destruction of the state was the only viable long-term solution. The struggle then became part of a self-fulfilling process in which an attempt to reform the state became transformed into one to end it.

There are, therefore, only limited opportunities for the development of poverty-oriented politics, with a greater scope at the informal rather than formal level, and even then there is the possibility of any initiative or campaign being intertwined with other central contradictions of the state. In this context, the issue of poverty can only be used to challenge the contending political forces in Northern Ireland in terms of evaluating the solutions they offer. The Northern Ireland Poverty Lobby has called for a strategy

> based on grassroots, community and claimant action ... the development of more co-ordinated, unified action among groups and interests ... [and the need for a charter of] key policy demands or changes on which a wider range of groups will agree.[11]

The establishment of a 'poverty' network able to develop programmes and then encounter established political parties and government offers perhaps the best opportunity for the growth of poverty-based politics. This remains an important project, for, as the next section demonstrates, poverty in Northern Ireland remains prevalent.

Poverty in Northern Ireland, the Current Situation

It has become conventional to comment on the exceptional levels of poverty in Northern Ireland. Such features as high-level, long-term unemployment, the prevalence of low incomes in a large number of households, high rates of unfit housing and the social and physical damage of nearly two decades of political and military conflict, suggest an area of concentrated disadvantage. Here we examine evidence on incomes, earnings and housing conditions to evaluate whether Northern Ireland experiences distinctively different social problems from other ailing regions in which levels of deprivation have been enormously multiplied by economic decline and the policies of the Thatcher government.

It should, however, be said in advance that attempts to describe the extent of poverty in a region like Northern Ireland encounter many problems. One major difficulty is that to compare Northern Ireland, with a population of around 1.5 million people, with a social formation like Great Britain, with approximately 50 million, can easily mislead. Concentrating only on British averages may conceal pockets of people in regions or smaller units with levels of poverty approaching that in Northern Ireland. The comparison must therefore be made with other regions rather than with national averages. Even then population differentials can mean that like is not being compared to like. However the virtual absence of sub-regional data precludes the possibility of comparing Northern Ireland with another geographical unit with a similar population structure. Consequently, the primary focus of comparison here will be with other UK regions, identifying where possible 'best' and 'worst' regions to be counterposed to Northern Ireland. Where that is not possible, comparison will be with the North-West, a heavily disadvantaged region with traditional links with Northern Ireland, and the West Midlands, which has suffered the most rapid rate of decline in recent years.

Another problem concerns the distribution of poverty within Northern Ireland. In particular, the regional average conceals systematic differences between different groups in the population. This relates most obviously to differences between Catholics and Protestants, and fortunately, data on a number of poverty indicators distinguishing between religions is now available. A recent investigation contends that differences internal to Northern Ireland may be more significant than those between Northern Ireland and other regions.[12] This internal dimension to deprivation will also be considered. The account begins with an analysis of comparative incomes.

Households and incomes

There are significant differences in household structure between
Northern Ireland and Great Britain which need to be taken into
account when comparing income differences. In 1984 57 per
cent of British households consisted of two persons or less,
compared to 45 per cent in Northern Ireland, while only 9 per
cent of British households were of five or more persons
compared to Northern Ireland's 21 per cent.[13] Thus household
size in the province tends to be larger, suggesting that differences
in average household income conceal a greater disparity –
household income has to cater for a larger set of needs. There
are, however, two aspects of household composition relevant to
the generation of poverty – single parenthood and retired heads
of household – for which Northern Ireland has a lower
proportion (11.4 per cent of single parents compared to 13 per
cent in Great Britain and 31 per cent with one or more adult
aged 60 or over compared to 34 per cent).

The following table provides data on UK and regional
incomes.

Table 1: Average Personal and Household Weekly Incomes, 1982-83

	Average Personal Income	Average Household Income
UK	£74.90	£182.10
Best region (South East)	£89.40	£210.50
Worst region (Yorkshire/Humberside)	£65.70	£163.30
Northern Ireland	£52.30	£144.70

Source: Regional Trends, 1985.

The exceptionally low average income levels in Northern Ireland
can be easily noted. In fact the Northern Ireland averages are a
lower proportion of the worst British region's than that in turn is
of the UK average. This suggests a level of disadvantage
unmatched elsewhere in the UK.

Information on the distribution of incomes also points to Northern Ireland having a disproportionate concentration in the lower income bands. With respect to personal incomes before tax, 11.7 per cent of people in Northern Ireland fell into the £1,350-£1,999 band compared to 6 per cent in the UK, 6.8 per cent in the West Midlands and 6.2 per cent in the North West (1981-82). In 1982-83, only 54 per cent of household incomes was derived from wages and salaries in Northern Ireland compared to around 65 per cent for other UK regions. In the same period Northern Ireland had 32.1 per cent of households with an average income of less than £75 weekly, the UK had 22.1 per cent, the West Midlands 21.1 per cent and the North-West 24.9 per cent. Further, Northern Ireland also had a greater proportion in the £75-£109 band, but a significantly lower proportion (27 per cent compared to over 40 per cent for each of the three comparative areas) of those earning £180 or more.

The condition of lower incomes in Northern Ireland is also reflected in levels of household expenditure and in the possession of consumer durables. In 1982-83 households in Northern Ireland were able to spend only 91 per cent of the UK average, and although accommodation occupied a lower proportion of household expenditure, fuel, light and power, food and transport all took up a greater proportion. Standardising for family size, the purchasing power of households in Northern Ireland was about three-quarters of the UK average. Similarly, a lower proportion of the population in the region had access to central heating, a washing machine, telephone, television and a passenger car than any other region. Additionally, Northern Ireland households consume less cheese, meat, fresh fruit and vegetables than in any other UK region.[24]

Earnings

Table 2 provides data on the distribution of gross hourly earnings for selected regions.

The rates given are for hourly earnings because of the difference in average hours worked between regions. Two features of the table are significant. First, for each decile and median earnings category, the rates in Northern Ireland are

Table 2: Gross Hourly Earnings, Full-Time Men and Women Whose Pay Was Unaffected by Absence, 1974, 1984

	Lowest Decile	Median	Highest Decile
1974			
MEN			
West Midlands	70.7p	103.2p	155.8p
North-West	67.4p	96.2p	154.1p
Northern Ireland	61.0p	86.7p	147.4p
WOMEN			
West Midlands	43.7p	62.0p	103.6p
North-West	42.1p	61.3p	93.6p
Northern Ireland	38.3p	58.8p	106.8p
1984			
MEN			
West Midlands	240.8p	361.7p	616.3p
North-West	238.9p	369.7p	657.1p
Northern Ireland	210.1p	332.4p	587.3p
WOMEN			
West Midlands	184.2p	263.3p	499.5p
North-West	184.6p	272.2p	490.4p
Northern Ireland	173.6p	248.2p	418.3p

Source: New Earnings Survey Great Britain and Northern Ireland 1974/1984

significantly below those for the other two regions. This applies to both men and women with the exception of the top decile of female earnings in Northern Ireland in 1974, clearly an anomalous result. Thus the whole range of earnings in Northern Ireland falls below that of two other disadvantaged regions. Further, if the bottom decile of male earnings in Northern Ireland is taken as a percentage of the same decile for other regions, it can be seen to have fallen between 1974 and 1984. In 1974 the bottom decile in Northern Ireland was 90.5 per cent of that in the North-West, but by 1984 it was 87.9 per cent. While the decline is marginal, it nevertheless suggests a worsening of the relative position of Northern Ireland's lowest earning men.

This is reinforced when comparison is made between the bottom decile male earnings and median earnings within Northern Ireland. In 1974 the earnings of the lowest decile were 70 per cent of the median. By 1984 this had declined to 63 per cent. At the same time, the earnings of the top decile had increased from 170 to 177 per cent of the median. Thus men at the bottom end of the earnings distribution are doubly disadvantaged. Their position has been declining relative to the worst earning men in other regions, and it has also been worsening within the earnings scale in Northern Ireland. The trend in female earnings is more ambiguous. The bottom decile increased from 90 to 94 per cent of the next lowest region, and from 65 to 70 per cent of median earnings within Northern Ireland, suggesting modest overall improvement. The anomalous result for the top decile in 1974 meant that the earnings for that category fell as a proportion of the median over the period, but little weight should be given to this statistic.

A more up-to-date picture is provided by the 1985 *New Earnings Survey*. In terms of gross weekly earnings including overtime pay, 29.2 per cent of male manual workers and 76 per cent of women in the same category earned less than £110 per week. The equivalent proportions for non-manual workers were 11.4 and 39.2 per cent respectively. Since £110 per week represents a low pay threshold currently accepted by a number of trade unions campaigning on the issue, these percentages give some idea of the extent of low pay among adult employees. Given that the *New Earnings Survey* samples 1 per cent of employees paying national insurance contributions, it does not cover those whose earnings are below the national insurance threshold. There has been some evidence that in certain occupations – hairdressing being the most obvious – there are significant numbers of workers who fail to reach that threshold, so, if anything, these percentages underestimate the real situation. In any event, all the indications suggest that substantial proportions of employees in the province are affected by low pay.

The Northern Ireland Family Finances Survey gives an insight into the relationship between low pay and family poverty.

This survey was conducted with a sub-sample of low income families drawn from a larger sample of families in receipt of child benefit. The measure of poverty employed was that of 'relative needs resources' (RNR) where the total family income minus housing and necessary working costs was divided by the amount available to the same family under short-term supplementary benefit scale rates. If a family was found to have a RNR of 100 per cent then its income was exactly equivalent to the state poverty line, and if greater than that, it was above the line. Because of the much discussed inadequacies of the state's definition of a poverty line, families with a RNR of up to 140 per cent were still considered to be poor.

When the RNR level was cross-tabulated with the economic position of the family head, the role of low pay in generating family poverty was demonstrated. Just over 30 per cent of the sample of poor families had a head in full-time work. If self-employed were also included the proportion rose to 41 per cent. To the extent to which this is representative of the population as a whole, a considerable number of Northern Ireland's poor are in employment. Nevertheless the employed did exhibit a certain advantage over other categories of the poor. Only 13 per cent had a RNR level of up to 100 per cent compared to 57 per cent of the unemployed and 40 per cent of the self-employed. Conversely 46 per cent were in the RNR band of 121-140 per cent compared to 12 per cent of the unemployed and 25 per cent of the self-employed. In other words, paid employment does not provide any necessary protection against poverty – families with employed heads constitute a substantial minority of all poor families – but the degree of deprivation is less than for either the unemployed or self-employed. The findings for the last group have to be treated with some scepticism owing to the extreme difficulties in obtaining accurate estimates of the income of the self-employed.

Housing

Since the Northern Ireland Housing Executive began its house condition surveys in the mid-1970s, data has been consistently available on the condition of the housing stock. The latest survey in 1984 revealed that 10.4 per cent of the stock was unfit with a further 1.3 per cent of fit dwellings lacking amenities. This compares to 6.2 and 2.2 per cent respectively for England in 1981. The overall condition of the housing stock is thus worse than for England as a whole.

The highest rates of unfit housing are found in the West of the province with a general rate of 20 per cent. Some areas, like Fermanagh with 27 per cent, are considerably worse. Nevertheless, the relatively high rates of housing expenditure in the province during the past decade have produced a rate of improvement in the housing stock greater than in other parts of the UK. In 1974, housing unfitness stood at 19.6 per cent; it is now half that figure. This underlines the importance of housing expenditure in Northern Ireland in inducing a set of housing standards consistent with those in other regions. It has been estimated that it would require £667 million at 1984 prices to bring the housing stock up to recognised improvement standards. Since house building creates a large number of jobs and generates extensive linkages with the rest of the economy, many would judge this to be an excellent form of investment, but recent cuts in housing expenditure suggest that the previous rate of improvement will not be maintained.

In the above overview, three indicators were used to evaluate the level of poverty in Northern Ireland compared with other regions of the UK. In every case the averages for Northern Ireland were below those of other regions and, where evidence was available, the overall range was again lower. It has frequently been claimed that higher levels of social expenditure compensate in Northern Ireland for higher levels of social malaise. As the Northern Ireland Economic Council has demonstrated however, much of the 'higher subsidy' consists simply of flows into the region which exist but are invisible for other regions. Thus the 'excess' social expenditure is largely an artefact of public expenditure accounting. Across a range of cash benefits including national insurance benefits, supplementary benefits, child benefit and war pensions, other regions do better than Northern Ireland. In 1982-83 expenditure per head on these benefits was £578.30 in the North, £569.50 in the North-West, £579.60 in Wales and £563.40 in Northern Ireland. Northern Ireland's share can hardly be regarded as exceptional.

In the light of the above data, it seems reasonable to conclude that a persistent and severe problem of poverty exists in Northern Ireland greater than for all other regions. However for some of its citizens the position is even worse.

Religion and the Distribution of Poverty

A debate at the heart of the political crisis in Northern Ireland has been that about discrimination in housing and jobs. The political subordination of Catholics, it has been argued, has also been manifest in an exclusion from economic and social resources both through conscious discriminatory decisions and through less direct mechanisms for reproducing their disadvantage. This process relates closely to the notion of relative poverty – the exclusion from normal social roles through an insufficiency of resources. The relative position of Catholics and Protestants is therefore important in any account of poverty in the region. It should be said immediately that Northern Ireland does not have a form of apartheid in which all Catholics are worse off than Protestants. Rather the situation is one in which Catholics tend to be over-represented among the unemployed, low paid and so on, and therefore can be said in general to be disadvantaged. There has always been a Catholic bourgeoisie and a whole set of professionals, like solicitors, serving the needs of their own community, and these people are unquestionably more affluent than many Protestants. But the existence of affluent Catholics does not contradict the proposition of disadvantage for Catholics as a whole.

Relevant data on this question is mainly available on unemployment and employment. The 1981 Census revealed that unemployment was unevenly distributed between religions. Catholic men had an unemployment rate of 30.2 per cent compared to the 12.4 per cent for Protestant men; the respective female rates were 25.2 and 10.2 per cent. The breakdown by age shows that only for the 16-25 age group is the general Protestant advantage marginally less. However the advantage is significantly less for some areas affected by de-industrialisation. For example in Carrickfergus, which suffered from substantial job loss in the early 1980s through the run-down and closure of several large multinationals, there was a more congruent set of figures. The rate for Catholic men was 20.5 per cent compared to 22.7 per cent for Protestants, and 8.9 and 10.6 per cent for women. While this result was partially the result of a differential age structure between religions, the relative convergence of rates was also due to economic change.

It is unfortunate that post-1981 data is not more widely available. If economic decline does produce a relative convergence of misery, then it should be exhibited in other areas like Antrim where the industrial base collapsed after the Census survey. Differences in the general structure of relative disadvantage at age and area level do not suggest that the overall superior position of Protestants is amenable to easy change. Rather it implies that on the edge of the labour market, perhaps for young people coming into it or for areas hard hit by closure and decline, traditional Protestant advantage is being eroded.

The Continuous Household Survey offers a more recent, but more limited picture of the relative position of the two religions.

Table 3: Economic Activity by Religion, percentages

	Unemployed	Full-time working	Part-time working
Catholics			
Males	35	62	3
Females	17	55	28
All	28	59	13
Protestants			
Males	15	82	3
Females	11	55	35
All	13	71	16

Source: Continuous Household Survey, 1984.

With respect to unemployment, there remains a clear Protestant advantage, though less so than in 1981, particularly with regard to women. That advantage is further reflected in employment but again with the major differences between men rather than women. However the Survey further provides data on the duration of unemployment and here a higher proportion of

Catholics was found in the long-term category, 60 per cent as compared to 50 per cent for Protestants.

Further differences were also recorded. In terms of occupational class, Catholics were less likely to be in the professional/managerial category and more likely to be in the semi-skilled and unskilled manual bracket. They had less chance of being owner-occupiers and more chance of being public sector tenants. A greater proportion of Catholics were living in overcrowded housing conditions, though differential family size influences that result. Finally, Catholics were less likely to possess a range of consumer durables such as fridge/freezer, dishwasher and telephone.

Clearly the respective profile of the two religions demonstrates that Catholics are more likely to occupy a subordinate place in the labour market and to have access to fewer resources. Arguably, this difference is more significant than that between Northern Ireland as a whole and other regions in the UK. Rowthorn has shown that Catholic men have the highest unemployment rate in the UK but that Protestant men would be eleventh in any league table of unemployment blackspots, but any assessment remains problematic because of the substantial economic changes since 1981 (the year for which the evidence is derived).[15]

The unequal distribution of disadvantage within Northern Ireland cannot be ignored and the pressure to ensure fair employment should be increased. However substantial change is improbable without some improvement in the overall economic and social position of the region. Additional resources are required to be targeted at the most deprived and of necessity that demands reconstruction. The best case for additional resources depends on demonstrating the very extreme forms of hardship that prevail. Nevertheless unequal access to resources has fuelled the political crisis in Northern Ireland which in turn has had significant effects on poverty and poverty programmes.

Poverty and the Political Crisis

For the last fifteen years the political crisis has been the context for the consideration of almost any issue in Northern Ireland. While the Northern Ireland state was previously subject to military challenge by the IRA, in no other period was the campaign so sustained, nor did it mobilise such mass support, nor did it have comparable impact. Perhaps the most striking feature has been the increasingly direct involvement of the British state, first manifest in the introduction of troops onto the streets of Belfast and Derry, and today in the form of a complete administrative and coercive apparatus. The relationship between the political crisis and poverty has to be seen at a number of levels. First the level of physical damage and human suffering has greatly exacerbated the problems already experienced by the poor. Those areas which most experience state repression and have been the location of extensive communal violence, have also had the highest unemployment and the greatest social malaise. This is not to suggest a causal relationship between the two, as the roots of violence run deeper than social deprivation, but to note the correspondence.

When the troubles broke out in Belfast, there was a flight of population into the Catholic West of the city as people sought safety. This caused intense overcrowding in an area already suffering from high rates of housing unfitness. In one area there were persistent public health crises, including fears of a polio epidemic, owing to a wholly inadequate sewerage system. Coupled with the general housing problem, the delivery of other services was disrupted or was carried out with inadequate staff.[16] West Belfast also has disproportionate rates of unemployment, the worst concentrations of low incomes and high rates of juvenile offence rates. The last would undoubtedly be greater were it not for the operation by paramilitary organisations of an informal system of physical punishments which reduces the numbers appearing before the courts. The crisis has thus created an additional burden in areas already affected by a multiplicity of social problems.

Secondly, the administrative response to the crisis was to reconstruct the local state. The twin arguments were about efficiency and the need for a local administration untainted by claims about political discrimination. The result was to create a structure of local services that is almost entirely unaccountable. Housing, health and education are the preserve of non-elected boards which operate without any real autonomy from Departments of State. The lamentable dilemma is to choose between technocratic, non-democratic agencies that act as the instruments of Direct Rule, and democratic local government where the sectarian character of politics would ensure a return to discriminatory practice.

The policies of these new structures, have been determined by three developments. Firstly, there was the adoption of social programmes being developed in Britain; secondly, extra provision was made available in certain areas of greatest need, housing expenditure being the obvious example; thirdly, in some instances social policies were employed to achieve local political objectives, in particular to further coerce those in opposition to the state.

One example of a straightforward adoption of a British programme was the inner city initiatives of the late 1970s. These initiatives launched by the British Labour government in 1977 involved an endorsement of a key research conclusion of many studies – that economic decline rather than community pathology lay at the root of inner city deprivation. Greater emphasis was to be given to local economic regeneration. A new form of co-ordination was to be established, both within central government and with local government in seven designated 'most deprived' areas. This new relationship was referred to as Inner City Partnerships.

A parallel development took place in Northern Ireland. A study examined areas of special social need in Belfast (22 of the 'worst' wards were identified and the key problems were seen as jobs and housing). The Belfast Areas of Need project was established as a result of the study, but its potential was not fulfilled. While an additional £2 million was made available for the designated areas, the funds were mainly allocated to community centres, play groups and to similar welfare provision. Many groups detected a tendency for money to be allocated to more 'respectable' organisations confirming for some the view that the government saw community work as a form of low level counter-insurgency by separating the respectable from the militant in the ghettoes.

The relationship between social programmes and social control in the exceptional conditions of Northern Ireland has been much discussed.[17] Two theories are advanced. One suggests that social programmes have been the 'velvet glove covering the iron fist'. In this account, the Northern Ireland 'problem' is disaggregated into its social deprivation and counter-insurgency components. These two componnents are seen to be complementary in that better social welfare provision has helped to legitimate repression. The development of poverty programmes, the argument goes, was not the product of the British state's altruism towards Northern Ireland's poor, but part of the overall project to defeat its guerrilla opponents. The other thesis is that Northern Ireland has been the testing ground for policies designed better to manage the poor which have been subsequently implemented in a similar form in Britain generally.

A clear example of this policy experimentation is the problem of debt.[18] In 1971 the Northern Ireland Parliament passed the Payments For Debt (Emergency Provisions) Act designed to enable deductions, principally from social security payments, to recoup rents and rates unpaid because of the rent strike against internment. Before very long this piece of legislation was being employed against rent defaulters generally, since it proved useful in the state's management of the poor's debts. Undoubtedly many features of recent British social security legislation designed to deal with the rent and electricity debts of claimants were modelled on the Payments For Debt Act. Here was an example of a piece of emergency legislation not just being employed in 'normal' circumstances but acting as a model for changes in social security generally.

A further aspect of the use of social policy in the management of the political crisis was the frequent claim by British army counter-insurgency theorists that the information amassed by social welfare agencies could be best employed to identify and capture terrorists. Evelegh, for example, argued that social security information would greatly help in the intelligence war against terrorism.[19] In Belfast social workers were concerned that the computerisation of their files might make them available for transfer to army computers where the confidentiality codes could be broken. As indicated earlier, there was at times considerable suspicion that community work in Republican areas could provide an information-gathering function.

A final aspect of the relationship between the political crisis and the politics of poverty was the way in which it spawned a proliferation of community groups attempting to address

directly their immediate social problems. In part this
development was a function of the fragmentation of, and a
disaffection with, traditional political forms. Many of the leading
participants of these groups invested great optimism in their
potential to heighten awareness of communal need, and to
prompt groups across the sectarian divide to recognise and
jointly address common social problems. It was even mooted
that community action could be one instrument to break the
paralysis of the formal sectarian political system. For a time the
possibility of a bicameral assembly with a second 'community'
tier was canvassed. Considerable statutory funding was
available to many groups, though the suspicion that these grants
were differentially allocated according to the 'respectability' of
the groups has already been indicated.

However the limitations of community action in redressing
poverty in Northern Ireland are very severe. Elsewhere we have
described these in the following terms:

> Community groups are limited with respect to size, operate within
> particular localities and tend to be organisationally weak. They
> operate defensively with limited powers of veto on the forces they
> oppose, tending to intervene in specific crises without some overall
> strategic conception. In that they often lapse into self-help, they
> have a potential to be incorporated within the systems that deliver
> social services. On many occasions, their arguments are about
> switching resources from other localities to their own advantage
> without challenging the total volume of resources available.[20]

Such limits are general to community action. But in Northern
Ireland the unequal distribution of resources between Protestant
and Catholic communities accompanied by the ways in which
insecurity intensified segregation and distance, were additional
problems. In terms of the methods of resistance available to
community groups, the crisis both encouraged direct action but
undermined its effectiveness. On the one hand direct action was
less effective in a situation in which full-scale riots and military
confrontation were taking place, and on the other hand there
was the fear that direct action was at the instigation of
paramilitary organisations. Moreover, even if a coherent
community movement had emerged, it would have needed to
align itself with the labour movement in order to effectively

address socio-economic issues. This would have been highly problematic not just because of the traditional mutual suspicions between the two – one characterised as bureaucratic and insensitive, the other as disorganised and unstructured – but also because of the weakness of a trade union movement in a region with high rates of economic decline and a constantly divided working class.

None of this is to dismiss the impact of community action as a form of informal politics since there have been instances of successful pressure for reforms and more resources, while community action has offered a demonstration of anti-bureaucratic prefigurative forms of local organisation. However neither is the solution to the paradox of high levels of poverty and the absence of a mass politics around the issue.

Overall, the context of political crisis exacerbated the difficulties encountered by the poor and brought them into new forms of contest with the state. Simultaneously, however, it opened up new spaces for a politics around issues of poverty though articulated in terms of the specific features of the situation in Northern Ireland. The most recent development in the political crisis has been the Anglo-Irish Agreement and the responses to it. We next offer some brief comments on whether that will create a sufficiently different situation to place poverty centrally on the political agenda.

The Anglo-Irish Agreement: A New Situation?

The thrust of the argument so far is that the persistent and widespread nature of the problem of poverty in Northern Ireland, coupled with the character of the local political system, has inhibited, at least at the formal level, the opportunities to develop a substantial politics around the issue. Our contention is neither that this impasse makes poverty an irrelevant issue nor that more fundamental questions will have to be solved before it can be adequately tackled. Rather we are claiming that the means need to be found to articulate poverty with other core contradictions so as to reinsert it as an integral element of political discourse. Since politics in Northern Ireland is currently dominated by the aftermath of the Anglo-Irish Agreement, it is sensible to ask whether this situation is one in which that kind of poverty project can become feasible. The answer depends both on the characterisation of the Agreement and on the specification of the programme required to tackle poverty.

The problem of poverty is so severe that it requires a massive programme of intervention. Central to that is the reconstruction of the local economy and the provision of jobs. Elsewhere we have argued that a popular planning alternative based on the economic development experiences of a number of Labour-controlled local authorities in Britain offers the best hope. This would maximise the participation of trade unions, community organisations and others in the development process, locate the programme firmly within a strategy led by the public sector and through enterprise planning agreements offer support to the private sector only under conditions which maximised community benefit. A second feature of an anti-poverty programme would be an improvement in the social welfare infrastructure through the reconstruction of social security and a massive investment in the housing programme.[21] Finally it would involve developing economic links with the Irish Republic, for example in the fields of industrial development, tourism, energy and agriculture, while examining the ways in which the social welfare system of the Irish Republic could match the changes taking place in Northern Ireland. It is clear that an Agreement which brings together two versions of monetarism would not willingly encompass such ideas. Thus both the reaction to the Agreement and the political composition of its architects make it improbable that this new situation is any more conducive to a politics around poverty.

Nevertheless the situation is not devoid of opportunity for political intervention. The Agreement cannot hope to convince nationalists unless it is able to address issues which are relevant to those areas where IRA strength is greatest and many such issues are poverty-based. Similarly any attempt to isolate the most rabidly sectarian Unionist politicians must involve being prepared to offer Loyalists some compensation for the process of transition they are experiencing. Opportunities may thus exist not to block the progress of the Agreement but to develop a politics around its agenda by demanding that this be broadened to include a perspective on economic and social reconstruction. The reference to external US funding as compensation for the costs of the political crisis suggests some limited thinking has already taken place in that direction. But rather than the small sum mentioned as charity from a globally dangerous superpower, the demand could be for appropriate financing for the kind of programme needed as an integral part of the agreement. The Irish Congress of Trades Unions at its 1986 annual conference has endorsed this approach. It remains to be seen whether anything practical will come of it.

Notes

[1] See, for example, E. Evason, *Family Poverty in Northern Ireland*, Belfast 1978 and P. Townsend, *Poverty in the United Kingdom*, Harmondsworth 1979.

[2] C. Driver and S. Parker, 'Capitalism in Ireland', *Bulletin of the Conference of Socialist Economists*, Vol.IV No.2, 1975.

[3] A Birrell *et al.*, *Housing in Northern Ireland*, London 1972.

[4] J. Ditch, 'The Development of Social Policy in Northern Ireland 1939 to 1950', unpublished PhD thesis, University of Ulster 1985.

[5] Examples of this view are M. Farrell, *Northern Ireland, The Orange State*, London 1974 and E. McCann, *War and an Irish Town*, Harmondsworth 1974.

[6] D. Greaves, *The Irish Crisis*, New York 1974.

[7] See Paul Bew *et al*, *The State in Northern Ireland*, Manchester 1979.

[8] B. Probert, *Beyond The Orange and Green*, London 1978.

[9] H. Patterson, *Class Conflict and Sectarianism*, Belfast 1980.

[10] D. Byrne, 'Northern Ireland and the Crisis', unpublished paper, 1981.

[11] Northern Ireland Poverty Lobby, *Northern Ireland: A Life of Poverty*, Belfast 1980.

[12] See R. Osborne and R. Comack, 'Unemployment and Religion', Appendix II, Ninth Report and Statement of Accounts for the Fair Employment Agency for Northern Ireland, Belfast 1986.

[13] See *Continuous Household Survey*, HMSO London 1984 and *Social Trends*, HMSO London 1986.

[14] All these figures and more can be found in *Regional Trends*, HMSO London 1985.

[15] B. Rowthorn, 'Unemployment, the Widening Sectarian Gap', *Fortnight*, December 1985.

[16] J. Darby and A. Williamson, *Violence and the Social Service in Northern Ireland* London 1978.

[17] See L. O'Dowd *et al.*, *Northern Ireland: From Civil Rights to Civil War*, London 1980 and J. Ditch and M. Morrissey, 'Recent Developments in Northern Ireland' in Baldwin and Brown (eds), *Year Book of Social Policy*, London 1979.

[18] See M. McWilliams and M. Morrissey, 'Debt and Debt Management in Northern Ireland', in I. Ramsie (ed.), *Creditors and Debtors*, Belfast 1986.

[19] R. Evelegh, *Peace Keeping in a Democratic Society*, Cambridge 1979.

[20] F. Gafikin and M. Morrissey, 'Community Action and the Economy', *Scope*, April-June 1986.

[21] M. McWilliams and M. Morrissey, *Divis: the Production of a Dreadful Enclosure*, Belfast 1984.

Paul Teague

Multinational Companies in the Northern Ireland Economy: An Outmoded Model of Industrial Development?

Introduction

Since the Second World War advanced capitalist economies have gone through phases of sustained economic growth and prolonged economic stagnation. These phases have been referred to as the 'virtuous' and the 'vicious' circles respectively.[1] In the virtuous circle economic growth caused investment and employment levels to rise, which in turn generated higher levels of output with the effect of starting the entire process once again. A key feature and a central dynamic of the virtuous circle was the growth and spread of multinational companies in the world economy.[2] But when economic growth declined in the mid-1970s an entirely different scenario unfolded at the national and international levels. A vicious circle replaced the previous virtuous one. During this phase, which many argue still prevails, the economic down-turn meant lower levels of output causing investment and employment to fall with the result of output being further reduced. Once again multinational companies played a key role, being both a casualty and an agent of the vicious circle. The new depressed economic environment forced these organisations to enact systematic restructuring plans which has led to a major reshaping of their operations world-wide. For example, between 1972-83 a sample of 58 UK multinationals shed 600,000 jobs at home while adding nearly 200,000 new jobs abroad.[3]

The fortunes of the Northern Ireland economy have

fluctuated with the virtuous and vicious circle phases of the post-war world economy. During the virtuous circle many major multinational companies invested in the province, helping to revive its faltering manufacturing base. Since the start of the economic crisis in the mid-1970s, however, many of these companies have withdrawn from the province. This essay examines the rise and fall of multinational companies in the Northern Ireland economy. After each phase is analysed in detail, we go on to assess the applicability of the present industrial policy which puts considerable emphasis on attracting inward investment.

Before the examination begins, however, several methodological points need to be made. Because no accurate balance of payments accounts are kept, a detailed picture cannot be developed of the economy-wide impact of multinational companies. For example, such accounts would allow an insight into the extent to which multinationals have used local firms as suppliers of intermediate goods and services. This problem is compounded by the Statistics of Trade Act (Northern Ireland) 1949 which prohibits disclosure of information on such things as the contribution of multinationals to sectoral output, etc. No similar restrictions exists in any other region of the UK.

The Virtuous Circle 1958-75

The Second World War gave Northern Ireland's traditional industries (shipbuilding, linen and textiles) a much needed boost, but with the outbreak of peace the performance of these industries slipped back once again. During the 1950s the indices for industrial output, employment and investment showed that Northern Ireland was faring worst of all the UK regions. This convinced economists, civil servants and the ruling Unionist Party that a major rejuvenation strategy was needed if the decline of the province's industries was going to be halted.[4] Such a strategy did emerge, and a key part of it was the attraction of inward investment.

There does not appear to be a particular point when attracting multinational companies became the explicit goal of industrial policy. It seems, rather, to have evolved over a period of two years, between 1957 and 1959. Before 1957 little emphasis had been given to this method of industrial development. Between 1945 and 1951 just one foreign firm opened in the province, and in the following eight years only another five were added to the list.[5] The indications of the new policy were increased visits abroad by politicians and civil servants on 'commercial missions', the publication of glossy brochures promoting Northern Ireland as an attractive location for international investment and the development of a wide-ranging set of financial incentives for overseas investors. These included investment grants and allowances, a government factory-building programme and a regional employment premium scheme.

Partly due to these instruments and partly for other reasons detailed later the number of internationally mobile investment projects attracted to the province grew substantially during the 1960s. The table below details the nature of this inward investment by country of origin.

Table 1: International Investment in Northern Ireland by Country of Origin, 1958-75

	USA	Canada	West Germany	Other European	South Africa
1958	7	–	–	6	–
1968	27	1	5	9	1
1975	26	2	11	11	1

Source: Department of Economic Development Northern Ireland, unpublished data on foreign owned units.

The table shows that before 1968 foreign investment increased markedly in the province, but after that date the rate of expansion was more modest. In the 1960s most of the multinationals came from the United States, the largest single source of international investment projects at the time, and after 1968 the number of European multinationals in the province increased significantly. This was also the result of global trends; from the late 1960s US multinationals were redistributing their stock across Europe, while at the same time the overall number

Table 2: Industrial Profile of Multinational Companies in Northern Ireland 1968-1975 (1968 Industrial Classification)

	1958	1968	1975
Food, drink and tobacco	3	4	4
Chemical and allied industries	–	2	3
Mechanical engineering	2	10	11
Instrument engineering	–	2	2
Electrical engineering	–	3	7
Vehicles	–	2	2
Metal goods	–	2	1
Textiles	5	9	9
Leather, etc	2	3	2
Clothing and footwear		1	2
Bricks, pottery, etc	1	1	2
Timber, furniture	–	–	1
Paper, printing	–	–	2
Other manufacturing	–	4	4

Source: Department of Economic Development Northern Ireland, unpublished data on foreign owned units.

of European multinationals was growing appreciably.

The industrial profile of the overseas-owned companies is shown in Table 2, which shows that foreign owned companies were concentrated in the mechanical engineering and textiles industrial sectors, with electrical engineering becoming more prominent towards the end of the period. Again there is little that is particularly significant about this industrial profile – it broadly reflects the trend at the time of national (mainly US) medium technology companies building up networks of subsidiaries and affiliates outside their home country in an attempt to exploit large economies of scale and to penetrate new markets. The profile lends weight to the theory that multinationals in particular industries tend to locate in regions where there is a heavy indigenous concentration in these sectors (there was a considerable number of local mechanical engineering companies in the province in the 1960s).[6] The only deviation from this was electrical engineering where the foreign share of employment was at least double the overall share of employment in the sector. This point is open to a double interpretation: it can be read as the industrial promotion agencies being able to attract transnationals in more advanced technical sectors, or it can be seen as the indigenous industrial structure becoming increasingly outmoded. This is not a pedantic point: it is an issue at the heart of the present industrial policy debate, namely, whether more emphasis should be placed on modernising local industries rather than trying to attract 'new' inward investment projects, particularly in the fields of electronics and high technology. This debate will be analysed in depth later.

Because the multinationals that came to the province in this period were seeking to exploit economies of scale, it is not surprising to find that the plants opened were large. Approximately 78 per cent of all multinational units established in the province between 1963 and 1975 employed more than 500 people. During the virtuous circle phase employment in foreign owned companies increased from 4,515 to 26,141. Smith suggests that Northern Ireland experienced the largest employment growth in foreign enterprises amongst UK regions – the estimated increase was 303 per cent, the next highest figure being 180 per cent for the North of England.[7] A Northern Ireland Economic Council Report shows that only about 10 per cent of all assisted new industrial jobs between 1946 and 1967 were in local firms. By the early 1970s multinational companies had clearly become the central dynamic economic force in the province, especially in the manufacturing sector.[8]

The factors motivating multinationals to invest in the province have been interpreted differently. Perrons suggests that the main motivating influence was Northern Ireland's low labour costs.[9] This is challenged by Moore and his colleagues, who suggest that this argument is undermined by the fact that the Republic of Ireland, where wages levels were similar, attracted six times as many foreign projects than Northern Ireland during the period under examination.[10] They argue, more plausibly, that the most important factor was the package of regional incentives on offer, but one suspects that even without these incentives Northern Ireland would have benefited from international investment, such was its scale at the time.

The socio-political impact of foreign owned enterprises in the province has received more attention than the economics of the issue. Two contrasting interpretations have been developed, both linking multinational investment to the central political issue of sectarianism and the Northern Ireland state. One thesis, put forward by Boserup, is that multinational companies have played a progressive role in the province as they have undermined the sectarian employment practices of many local Unionist employers.[11] The opposite conclusion is reached by O'Dowd and his co-authors who argue that the multinationals conformed to these discriminatory practices, thereby reproducing the material base of Unionist hegemony.[12] At the level of academic debate, there is little that is peculiar about this sharp difference in interpretation: the question of whether multinationals assimilate into or diverge from the prevailing pattern of industrial relations in a host country is a long standing debate.[13]

It is a crucial weakness of both accounts, however, that no empirical evidence is provided to substantiate their theoretical assertions. In the absence of such evidence both arguments rest on highly questionable assumptions. Firstly, both analyses assume that the multinationals in the province were sufficiently strong to make a telling impact on the social and political environment, and in particular on the sectarian practices which undoubtedly existed. But this assumption can be challenged. Although multinationals made up a sizeable proportion of the province's industrial structure, local industry and public services still remained the largest employer during the 1960s and 70s. This suggests that irrespective of the employment practices of dominant multinationals, the trend in this area would have continued to be set by local employers. Secondly, both Boserup and O'Dowd and his collaborators write about multinationals as if they were a homogeneous grouping. For example, they make the highly questionable assumption, although only implicitly, that these companies adopt similar employee relations policies although one study, by Buckley and Enderwick, concluded a survey of the industrial relations practices of foreign firms in Britain by suggesting that there is little similarity amongst them.[14] In other words, some multinationals fit into the established system of industrial relations while others challenge it.

It would appear, therefore, that both accounts make conclusions which are too sweeping given the paucity of the evidence. This is far from satisfactory, especially given the political sensitivity of the topic. The impression is that both analyses were too eager to establish a connection between the multinationals and the political issue of Unionist dominance. At the same time, it would be wrong to conclude that multinationals made no impact on the social and political environment. In assessing the nature of their impact it is perhaps best to use the 'eclectic theory' developed by John Dunning which emphasises the need to examine multinationals on a case-by-case basis, an approach which at least reduces the risk of making excessive and unsubstantiated conclusions.[15]

Thus, during the virtuous circle there was a continual increase in the number of multinational companies entering the province, which was largely a by-product of the rapid increase in the number of mobile international investment projects at the time. Important positive benefits accrued from these foreign owned enterprises, particularly in terms of employment. The only extensive analysis that has been made of these multinationals relates to their impact on the province's socio-political environment; these studies have attempted to draw some type of connection between the arrival of multinational companies and the political issue of Unionist dominance in the province, but are unconvincing mainly because they are too reductionist.

A Vicious Circle

It is widely accepted that the vicious circle started properly around the mid-1970s. The oil price shocks, accelerating inflation and burgeoning public deficits had worked their way through the world economy by this time, giving birth to the new phenomenon of stagflation. The result was a significant fall in output amongst the advanced industrialised countries (average growth for these countries during the 1960s was 5 per cent. By the mid-1970s it had fallen to 2.5 per cent). This led to lower levels of investment, higher unemployment, and a fall in demand largely caused by governments attempting to reduce their public expenditure. The vicious circle was now in full operation, and some argue that the industrialised countries have yet to break out of it.

At the same time, the rate of new multinational openings was slowing down. This was only to be expected for in hindsight the sheer scale of internationalisation during the 1950s and 60s was extraordinary. During that period the nature of the internationalisation of firms changed significantly. At the start of the period subsidiaries opened were frequently the first overseas operation of the parent and were relatively free-standing concerns, but by the end of the period they had become integrated into complex international commercial networks. Very often a key feature of these networks was that similar products were spread over a number of affiliates, thereby reducing the dependency of the group on one subsidiary. Of course, this meant that many subsidiaries, especially in peripheral areas like Northern Ireland, became more vulnerable when the new economic environment of the vicious circle started to have an impact on the multinationals.

Since the mid-1970s there has been a continual reduction in the importance of multinational companies in the Northern Ireland economy. The next table gives some indication of the extent of this decline in the early 1980s. Unfortunately no similar information is available for the late 1970s, or for the years after 1983.

Table 3: Foreign-owned enterprises in Northern Ireland 1981-83

	Employment		Net capital expenditure		Gross value added	
	Percentage	Thousands	Percentage	amount	Percentage	amount
1981	23	25.6	43	£53.1 million	30	£312.6 million
1983	16	16.8	36	£52.6 million	19	£218.8 million

Source: Regional Trends 1985 and 1986.

The table indicates that there has been a decline in the numbers employed in multinational companies both in absolute terms and as a percentage of all manufacturing employees in the province.

Table 4: Openings and Closures of Foreign-owned Units in Northern Ireland by Country of Origin

	USA	West Germany	Eire	Other European	Asia	South Africa
			Openings			
1976	–	–	1	1	–	–
1977	1	–	–	–	–	–
1978	2	–	–	–	–	–
1979	2	1	–	–	–	–
1980	7	–	–	–	–	–
1981-5	5	3	9	8	3	1
			Closures			
1976	–	1	–	2	–	–
1977	1	–	–	2	–	–
1978	1	–	–	–	–	–
1979	–	–	–	–	–	–
1980	3	2	–	2	–	–
1981-5	12	4	1	5	–	–

Source: Unpublished figures from the Statistics Branch of the Department of Economic Development in Northern Ireland.

This is due mainly to the withdrawal of many of the major older multinationals from the province. The figures on capital expenditure and gross value added should be read cautiously, as they are slightly distorted by the high inflation rates and by the constantly changing exchange rate relationships during the late 1970s and early 1980s. But these distortions do not alter the overall downward trend of multinational investment in the province.

The next tables outline the trends in more detail. Table 4 shows the multinational openings and closures by country of origin, while Table 5 does a similar exercise on an industry basis. It needs to be pointed out again that the figures should be interpreted warily. The tables show that in the vicious circle there has been a net increase of ten multinationals in the

Table 5: Openings and Closures of foreign-owned Units in Northern Ireland by Industrial Sector, 1976-85 (1968 Industrial Classification)

	Openings		Closures	
	1976-80	1981-85	1976-80	1981-85
Manufacture of non-metallic mineral products	1	2	–	1
Food, drink and tobacco	1	9	1	–
Chemical and allied industries	1	1	1	2
Mechanical engineering	3	3	3	4
Instrument engineering	1	–	–	2
Electrical engineering	3	4	4	5
Vehicles	2	–	–	2
Metal goods	–	1	–	1
Textiles	2	4	2	5
Leather	–	1	–	–
Clothing and footwear	–	–	2	–
Bricks, pottery, etc	–	–	1	–
Timber, furniture	–	1	–	–
Paper, printing	–	1	–	–
Other manufacturing	2	1	–	–

Source: Unpublished figures from the statistics branch of the Department of Economic Development Northern Ireland.

province which appears to be at variance with the above observation that the importance of these companies declined during this period. This apparent discrepancy is resolved when it is realised that over the past ten years multinationals have used the acquisition method (the purchase of existing local or transnational companies) rather than the direct entry method as a means of establishing an operation in Northern Ireland. Research has shown that the acquisition method of entry generates only minor positive spin-offs for the host country in terms of employment creation and capital expenditure.[16]

Thus a dynamic picture emerges about multinational investment in the province during the vicious circle: on the one hand, some of the more mature multinationals which had been major employers started to withdraw from the province, particularly in the textile sectors: meanwhile, on the other hand, different multinationals entered the province via relatively small scale acquisition investments. The net result has been that although there are now more multinationals in the province than before, their overall economic significance has decreased. This conclusion is somewhat different from the conventional view which sees multinationals as simply retreating from the province. The reality is that the vicious circle has had the effect of inducing new forms of internationalisation, leading to much higher activity *rates* on the part of multinationals.[17]

The most significant figure in Table 4 is the one which shows the rapid increase in multinationals originating from the Republic of Ireland, most of which took the form of acquisition investments: during these late 1970s increasing numbers of profitable businesses in the Republic began to look towards the North for suitable companies to take over.[18] This development apart, there has been little net change in the originating country of international investment in the province, but there has been some change in the industrial profile of foreign owned enterprises. In particular, the number of multinationals in the food, drink and tobacco sector has increased while the textiles sector has been affected the most by disinvestment. The highest overall flow of activity has occurred in the engineering sectors, resulting in a small decrease in the number of multinationals in these industries. The industrial profile also shows that few high technology multinationals have been attracted to the province in recent years.

It is difficult to get a more in depth picture than the above due to the restrictions on the publication of related statistics mentioned earlier, but a recent large scale survey of multinational companies in the British Isles allows for further insight into the nature of international investment in the province.[19] From the survey a comparison was made of multinational activity within the assisted areas of the UK. Multinationals in Northern Ireland registered below-average scores in the following variables: size of plant; incidence of administrative functions at the plant; number of other group plants; incidence of single source activity; UK orientation of output; percentage of inputs from within the region; proportion of skilled workers on the pay-roll. Scores above the average were noted in the following areas: incidence of greenfield entry; capital employed per employee; decline in costs with larger plant size; direct labour costs as a percentage of total costs; net exports; percentage of labourers and other manual workers; proportion of managerial and professional personnel; incidence of unionisation and strikes and stoppages.

These results suggest that important changes have occurred in the nature of international investment during the vicious circle. Previously, multinationals were situated in large plants and were part of international networks; now they appear to be relatively small scale concerns. Moreover, the newer multinationals appear to have even fewer backward linkages with local producers than their earlier counterparts. Only a small proportion of these companies' exports are destined to local or UK markets, which suggests that most of their output is related to inter-company production. All these features bear the hallmarks of acquisition investments.

To get a more detailed picture of the characteristics and peculiarities of this survey of overseas investment in the British Isles, Young and Stewart conducted a series of discriminant analyses on the data.[20] One of the main conclusions from this exercise was that international investment was highly distinctive in Northern Ireland in comparison with other UK regions. In particular, the tests showed that multinationals in Northern Ireland tended to be low technology concerns requiring a semi-skilled workforce, while other UK regions had more high technology, capital intensive multinationals. To a certain degree this is explained by other UK regions, especially in Scotland and Wales, being successful in attracting new modern forms of international investment; the 'Silicon Glen' development in Scotland (consisting mainly of US high-tech companies) and the cluster of Japanese multinationals in Wales are particular cases in point.[21]

Of course, the policy of attracting new direct entry international investment continued during the vicious circle, but did not meet with much success. As the amount of new mobile international investment declined and as Northern Ireland became a less attractive location – a recent survey of US executives of multinational companies placed Northern Ireland 49 in a list of 50 of the most attractive overseas sites for investment – the ventures established have become more precarious. The spectacular failures of De Lorean and, more recently, Lear Fan are examples of this. Furthermore, while Japanese companies are now increasing their international activities more than any others, Northern Ireland has been able to attract only one company from this source.[22]

Thus the nature of international investment in the province changed during the vicious circle. In particular there was an exodus from the province of many of the larger multinationals. In their place have come relatively small scale foreign enterprises, entering the province through the acquisition method. The net result of all this activity has been a reduction in the importance of multinationals in the province. Despite efforts to attract new modern forms of international investment to Northern Ireland, few such companies have come. The 'troubles' undoubtedly tarnished the image of the province in the eyes of overseas investors, and it is unlikely that there will be an improvement in this respect in the foreseeable future. Indeed, it can be argued that the province has missed out in the recent phase of 'high-tech' international investment projects that have come to the UK.

Industrial Policy and Transnational Companies

The preceding analysis suggests that the policy of attracting inward investment is meeting with less and less success. The response of the present and past governments has been to try and reinvigorate the policy. The amount and range of incentives on offer to overseas investors have been increased in the 1980s, and Northern Ireland has now probably the best package of industrial incentives in Europe. The Industrial Development Board (IDB) currently finances fourteen separate offices abroad, stretching from the Scandinavian countries through the USA to Singapore. A concerted drive has been made to 'improve Northern Ireland's image abroad'. In 1983, for example, £500,000 was spent on advertising promotions in American financial magazines. A group calling itself Northern Ireland Partnership has been established consisting of business people, academics and others prominent in public life in the province. The body organises overseas 'commercial missions' to promote the province as a location for inward investment, but has produced few tangible results so far.

The continuation of the policy means a high level of resource and financial allocation. An examination of IDB overseas activities in 1984-85 gives an indication of the staffing and administrative resources required to maintain the policy. During that year staff undertook 1,627 promotion visits while others arranged 105 commercial visits to the province. In order to get these 105 visits, 1,600 telephone calls had to be made, and from this group only five realistic prospects emerged. Given this situation it is hardly surprising that inward investment is the most expensive form of job promotion undertaken by the IDB.

All this has led organisations such as the Northern Ireland Economic Council to argue for a change in industrial policy so that greater emphasis is placed on developing local businesses. But, despite all its shortcomings, abandoning the inward investment strategy would be inappropriate.[23] There are good reasons why the overseas activities of the IDB should continue, although perhaps in a revised form. At this point it is necessary to make the distinction between international investment as a model of industrial development, and the role of governmental agencies as actors in the new international system of production. A key feature of this new system, as seen earlier, is the ability of multinationals to shift factors of production, particularly capital and technical knowledge across frontiers with relative ease, and government action is an important influence on such decisions.[24]

By the construction of wide ranging incentives for inward investment, governments have unwittingly created an awkward dilemma at the international level. The rules of the game are that if a government participates by developing incentives there is no guarantee of success, but if it does not participate then it will lose out and have virtually no possibility of obtaining any new international investment, and will also face the possibility of existing multinationals being lured elsewhere by the offer of advantageous subsidies.

It is, therefore, imperative for the IDB to continue some form of international activity, but this should become more discretionary and flexible. The 'jobs at any price' strategy towards inward investment has ended up in embarrassing failures which have only served to further tarnish the image of the province. There are signs that the IDB is revising its approach on this point. The Board appears to have developed a more targeted strategy, concentrating more on market research and on identifying companies and sectors which are likely to grow and which might regard the province as a suitable location.[25] This should be welcomed, but even greater flexibility needs to be introduced.

Complementing the above action, more effort should be made to upgrade the performance of existing multinational companies within the province's economy. This should involve encouraging multinationals in mature sectors to modernise their capital equipment, promoting closer integration between these companies and Northern Ireland's research bodies, making more long-term development and venture capital available, and encouraging more interaction between local and overseas owned companies. The goal must be to entrench the existing multinational enterprises within the province to reduce the possibility of their withdrawal, while at the same time maximising the economy wide benefits from their operations.

But as the existing multinationals in the province spawn few positive economy-wide benefits at present, and given that this will continue to be the case for the foreseeable future, it is questionable whether the strategy of attracting inward investment should remain the central objective of industrial policy in the province. A new rationale for industrial policy needs to emerge, and it is argued here that this should be the establishment of a dynamic economy both within Northern Ireland and Ireland generally. The logic behind this new policy direction is summed up by Kindleberger when discussing the future prospects of the Southern Irish economy: in his words: 'The more central question is whether the Irish society conforms more to the patterns of adaptable and transforming economies and societies like Sweden, Denmark and the Netherlands, at least as they were some years ago, or nearly to that of Puerto Rico.'[26]

A similar type of logic applies to the Northern Ireland economy. As the role of the multinationals has declined in the province, the economic problem of its geographically peripheral position has come increasingly to the fore. A recent study of regional economic development in the EEC shows Northern Ireland to be one of the worst affected regions in Europe in this respect.[27] There are distinct economic disadvantages associated with peripherality: high transport costs, resulting in higher prices and/or limited markets; poor quality transport links, resulting in the risk of delays and inconvenience; limited accessibility to urban centres which are large enough to generate specialised services and other economies of scale; and distance from market information and customer contact.

While the case for constructing a dynamic internal economy may well be compelling, its achievement will be far from straightforward. One of the main barriers is the fact that Northern Ireland is by and large a satellite economy of Britain. At one level this is of undoubted benefit to the province: the standard of living would drop significantly if the British exchequer stopped its subvention to Northern Ireland, and without public contracts from Britain many producers in the province would go bankrupt. More generally, the vast majority of Northern Ireland exports go to the British mainland. The now conventional wisdom that Britain shores up the Northern Ireland economy is undoubtedly true.

However there is another, less positive, dimension to this British link. Being, in effect, an appendage to the British economy means that when the chill winds of the economic recession hit the UK mainland they also blow over Northern Ireland. In fact, some argue that the fortunes of the Northern Ireland economy are so bound up with those of the British economy that economic recovery in the province will only occur when the UK generally experiences an upturn.[28] This argument appears logical enough, but history suggests that while the effects of economic decline are transmitted from the British to the Northern Ireland economy, the reverse is not the case in times of economic expansion. Previously, Northern Ireland has not benefited greatly from economic expansion in the rest of the UK; in the 1950s, for example, before the arrival of multinationals, while most parts of the UK were enjoying the fruits of unprecedented growth rates, manufacturing industry in the province was actually declining.

There is a further issue. Because mainland Britain is a source of almost fixed markets (via subcontractual relationships, etc.) for some Northern Ireland producers, and because public contracts have given others a secure source of orders, it has been argued that entrepreneurial activity in the province has atrophied: the business community has become satisfied with its present circumstances and as a result has not given any priority to opening up new markets outside the UK.[29] There is some evidence to support this argument: O'Dowd's essay in this book shows that the level of producer services – an indication of a dynamic and innovatory business structure – is low in comparison to other regions in the UK; Kenneth Cork, the noted City accountant who headed the De Lorean liquidation team, commented on numerous occasions that the Northern Ireland business community has become too dependent on outside help and should be doing more for itself.

There appears to be sufficient grounds to conclude that while the British contribution to the province is essential if a major economic crisis is to be prevented, it also has a smothering effect on a dynamic economic framework emerging within the province. The central economic project is therefore to work towards the creation of such an economy while the British contribution continues. (It would be sheer folly to argue for an economic programme for the province without the British contribution to the province continuing at its present level.) Moreover, the establishment of a dynamic economy in the province should not be interpreted as essentially promoting indigenous small and medium sized companies. This to a large extent is already being done by the Local Enterprise Development Unit (LEDU). However, the results from this activity have been lacklustre, and a recent study shows that the performance of small businesses in Northern Ireland is mediocre in comparison with small firms in other parts of the UK.[30]

The objective of industrial policy, and economic policy more generally, needs to be more far reaching. It should be nothing less than the integration of the economies of Northern and Southern Ireland. Unfortunately, the notion of integration is heavily loaded given the nature of politics in the province after the Anglo-Irish Agreement. This is made worse by the fact that existing discussions on economic integration in Ireland have linked this idea with some degree of political unification. A case in point is the economic material prepared for the New Ireland Forum: the consequences of an integrated economic policy in Ireland are only discussed in these documents in relation to three different political arrangements – a unitary Irish state, a confederal state and joint authority.[31] But it is highly misleading to assume that economic integration has necessarily to involve some diminution of political sovereignty. There are several successful examples of economic integration in West Europe which have not involved political matters: the Belgium-Luxembourg Economic Union and the Benelux Economic Union.[32] To advocate economic integration in Ireland with a strong political component would, in the present climate, obviously put the entire policy in jeopardy.

Another shortcoming of existing discussions is that they assume economic integration must involve some formal arrangements. Again this definition of economic integration is too narrow. For example, the process of integrating the economies of Benelux took place over a period of fifteen years, involving individual agreements, protocols, ministerial decisions and so on, in specific spheres of the economy. This was unlike other instances of economic integration which began with the signing of a treaty which foresaw the path of integration, defined the scope and extent of the transitional phase, and set out the model of economic association which the partners would like to reach. Economic integration is not a narrow concept, and the literature on the subject is full of different and sometimes contradictory definitions of the term.[33]

The path towards greater economic integration between Northern and Southern Ireland can take whatever form the administrations in both parts of the island deem fit, and any strategy developed does not have to be shackled by issues which could hamper the active pursuit of the policy. The author's preferred option is for some form of informal rolling economic integration pursued on a case-by-case basis. This approach would avoid the political problems which could arise from a more formal strategy, and it would also be more effective in tackling the peculiar barriers to integration in each economic sphere. Of course, this would mean that the level of integration would be uneven, but this is only to be expected as some areas are more conducive to harmonisation than others.

Encouraging the formation of a single market is often seen as the central objective of economic integration, but it would bring few benefits. Since the Anglo-Irish Trade Agreement in 1965 which removed many of the existing tariffs, trade between

Northern and Southern Ireland has increased considerably. Beyond creating better channels of contact and communications on market opportunities, further progress in this area would entail harmonising indirect taxes both sides of the border, which is hardly realistic in the foreseeable future given the present wide divergence.[35] But another area of economic integration – monetary arrangements – could once again be integrated if Britain made the political decision to join the European Monetary System (EMS). This area had been integrated until 1979 when the Republic decided to join the EMS, while Britain chose to remain outside the arrangement, which led to unnecessary currency upheavals resulting in diverging exchange rate policies either side of the border. However monetary arrangements are the only aspect of central economic policy-making which is relatively open to integration. It would be much harder to achieve closer harmonisation in other areas such as fiscal and budgetary policies. A more long-term and gradual approach needs to be taken in these areas.

Given this situation more focus must be placed on other economic spheres such as industry and agriculture. Some possible initiatives are foreshadowed by existing schemes. One example is the Border Area Development Plans which attempt to improve the infrastructure of border areas 'unnaturally' divided by the creation of two separate states. These plans could be more extensive, covering such points as local economic development (tourism, for example), more integrated local planning, better transport provision, etc. Other major joint infrastructural projects could be initiated. Of particular significance is the construction of a modern road link between Belfast and Dublin. In no other European region is the road network between two major capitals so outmoded. Such schemes would have the added advantage of quickly creating large numbers of jobs in the construction industry (a sector in which there are a large number of unemployed workers both sides of the borders).

But perhaps the area that needs to be given most immediate attention is industrial policy. By no means is the idea of a more co-ordinated policy widely accepted. For example, McCarthy and Blease conclude in relation to multinational companies that:

It is not at all clear that cross-border co-operation in attracting investment is a very practical idea. A joint approach by both administrations to overseas investors would require some element of agreement in advance in relation to terms, some harmonisation perhaps, but this would have the disadvantage of reducing flexibility and the capacity to bargain. But even if such harmonisation were to take place, the differences between the states are far greater and more pervasive than industrial grants and other aids. The social systems are different and so also are the style and form of work regulations. Even if a firm were to respond to a joint approach from the two administrations, it must establish itself either in the North and South and therefore would accord either with the arrangements of the North or South not an amalgam of both.[36]

From this the authors conclude that any co-operation on industrial matters is not feasible. Unfortunately this view is caught in the conventional logic of seeing industrial policy revolving essentially around attracting internationally mobile investment projects.

Even allowing for this shortcoming the above statement is not very helpful. Of course there will be some degree of competition between Northern and Southern Ireland in attracting inward investment, but this also applies to the North and South of England where it does not exclude simultaneous pursuit of a wider industrial policy. In other words, competing interests are not necessarily impediments to a co-ordinated policy, especially if these are allowed for. Moreover, although it is true to say that there are diverging competitive interests in relation to attracting overseas investments, there are also important areas where there could be meaningful collaboration. Take for example the widely noted problem of few multinationals in Southern Ireland having backward linkages with local producers. One of the main reasons for this is simply that there are few local businesses in the South which could act as suppliers to the multinationals. But this is not the case in relation to Northern Ireland where many suitable medium technology firms exist which could act as subcontractors. If greater co-ordination between the IDA and the IDB was established then there is no good reason why such companies could not perform this role.

A number of reports outline other areas where industrial co-ordination and integration could be secured. For example, a report written for 'Co-operation North' on business co-operation between Northern Ireland and the Republic indicates a whole range of initiatives that could be pursued, particularly in the field of small and medium sized enterprises. Suggestions include greater co-operation in marketing and distribution overseas, more joint ventures geared towards export markets beyond Britain, and an all-Ireland drive to increase innovation and technical expertise of businesses. These and similar initiatives, although small in their own right, have the potential to bring about a new collective repertoire of policies which could result in the creation of a dynamic economy in Ireland. The picture is one of rolling integration going at different speeds in individual spheres of the economy. The objective is invariably long term but it should be the priority of the policy-makers and administrators in both Northern and Southern Ireland.

Notes

[1] For a full discussion of the dynamics of the 'virtuous' and 'vicious' circles, see M. Aglietta, 'World Capitalism in the Eighties', *New Left Review*, No.63, November/December 1982.

[2] For a detailed survey of the rise of multinationals since 1945, see J.H. Dunning and S.M. Stopford, *Multinationals: Company Performance and Global Trends*, London 1983.

[3] J.M. Stoppard and L. Turner, *Britain and the Multinationals*, Geneva 1985, p.12.

[4] See K.S. Isles and N. Cuthbert, *Economic Survey of Northern Ireland*, Belfast 1957.

[5] B. Moore, J. Rhodes, and D. Tarling, 'Industrial Policy and Economic Development: the Experience of Northern Ireland and the Republic of Ireland', *Cambridge Journal of Economics*, Vol.2 No.2, 1978.

[6] R.E. Caves, *Multinational Enterprise and Economic Analysis*, New York 1982 and G. Yannaopoulos and J.H. Dunning, 'Multinational enterprises and Regional Development: An Exploratory Paper', *Regional Studies* Vol.10, No.4, 1976 pp.389-99.

[7] I.J. Smith, 'Some Aspects of Inward Direct Investment in the United Kingdom, with Particular Reference to the Northern Region', Discussion Paper No.31, Centre for Urban and Regional Development Studies, University of Newcastle 1980.

[8] See Northern Ireland Economic Council, *Economic Strategy: Historical Growth Performance*, Belfast 1983, Section 4.

[9] D.C. Perrons, 'The role of Ireland in the New International Division of Labour: A Proposed Framework for Regional Analysis', *Regional Studies*, Vol.15 No.2, 1981, pp.81-100.

[10] Moore *et al.*, op cit; for a similar view see N. Hood and S. Young, *Multinational Investment Strategies in the British Isles*, London 1983.

[11] A. Boserup, 'Contradictions and Struggles in Northern Ireland', *Socialist Register* 1972.

[12] L. O'Dowd, B. Rolston and M. Tomlinson, *Northern Ireland: Between Civil Rights and Civil War*, London 1980.

[13] See R.F. Banks and J. Stieber (eds), *Multinationals, Unions and Labour Relations in Industrialised Countries*, New York 1977.

[14] P.J. Buckley and P. Enderdrick, *The Industrial Relations Practices of Foreign-Owned Firms in Britain*, London 1985.

[15] J.H. Dunning, 'Explaining Changing Patterns of International Production: In Defence of the Eclectic Approach', *Oxford Bulletin of Economics and Statistics*, Vol.41, 1979, pp.269-95.

[16] See B. Wilson, 'The Propensity of Multinational Corporations to Expand through Acquisitions', *Journal of International Business Studies*, Spring/Summer 1980, pp.59-65.

[17] R. Vernon, 'Multinationals are Mushrooming', *Challenge*, May-June 1986 pp.41-8.

[18] Interview with an official from the Department of Economic Development Northern Ireland.

[19] Hood and Young, op. cit.

[20] S. Young and D. Stewart, 'The Regional Implications of Inward Direct Investment' in A. Amin and J.B. Goddard (eds), *Technological Change, Industrial Restructuring and Regional Development*, London 1986.

[21] See N. Hood and K. Ingham, 'Foreign Multinationals in Scotland and the Attraction of Multinationals', IRM Working Paper, Geneva 1986.

[22] See *Hansard*, Vol.88 No.7, p.1055.

[23] Northern Ireland Economic Council, 'Economic Strategy and Industrial Development Linkages', Report No. 56, February 1986 p.48.

[24] John Dunning (ed.), *Multinational Enterprises, Economic Structure and International Competitiveness*, Geneva 1985.

[25] Northern Ireland Industrial Development Board, *Encouraging Enterprise, a Medium-Term Strategy for 1985-1990*, Belfast 1985.

[26] C. Kindleberger, *Multinational Excursions*, New York 1984, p.109.

[27] D. Keeble, P.L. Owens and C. Thompson, *Centrality, Peripherality and EEC Regional Development*, London 1982.

[28] See for example J. Simpson, 'Must there be any Good News for the Economy?' *Fortnight*, 4 November 1985.

[29] S. Harvey and D. Rea, 'The Northern Ireland Economy with Particular Reference to Industrial Development', Ulster Polytechnic Innovation and Resource Centre, 1982.

[30] O. Hitchens and P. O'Farnell, 'Inter-Regional Comparisons of Small Firm Performance: The case of Northern Ireland and South-East England', Working Papers in Economics, Occasional Papers No.4, Queen's University, Belfast, 1985.

[31] New Ireland Forum, *The Macroeconomic Consequences of Integrated Economic Policy, Planning and Co-ordination in Ireland*, Dublin 1984.

[32] J. Meade, H.H. Liesner and S.J. Wells, *Case Studies in European Economic Union: The Mechanics of Integration*, Oxford 1962.

[33] F. Machlup, *A History of Thought on Economic Integration*, London 1977.

[34] E. O'Mally, 'Industrial Development in the North and South of Ireland: Prospects for an Integrated Approach', *Administration*, Vol.83, No.1, 1985.

[35] C. McCarthy and W.J. Blease, 'Cross-Border Industrial Co-operation Limits and Possibilities', *Administration*, Vol.26 1979 p.362.

[36] Co-operation North, 'Business Co-operation between Northern Ireland and the Republic of Ireland', Belfast and Dublin, December 1985.

Liam O'Dowd

Trends and Potential of the Service Sector in Northern Ireland

As the violent political struggle over the role, and even the presence, of the British state in Northern Ireland drags on, that same state has become ever more crucial to everyday economic life in the province. In two key areas, public expenditure and public service employment, the British state is now the lynchpin of the Northern Ireland economy. Public expenditure accounts for 70 per cent of GDP while public services directly account for 45 per cent of all employees. The comparable figures for Great Britain are 44 and 32 per cent respectively. In addition, 21 per cent of the workforce are in receipt of state unemployment benefits – the highest regional percentage in the UK; the two major manufacturing companies, Shorts and Harland and Wolff, are in public ownership; and employment in the private sector is heavily subsidised by monies channelled through state institutions.

This essay focuses on the political economy of the service sector – the most under-analysed sector of the Northern Ireland economy, yet, in employment terms, by far the most significant. Approximately 70 per cent of all employees (under the 1968 industrial classification) are now in this sector. By 1981, Northern Ireland had a higher proportion of employees in services (defined narrowly as 1981 Census Divisions 8-9) than any other UK region. Service employment is particularly concentrated in three key areas – health, education and public administration and defence.

We will argue that it is not sufficient to see the political economy of the Northern Ireland service sector simply as a regional instance of that of the UK as a whole. Of course,

183

British debates over public expenditure and services, as well as over general economic strategy do have major implications for the province, but, analysis of these implications in aggregate economic terms does not take us very far. It is necessary to examine how the specific politics of service employment and service provision within Northern Ireland influence, and are influenced by the wider British economy and polity of which the province is a part. The focus here is on the way which Northern Ireland's polity and economy articulates with that of the UK generally. Furthermore, the British state must not be seen as some kind of external force making periodic interventions in Northern Ireland. The contrary is the case: it is continually and actively engaged in the shaping and reshaping of political and economic relations within the province. In this sense, it is not simply a referee or political manager of the Northern Ireland problem – it is part of the problem.

It is important here to distinguish between the British government and the British state. British governments have not been influenced to any significant extent by the party system in Northern Ireland.[1] The legislative programmes of these governments are primarily shaped by the balance of political forces in Great Britain, not by those within Northern Ireland. In most areas the tail does not wag the dog.[2] But, in implementing decisions in Northern Ireland however, the government must work through the particular form the British state takes in the province. As shown below in relation to the (public) service sector, the two religious communities interact with each other via this state. The nature of this interaction is shaped to a significant degree by the way in which elements of both communities are incorporated into the state, albeit in different ways – Protestant police, Catholic nurses, Protestant senior civil servants and electricity workers, Catholic teachers and clerical workers. Beyond these occupational categories are the different class profiles of both communities, and the different ways in which both classes and communities relate to the state.

The discussion of the service sector is organised as follows: the first section locates the service sector within the broad context of economic change in the province. The next section briefly specifies the political context in which the expansion of service employment occurred. The next two sections examine the structure of growth of the service employment in more detail, distinguishing between private and public services and comparing Northern Ireland with the rest of the UK. The effects of service growth on spatial and Protestant/Catholic disparities in employment are then analysed. Finally, the conclusions draw out some of the political implications of the changing dimensions of service employment and particularly of the state's greatly expanded role as an employer and provider of public services.

Economic Change and the Service Sector in Northern Ireland

Northern Ireland's economy has been transformed over the last two decades – a transformation which has gone relatively unnoticed compared to the upheavals generated by violent conflict in the same period. Three interrelated trends have contributed to this transformation. Firstly, there has been a dramatic loss of employment in what have traditionally been seen as the productive sectors – agriculture and manufacturing industry. Northern Ireland still retains a higher proportion of employment in agriculture than any UK region but this had shrunk to 5.4 per cent of civilian employment by 1981. The loss of manufacturing jobs has accelerated in the 1970s and 80s. Since 1966, the province has slipped from fifth to ninth place of the eleven UK regions in terms of the proportion of its employees in manufacturing. By 1984, proportionate employment in engineering, metals and chemicals was less than in any other region. The rate of de-industrialisation in Northern Ireland has been among the highest of any region within the EEC.[3]

The second trend has been a return to levels of unemployment approaching those of the 1930s. Northern Ireland has the highest unemployment rates in the UK. But, a rate of over 20 per cent masks significant spatial variations within Northern Ireland, with rates of over 50 per cent for male unemployment in the West of the province and in parts of Belfast. Catholic male unemployment has remained almost two-and-a-half times the Protestant rate since the early 1970s. A growing population, rising female activity rates and a relative lack of emigration opportunities are important 'supply side' factors in the rise of unemployment, and some argue that these are the principal causes.

Finally, as employment has declined in other sectors, the service sector, and particularly the public services, has assumed an overriding importance. Historically, service employment in Northern Ireland had lagged behind that in the UK as a whole.[4] By 1981, however, services accounted for 62 per cent of civilian employment in Northern Ireland as compared with 60.6 per cent in Great Britain. This reversal was largely due to the dramatic growth in public services employment between 1974 and 1979. This growth was concentrated in three areas, public administration, defence, and health and education. It was also heavily female and part-time in character. Since 1981, however, the growth of service employment has not been sufficient to offset the overall decline of employment in the province. Approximately 56,000 jobs have disappeared – 11 per cent of the total – between 1981 and 1986. In 1986 manufacturing employment went under 100,000 to less than 70 per cent of its 1981 level.[5] The numbers employed in services also now show a slight decline. An important factor in this has been Tory policy of checking the expansion of public services.

It is tempting to argue that the development of the services sector generally, and the public services in particular, merely reflects international trends. In this view, the recent expansion in public service employment would be represented merely as a process of catching up with the rest of the UK – the administrative application to the province of the principle of 'parity of social provision' with the rest of the UK. But such a view both ignores the particular nature of service employment expansion in Northern Ireland (to be discussed more fully below), and its wider political significance.

In a recent book on the international service economy, Petit has observed:

> State intervention in health and education has neither followed a single model nor been pursued with the same vigour in countries with markedly different social systems.[6]

In Northern Ireland, the peculiarities of a third sector – public administration and defence – is at least as significant as health and education. To understand the specific political economy of the service sector in the province, it is necessary first of all to outline the political forces which shaped it and secondly, to look more closely at its composition and spatial distribution.

The Service Sector in Political Context

In terms of the politics of economic management, Northern Ireland has always belonged to the wider UK system. From its inception, the Stormont regime had few fiscal powers – its role was largely confined to the local administration of public expenditure. This included the control of employment in the public services and the allocation of resources between the Unionist community which it represented and the nationalist minority. These powers gave rise to many of the notorious discriminatory and sectarian practices during this period. Another feature of the Northern Ireland state was the way in which the Unionist Party blended UK-wide initiatives with these sectarian practices to sustain and invigorate its political base. A case in point is the welfare state.

The extension of the welfare state to Northern Ireland and the acceptance (if not the full implementation) of notions of parity of social provision had far-reaching implications for Northern Ireland.[7] The particular nature of Stormont's devolved powers, and the Unionist Party's need to maintain its working-class support, ensured that after 1945 the Stormont government adopted a step-by-step policy with the rest of the UK with respect to the introduction of welfare state measures. While the party was ideologically opposed to many of these measures, it adopted and even claimed credit for them.[8] In this way the imperatives of a politics dominated by the national question and Unionist supremacy were married to a politics of welfare provision.

Two factors conspired to undermine the political stability of the post-war marriage of the Unionist Party and the expanding welfare state. The first was the continued decline of the traditional manufacturing sector which forced the Unionist Party to sponsor multinational investment in the province to replace both the local Unionist employers and the jobs lost by Protestant workers. This was to make industrial location politically contentious, and it contained the seeds of a new relationship between Stormont and incoming multinational capital.[9] Secondly, the growth of public expenditure and state employment began to undermine the relationship of the state to the Catholic minority. As state institutions expanded in size and in their regulation of everyday life in the 1960s, Catholics came into ever closer contact with the local administration. The extent of Protestant control became evident and challengeable. Protestant monopolisation of local government, the civil service, the security forces and judiciary was now exposed. Some of the universalist principles enshrined in much social provision were at odds with state employment practices and discrimination in housing, policing and electoral legislation. These issues, combined with the emergence of a Labour government in Britain, gave the civil rights movement leverage to mount its campaign.

The subsequent history of the Northern Ireland conflict has been well documented elsewhere, but the ensuing political upheaval should not be allowed to mask the underlying continuities between the periods before and after 1968 with respect to service expansion. Public expenditure and state service employment continued to expand. Local politics remained dominated, more than ever, by the national question and the ethnic-sectarian divide. There were also discontinuities, of course, as Unionist politicians lost their direct control of local administration and public sector jobs. The British government and the central British state became more deeply implicated in overseeing an increasingly bureaucratic and centralised administration.

Local politicians were transformed into lobbyists concerned with influencing the communal share-out of services and jobs.[10] After 1974, all parties, with the exception of Sinn Fein, were implicated in successive, and fruitless, consultations over the future governance of the province. As before, the politics of the national and ethnic-sectarian questions were not separated from those of welfare provision and employment. Ian Paisley's Democratic Unionist Party and Sinn Fein who were most intensely polarised on the national question, both advocated more public expenditure, services and jobs for their respective communities.

With the deteriorating employment situation, even the most conservative elements in the Official Unionist Party were silenced as all parties advocated more state intervention.

Simultaneously, however, they were fundamentally at odds over the same state's policies on constitutional reform, law and order and inter-communal relations. From 1975 onwards British governments concentrated on two policy objectives – first the elimination or at least the containment of terrorism. The means used were the criminalisation of paramilitary activity aimed mainly, if not exclusively, at the IRA, and secondly, the alleviation of economic decline. Both Labour and Tory governments portrayed these twin objectives as distinct if not unrelated. On the other hand, local political parties, split on communal grounds, emphasised their interpenetration.[11]

There were differences in strategy between the Labour government of 1974-79 and the subsequent Conservative administration. These did not extend to security policy where there was remarkable continuity, but they were evident in the relative stress laid on 'political progress' and 'socio-economic progress'. Under the Rees and Mason administrations, there was considerable disillusionment with the prospects for agreement among the local political parties – parity of social provision with the rest of the UK was stressed instead, as was the creation of jobs. Underlying this approach was a rather traditional Labour view that progress on these fronts would make political progress easier in the longer term. The Tories reversed this thinking. They emphasised the need for some political progress and stability as a pre-requisite to improving the economy. Plans for 'rolling devolution', the creation of the Northern Ireland Assembly and, ultimately, the Anglo-Irish Agreement were directed to this end. This also fitted with the Thatcherite policy of cutting back state involvement in the economy and the social services.[12]

This then was the political setting for the development of the service sector in Northern Ireland in the 1970s and 80s. It was one which was significantly different from any other region of the UK, or indeed any other area in Western Europe. The official statistics of service employment need to be interpreted against this backdrop.

Service Employment: Private Services

Service employment is very diverse and includes much more than public service employment as such. Firstly, a distinction must be made between private and public sector services. The former includes banking and other financial services, distribution, and hotel and catering services, while the latter is dominated by health and education services, public administration and defence. Secondly, a distinction can be made within the private services between producer and consumer services. Producer services include advertising, market research, accountancy, and research and development, other business services, road haulage, and dealings in industrial materials and machinery. Consumer services include distribution, recreational services, catering, garages, hairdressing and laundry work. There is also a category of mixed services serving both final customer demand and intermediate consumption; this includes, *inter alia*, banking, insurance, wholesale distribution, property management and legal services.

The growth of service employment in all advanced capitalist countries has involved expansion of public and private services. Much of the post-war UK growth of service employment has been in producer-related activities. The official figures hide the true extent of this expansion, as they fail to take account of the rapid increase in 'non-production' service employment *within* manufacturing industries, for example, public relations and financial services departments. It is estimated that about 40 per cent of jobs in manufacturing in the UK are now in this area.[13] These 'in-house' 'non-production' workers carry out the same types of tasks as independent service companies. The evidence suggests that a firm's decision to buy in or establish its own producer services is arbitrary. At the aggregate level, the increase in total producer services has been interpreted as an important new source of economic activity given their 'value-added' potential, their employment creation potential and their ability to develop a modern complex business-support infrastructure.

In Northern Ireland, there is a relative weakness of producer service activity in the economy. For example, although 'non-production' employment in manufacturing has grown substantially in the post-war period, the Northern Ireland proportion remains considerably below the general UK level. A Northern Ireland Economic Council (NIEC) report estimated that non-production employment accounted for only 25 per cent of the manufacturing total in the province compared with 35 per cent in the UK generally (based on 1971 figures).[14] This shortfall was spread across nearly all manufacturing and was especially noticeable in those manufacturing industries attracted to Northern Ireland in the 1960s.

Table 1 is based on 1981 census figures and reveals a shortfall in key service occupations in Northern Ireland manufacturing compared with that of Great Britain. Only in one major sector, which includes the heavily subsidised Shorts aerospace enterprise, does Northern Ireland have a more favourable profile. The gap, although significant is not so large in private services such as banking and finance.

Table 1: Percentage of High Level Professional, Managerial and Technical Occupations in Selected Industries in Northern Ireland and Great Britain, 1981

	Northern Ireland	Great Britain
Food, drink and tobacco	8.7	12.9
Textiles, clothing and footwear	6.8	10.2
Mechanical engineering	12.3	20.3
Instrument engineering	9.2	24.6
Electrical/electronic engineering	11.2	23.6
Vehicles and other transport equipment	13.1	12.6
Banking, insurance and finance	28.9	34.2

Source: NI Census, 1981, Economic Activity Report.

This deficiency in 'non-production' service occupations in manufacturing is compounded by a shortfall in independent producer services in the province. As the same NIEC report notes, the absence of a fully developed business service infrastructure is a major weakness of the Northern Ireland economy. The province is particularly deficient in tradeable producer services such as research and development, advertising and market research, and 'stand-alone' administrative head-quarters. Only 3.5 per cent of total employment in Northern Ireland is provided by producer services generally, compared to a UK average of 5.9 per cent and 8.4 per cent in the South-East of England. In light of this deficiency, industrial policy in Northern Ireland has been modified (on the urgings of the NIEC) to include the promotion of employment in private services, especially in exportable services and in areas of service-import substitution, but this has met with little success. In 1974, private services accounted for 20 per cent of all employees in the province compared with 26 per cent in the UK as a whole. By 1983, the gap had widened to 25 and 33 per cent respectively.[15] In 1985, employment in private services actually fell.[16] Growth in this sector has been concentrated in consumer services such as retailing, recreational and cultural services, rather than in tradeable producer services.[17]

Four important influences have contributed to the relatively low level of producer services employment in Northern Ireland. The first is the disproportionate concentration of producer services in the South-East of England.[18] This is mainly due to London being the capital of the world's financial markets, and the location for the administrative headquarters of UK transnational companies. Gravitation towards the centre has obviously worked to the detriment of Northern Ireland. The second is that much of Northern Ireland's manufacturing sector (at least until very recently) suffers from the 'branch plant syndrome' in which the demand for producer services diminishes the more decision-making is located outside the region.

Thirdly, the Northern Ireland industrial structure is deficient in industries which have a greater propensity to make use of producer services, namely, chemicals, instrument and electrical engineering. This is compounded by the relatively small size of Northern Ireland's manufacturing companies. A fourth and more speculative influence is that local entrepreneurs have not regarded it necessary to complement their production processes with producer service functions given that they have been tied via subcontractual relationships and other forms of close association to guaranteed markets either locally or in Britain. This lends support to the argument advanced by both Rowthorn and Teague in this volume that while the British market has been crucial to Northern Ireland's manufacturing output, the link has operated in such a way as to stifle entrepreneurial creativity in the province.

Service Employment: Public Services

It has been public services, especially in the 1970s, which have prevented a major collapse in the Northern Ireland economy, and as a result the province has become ever more dependent on the central British state. In 1953, Northern Ireland and the UK generally had roughly the same percentage of employees in public services – 13 and 14 per cent respectively. By 1974, Northern Ireland had 35 per cent in the sector compared to 30 per cent in the UK; nine years later that gap had widened dramatically from 5 to 13 per cent.

Yet, despite the impact of public service employment, there is little evidence that the British government conceived it as part of an overall economic strategy for the province. At one level, under Direct Rule, there has been a broad commitment to parity of service provision with the rest of the UK. During the 1970s this had the effect of eliminating the shortfall in service employment in Northern Ireland and ultimately reversing it. In practice, however, implementation of state policy in this area is best understood as a set of responses to local class and political pressures. Just as the administration of the post-war British welfare state in the province was shaped by the political requirements of the Unionist Party prior to 1972, so public service policy after 1972 was tailored to the 'containment' strategies of the Direct Rule administration.

The Labour government of 1974-79 was mainly responsible for the growth in the public sector. In this period, it increased by an average of 6,800 jobs per annum compared with a growth of only 1,400 per annum in the first five years of the Thatcher government. More recently, public service employment has stabilised and, in fact, certain segments have even shown a decline. Employment growth was concentrated heavily in health, education and public administration and defence. A notable feature of Labour's strategy was 'Ulsterisation' which led to a marked increase in security force personnel. This has been the main area of growth in male public sector jobs, and it has benefited Protestants almost exclusively. In addition, Labour's disillusionment with local politicians meant that, under the Mason administration in particular, it was more responsive to the trade unions and voluntary groups lobbying for increased social provision which led to the increase in 'civilian' public service employment.

Yet the growth of service employment and public expenditure needs to be qualified. The rise in state (and other) service employment largely meant more part-time jobs for women. Part-time workers doubled between 1971 and 1983, increasing at an average rate of 5,644 per annum between 1971 and 1978 and by 2,332 per annum subsequently. Since 1973-74, public expenditure in Northern Ireland has grown by twice as much as in the UK as a whole, but most of the divergence arose under the Labour government. The composition of expenditure has shifted considerably. Health expenditure increased substantially by almost £100 million and proportionally from 13.4 to 16.4 per cent of the total. Similarly, law and order and housing programmes have grown in absolute and relative terms. Education on the other hand declined as a proportion of the total despite an absolute increase of £44 million.

The most spectacular shifts were in those areas that best illustrated the failure of overall economic policy. Between 1973-74 and 1984-85, spending on industrial development and job promotion has declined by £50 million (1975 prices) or from 18.4 to 10.2 per cent of the total programme. The increasing desperation of the industrial promotion agencies and the Labour government to promote and maintain large manufacturing plants was demonstrated in costly and controversial failures in Courtaulds, De Lorean and Lear Fan aerospace.[19] Subsequently, industrial expenditure and job targets became much more modest. Social security payments rose by £20 million or from 21 to nearly 30 per cent of total public expenditure.[20] These payments were, of course, largely non-discretionary and reflected the doubling of unemployment between 1970-79 and a further doubling between 1979 and 1982.

Much of the growth in services and public expenditure, then, was an unplanned, piecemeal response to changing political and economic forces. Simultaneously, however, the British government introduced a series of administrative reforms directed at modifying the exclusion of the minority from political power in Northern Ireland. It failed to establish an internal power-sharing framework but did initiate reforms of the security forces, local government and housing. The Fair Employment Agency (FEA) was set up to investigate and monitor discrimination and unequal opportunity in employment. The Agency's remit was limited, but it did help to underline the systematic and deep-rooted economic inequalities between Protestants and Catholics. In theory, at least, the expansion of state employment and public expenditure offered an opportunity to redress Catholic disadvantage.

Spatial Inequalities

The national question and the inter-communal struggle in Northern Ireland has typically taken the form of a struggle over territory and space. From the plantation to partition and after, this struggle may be seen in the bid to control territory, through the ownership or renting of land, through military control and policing, marching and intimidation, access to jobs, and political and electoral manipulation. To this may be added attempts to control housing estates and the nature and location of employment opportunities. The intensity of the struggle has waxed and waned – ranging from attempts at total exclusion, to seeking effective control of opponents. Partition resolved these struggles within Northern Ireland on Protestant terms – a resolution which was not seriously challenged until the 1960s.

Catholic disadvantage has a clear cut spatial dimension which is reflected in the distribution of employment and unemployment within Northern Ireland. Economic activity, especially manufacturing employment, has historically been concentrated in the East, which is dominated by the Belfast region. Unionist Party policy, prior to the abolition of Stormont, was to consolidate, not surprisingly, the economic advantage of an area where almost 80 per cent of its supporters lived. Catholics were in a majority in the West, although approximately half of all Catholics live in the East, heavily concentrated in West Belfast – an area which has suffered more from de-industrialisation than any other part of Northern Ireland. This East-West division has an even more fundamental significance in that it could form, a new and smaller Northern Ireland if repartition was to result from the current conflict.[21]

During the 1960s, as Stormont sponsored multinational investment in the province, the location of manufacturing industry, growth centres and other physical infrastructure projects was the subject of intense political controversy. In 1976, the Quigley Report on the Northern Ireland economy provided the most tangible official recognition of the East-West divide by referring to a dual economy in the province. It advocated a more interventionist state strategy for employment blackspots. The regional physical plan of 1975 moved away from a 'growth-centre' strategy which stressed developing the East of the province. Little attention was devoted to the spatial effects of growth in the service sector however, despite the Quigley Report's recognition that the regional effects of national policy might be more important than specially conceived instruments of regional policy.[22]

Table 2 indicates the overall distribution of population, employment and unemployment in 1981. It divides Northern Ireland into four sub-regions: Belfast, Belfast suburbs (predominantly Protestant post-war housing), the rest of the East and finally the West of the province – roughly the area west of the Bann with a Catholic majority.

Table 2: Percentage Distribution of Population, Industrial Sectors and Economically Active in Four sub-regions of Northern Ireland, 1981

	Belfast	Belfast Suburbs	Rest of East	West	Total
Population	21.1	23.7	23.7	31.5	100
Percentage Catholic*	20.5	7.9	22.0	49.6	100
Agriculture	.5	12.2	32.8	54.5	100
Manufacturing	33.8	21.2	25.0	24.0	100
Services	35.7	20.2	21.1	24.0	100
Percentage Economically Active	21.0	26.6	23.7	28.7	100

Source: Northern Ireland Census 1981.
* Percentage of Catholics are based on figures for population and denominational breakdown which included estimates of non-respondents as calculated by D. Eversley and V. Herr, *The Roman Catholic Population of Northern Ireland in 1981: A Revised Estimate*, Belfast 1985.

In Table 3 the base figure is the proportion of the total economically active (including the unemployed) residing in each region (as in Table 2). The figures in the other columns measure the degree of spatial concentration (or dispersion) of various industries and occupations among the four regions. The proportion of the total employed in each industry/occupation was calculated for each region. This proportion was divided by the proportion of the total economically active population residing in each region to give a measure of relative concentration. So, for example, a figure of 1.0 for banking and finance in Belfast would indicate that the number working in this sector was the expected one in view of the proportion of economically active people residing in the city. Scores greater

Table 3: The Relative Distribution of Selected Industries and Occupations Among the four Sub-Regions of Northern Ireland, 1981

	Belfast	Belfast Suburbs	Rest of East	West
Services	1.70	.76	.89	.84
Manufacturing	1.60	.80	1.05	.70
Agriculture	.02	.46	1.38	1.90
Metals/engineering	2.62	.85	.61	.28
Other services*	1.59	.79	.88	.87
Public administration etc.	1.78	.77	.81	.80
Banking/insurance	2.40	.76	.49	.63
Distribution	1.50	.89	.92	.80
Doctors	1.50	1.10	.81	.70
Nurses	.90	.94	1.15	1.00
Teachers	.90	.94	1.03	1.11
Catering/cleaning	1.27	.94	.98	.88
Clerical and related	1.21	1.29	.99	.59
Part-time workers	1.17	1.18	.93	.77
Out of employment	1.09	.62	.87	1.39

Source: Calculated from Northern Ireland Census, 1981.
* Other services (Census Division 9) is mainly public services and includes, public administration and defence, health and educational services.
N.B. The last seven categories in the table refer to residence rather than workplace.

than 1.0 indicate an over concentration of employment and scores less than 1.0 a shortfall in a particular sub-region.

Perhaps the most striking feature of Table 3 is the dominance of Belfast as a location for jobs within Northern Ireland. Although, it lost 25 per cent of its population, between 1971 and 1981, mainly to surrounding areas, it remains the main centre of employment.[23] It also has a slightly larger than expected share of unemployment – a figure which masks the huge unemployment disparities between Catholic West Belfast and the rest of the city. The table also shows that the rapid expansion of service employment has been concentrated in the Belfast area. In fact, Belfast is as dominant a location for service employment as it is for manufacturing. The degree of concentration of banking and finance is only slightly less than for metals and engineering (which includes shipbuilding and aerospace).

There are two main reasons why the expansion of the service sector in the province has clustered around Belfast. The first is simply that Belfast is the administrative and commercial capital of the province. In this respect, concentration is not a peculiar trend: all disadvantaged regions in the UK have such centres in which the lion's share of service employment is located, even if few are so dominated by one city. Clearly, it makes sense, for example, for the Head Office of the Northern Bank to be in Belfast rather than in Omagh or Enniskillen. But there are certain service sub-sectors, particularly in the field of public administration, where the opportunity cost of situating such jobs in the centre is to deprive the more peripheral Western sub-region of a possible source of employment. The concentration in Belfast of hospital services and routine clerical and administrative jobs are cases in point.

The second reason is equally straightforward – Belfast has enjoyed a disproportionate share of service sector employment as a direct result of it being the only conurbation in the province. A lot of service activity like distributive activities, transport, leisure industries are very much dependent on local demand. The fact that Belfast and its suburbs has a large population more of whom are in work than any other sub-region means that it is going to have a higher incidence of service sector activity. The net result of all this is that service employment expansion does not seem to have remedied the relative disadvantage of the West to any significant degree. The West as a *location* for jobs has a relative advantage in only one, rather predictable, area – agriculture. The only other areas in which it scores higher than 1.0 is in unemployment and in the proportion of teachers and nurses living in the area. This reflects the occupational bias of the Catholic majority in the West towards the education and medical services which we discuss below. Significantly, the West has relatively few of the part-time, clerical and clerical related jobs which were a major element in the expansion of service employment.

On the other hand, the suburban location of government offices and retail outlets is reflected in a high concentration in part-time clerical work in the Belfast suburbs. The low scores of the Belfast suburbs in most sectors should not be taken as evidence of a lack of employment opportunities in the area. On the contrary, this sub-region belongs to the Belfast travel-to-work area and workers commute in large numbers to the city. This picture is confirmed by the suburbs having the lowest concentration of people out of employment of any of the four sub-regions.

The rest of the eastern region shows a relative concentration of jobs in agriculture and manufacturing. The region has traditionally had a strong agricultural economy, and in the 1960s benefited from the location of new multinational investment, most notably in Craigavon and Ballymena. Although both these towns have since lost their major employers (Goodyear and Enkalon respectively), this sub-region has remained second to Belfast as a manufacturing area. Services are rather less concentrated in this area, although it benefited from the location of the new university in Coleraine and retains an advantage over the west region in terms of most service sectors.

The figures in Table 3 must be read in the light of considerable loss of manufacturing employment between 1979 and 1982, and rising unemployment in the three eastern sub-regions, especially in areas such as Carrickfergus, Craigavon, Antrim, Larne and Newtownabbey. Service employment does seem to have made good some of this loss however, meaning the East still retains a considerable advantage over the West. It would also appear that the growth of public service employment (covered here under public administration/ defence and 'other services') has assumed the spatial characteristics of the manufacturing sector. The private services are even more concentrated, however, than the public services.

Protestant-Catholic Differentials

There are clear signs that the growth of service employment has failed to reduce patterns of spatial inequality already existing in Northern Ireland. This will remain the case until the British government introduces a full-scale employment regeneration programme for the western sub-region. Some employment gains could be made by decentralising service employment, but, these would not be significant, and at this stage would probably mean displacing workers at the centre. A more effective strategy would be to launch a major infrastructural programme for the sub-region, the benefits of which would be more substantial and immediate. Moreover, local cross-border co-operative projects should receive more vigorous support from both the British and Irish governments.

Apart from Unionist objections to such schemes, the commitment to regional strategies of this type has diminished greatly under the Tory government. In the wake of a collapse of external investment in Northern Ireland, and increased competition from other UK and EEC regions, intra-regional inequality has slipped down the government's agenda. On the other hand, a generalised commitment to ending discrimination and encouraging equality of opportunity between Catholics and Protestants has remained a prominent element in the stated policies of all British governments since the early 1970s. The existence of the Fair Employment Agency (FEA) and, more recently, concerted Irish-American attempts to make investment contracts conditional on fairer employment practices, has ensured that the issue has remained politically significant.

Three questions may be asked with respect to Protestant-Catholic employment differentials. Firstly, has the broad sectoral shift towards services improved employment opportunities for Catholics? Secondly, has the growth of state employment effected any shifts in favour of Catholics? Thirdly, have there been any changes in the higher level service occupations responsible for important policy decisions?

Limitations of data preclude more than preliminary and qualified answers to these questions. There are serious problems of comparability between the 1971 and 1981 census figures. Firstly, the standard industrial classification and many of the occupational categories were revised in the interim, making comparison difficult. Secondly, and more significantly, there were major problems of differential non-response. In 1981 a substantial number of people did not return a census form in protest against government policy on H-Blocks. Current estimates suggest 45,000 people concentrated in strong Republican areas did not respond. Thirdly, of those who did return the census form 18.5 per cent did not answer the question on religion compared to 9.4 per cent in 1971. The result was that the number of Catholics was substantially underestimated. Two studies of overall non-response suggest that the Catholic proportion of the population was in the region of 38 or 39 per cent compared to 28 per cent enumerated in the census.[24] Estimates are not available, however, for industries and occupations.

Sectoral Shifts and Sectarian Imbalance

Industrial and occupational comparisons between 1971 and 1981 must also be subject to major qualifications. Chief amongst these is that industrial affiliation and occupations were distributed among non-respondents in the same proportion as among respondents. In any event, direct comparisons of the 1971/1981 proportions in the various occupations and industries are relatively meaningless. It is possible, however, to calculate the distribution of Catholics among the three major sectors and how the proportion in each sector diverges from the expected proportion for each year.

Table 4 suggests that Catholics (especially women) are better represented in services than in any other sector in both years. The slight loss of ground by Catholics in the service sector in 1981 is probably due to the dramatic contraction of the construction industry where Catholics are over-represented. On the other hand, the strength of Catholic women in services is

Table 4: Percentage Economically Active Catholics and their Relative Concentration among Major Industrial Sectors

| | 1971 | | | 1981 | | |
	Males	Females	Total	Males	Females	Total
Percentage Catholic Economically Active	28.3	27.4	28.2	25.8	25.5	25.7
Agriculture, etc.	1.10	.74	1.10	.87	.61	.86
Manufacturing	.71	1.10	.82	.71	.87	.76
Services (including construction)	.98	.99	.98	.90	.96	.93

Source: Calculated from Northern Ireland Census, 1971, 1981.

offset by a loss of employment in manufacturing. Apart from women working in agriculture, where numbers are insignificant, the main area of Catholic disadvantage remains male manufacturing employment. This position has remained static between 1971 and 1981. Overall, then, the major sectoral shifts in the Northern Ireland economy do not seem significantly to have improved the relative employment position of Catholics. Nevertheless, the growing proportion in the service sector has clearly provided the best prospects for Catholic employment in absolute terms.

Catholic Employment in the Public Services

There have been three main areas of public sector expansion: public administration, defence, health and educational service. In 1971, health and education showed over-representation of Catholics relative to their proportion of the economically active. There were two reasons for this – the existence of a separate Catholic school system and the large numbers of Catholic schoolchildren (approximately half the Northern Ireland total in 1980).[25] This system provided employment for large numbers of Catholic teachers and ancillary staff. In the case of the health service, Catholic women have traditionally been prominent in nursing (accounting for 43 per cent of the total in 1971). The 1981 figures show a considerable expansion in employment in health and education services, and indicate that Catholics have retained their relative advantage in these areas – accounting for 30 and 29 per cent of educational and health services respectively, compared to 23 per cent of the economically active. Similarly, Catholics accounted for 34 and 38 per cent of teachers and nurses respectively which, allowing for non-response, appears to maintain the 1971 position.

The case of public administration and defence is rather different. Here state control of employment is direct rather than in partnership with the churches or other voluntary bodies, as in education. Total employment in this area almost doubled between 1971 and 1981. Only 19.6 per cent of total employment was Catholic in 1971 compared to 17 per cent in 1981. This represents .69 of the expected Catholic proportion in 1971 and .74 in 1981. This seems to reflect an improvement in a sector which had been restructured under Direct Rule. Yet, the relative improvement in Catholics' position is marginal in the context of the overall doubling of employment. The stabilisation, even reduction, of employment in this sector in the 1980s suggests that an opportunity has been lost significantly to reduce Catholic disadvantage in this area.

The Northern Ireland Civil Service is a crucial part of this sector and has been the subject of a FEA investigation, which prompted the setting up of an internal system to monitor equality of opportunity. The FEA investigation revealed that there had been a shift from the old Stormont practices. Under Unionist control, the employment of a Catholic gardener or telephonist could provoke a mini-crisis in ministerial relationships, and accusations of Catholic infiltration made by the Orange Order. By 1980, there had been a considerable intake of Catholics into the Civil Service – this was unevenly distributed however in terms of department and grade. The total proportion of Catholics in the (non-industrial) civil service (21,100 employees) was 26.6 per cent compared with an estimate of 37.5 per cent in the economically active population, which amounts to .71 of the expected proportion. Proportions ranged from a high of 39.7 per cent in health and social services to a low of 10 per cent in the police authority.

Unionist control of housing allocation was one of the main objects of Catholic complaint under Stormont. The removal of housing from local authority control and the establishment of the Northern Ireland Housing Executive has given Catholics greater opportunity to influence housing allocation, even if building programmes have suffered under government cut-backs. The FEA investigation of the Executive in response to Protestant allegations of Catholic bias revealed that its staff reflected fairly the sectarian composition of the population. This clearly marks an advance from the pre-1972 period.[26]

Sectarian Imbalance in Key Occupations

General analyses of employment ignore the widely disparate political weight of certain key occupations and groups of workers. The upper echelons of the Civil Service, for example, are an important decision-making group. The FEA investigation showed greater recruitment of Catholics between 1975 and 1980, but low representation of Catholics at the key policy-making grades.[27] In 1980, only eight Catholics were in posts of Assistant Secretary or above out of a total of 121 in these grades. Overall, the higher the salary range the lower proportion of Catholics in each grade – Catholics had slightly higher representation than expected in one range only – the lowest salary grade of less than £5,100 p.a. in 1980. It seems clear that Catholics have come into the lower grades in greater numbers. More doubtful is the claim of the investigation that a long-term structural improvement is taking place at the upper levels. One of the consultants to the investigation has challenged this claim – pointing to promotion anomalies favouring Protestants in recently appointed grades, and arguing that Catholic under-representation at the upper levels will reproduce itself well into the next century – even with complete equality of promotion.[28]

The 1981 census figures confirm the under-representation of Catholics in key economic and political decision making occupations. The 1971 census showed an under-representation of Catholics among senior government officials (13 per cent), managers (12 per cent), company secretaries (7 per cent) and engineers (11 per cent). They were over-represented among publicans (73 per cent), waiters/waitresses (50 per cent), hairdressers (49 per cent), domestic housekeepers (48 per cent), nurses (43 per cent) and teachers (39 per cent). Allowing for the additional non-response/non-enumeration problems and a changed classification system, the same pattern is visible in 1981. Catholics are again under-represented among senior government officials (13 per cent) and in science and engineering (14 per cent) as well as in key business occupations – personnel managers (13 per cent), marketing/sales management (12 per cent). In the category covering shipbuilding and aerospace industries, Catholics accounted for less than 5 per cent.

Two further areas of Catholic under-representation are of crucial political significance. The first is the power industries, notably electricity. The role of the power workers has proved critical in three political strikes by Unionists – the 1974 Ulster Workers' Council strike which brought down the power-sharing executive, the abortive strike in 1977 when Ian Paisley failed to bring out the electricity workers, and the one-day strike against the Anglo-Irish agreement in 1986 in which the electricity workers again played a leading role. The industrial category covering the latter employed only 13 per cent in 1981. This is a product of Catholic occupational disadvantage and the location of the main generating station in East Antrim. The FEA investigated the Northern Ireland Electricity Service and found only 4 per cent to be Catholics among the 250 senior management posts. Fewer than 10 per cent of the engineers were found to be Catholic.[29]

The other key group includes the police and prison officers. Between 1974 and 1986, employment in this area doubled from 9 to 17 per cent of male public sector employment. In the same period, male public sector employment increased by only 1.2 per cent. In the category covering policemen, firemen and prison officers, only 5 per cent were Catholic in 1981, if anything a decline on the 1971 proportion. Since the 'Ulsterisation' of security in the mid-1970s, the police force has borne the brunt of the IRA campaign – especially its few Catholic members. The police are excluded from fair employment legislation and its overwhelmingly Protestant composition presents the Northern Ireland problem in its starkest form. This has been further highlighted by the tensions within the police over the Anglo-Irish Agreement sharpened by increased Loyalist hostility to them as upholders of the Agreement. Nevertheless, the expansion of jobs in 'security' occupations represents a large economic subsidy to the Protestant population.

Conclusions

The foregoing evidence has revealed the central role of the service sector, and public services in particular, in Northern Ireland. Yet, the sector shows structural weaknesses *vis-à-vis* Great Britain, and most especially a shortfall of high-level occupations in manufacturing and producer services. It is clear also that the growth of the service sector has done little to eradicate spatial disparities associated with manufacturing in the past within Northern Ireland. Catholics, especially women, have benefited from the expansion of service employment. Nevertheless, Catholics remain disadvantaged in areas of key political and economic significance – the police, power generation, shipbuilding and aerospace, banking, insurance and finance, and top civil service jobs. This is the result of the class profile of the Catholic community and the political and spatial framework of the Northern Ireland state.

There are few signs that Direct Rule has altered the underlying structural position of both communities, but it seems likely that Catholic disadvantage would have greatly widened without the growth in public services, especially health and educational service employment. A Catholic professional middle class has been strengthened, mainly in areas which service its own community. The growth of the services has now tapered off, however, which will make much more difficult any Catholic advance in employment equality.

It would be misleading to suggest that the British state has simply reproduced the class and sectarian relations of the Stormont system, but there is little evidence, as it has been increasingly drawn into the day-to-day running of Northern Ireland, that it has the will, or perhaps the capacity, to alter them fundamentally. The British government has been willing to take exceptional legislative and security measures to combat paramilitary violence which have done little to reduce, and have often increased communal, especially intra-working class, violence. The government's employment strategy has been much less radical. In the service sector it has incorporated rather than radically altered sectarian imbalance. Nevertheless, the Tory government has been forced, mainly by pressure from American investors, to make more explicit its commitment to fair employment.[30]

The greater the Catholic role in state institutions, the less the tendency of Protestants to identify the state as their state. The Protestant monopolisation of state power no longer exists, but Catholic participation does not guarantee Catholic compliance although it may presage increasing political assertiveness. Meanwhile, high unemployment and saturation policing leave large sections of the Catholic working class as alienated as before. The economic position of working-class Protestants, while clearly stronger, is still precarious and they are increasingly alienated from a state in which their political leverage has been reduced. There is a sense, however, in which the economic pre-eminence of the state service sector has acted as a prophylactic on sectarian conflict and reduced the attraction of UDI or re-partition. There seems little doubt that it has also reduced Catholic support for a united Ireland in the short term as well as weakened Loyalists' capacity to mount a coherent opposition to British political strategy.

British governments have taken little coherent action to increase the mutual economic interdependence of both communities.[31] Such interdependence should not be confused with physical integration of housing estates or shopfloors. The building of interdependence would appear to be a necessary, if not sufficient, prerequisite for a long-term solution. The most direct approach may well be via a much more spatially oriented employment strategy. This might involve more active cross-border initiatives to develop links between the area West of the Bann and the border counties in the Irish Republic. Here, the Anglo-Irish Agreement could have a role in mobilising EEC funds and co-ordinating the efforts of industrial promotion agencies. The direction of service employment to areas worst hit by unemployment might be combined with an attempt to get manufacturing firms to operate at more than one location.[32] Such an approach runs counter to the economic strategy of the Tory government which is prepared to see new concentrations of service and manufacturing employment in the South-East of England at the expense of other regions. It might however commend itself to a Labour government as a special Northern Ireland version of a broader spatial strategy for the UK. Any such strategy, however, must pay particular attention to the service sector.

Notes

[1] Since the signing of the Anglo-Irish Agreement the campaign within Unionism urging British political parties to organise in Northern Ireland has become more vocal. This reflects, in part, a desire to counteract a perceived weakening in the political negotiating position of the Unionist parties, and a strengthening of nationalist parties, arising from the Agreement. In some cases, it reflects Unionist attempts to avoid any substantial compromise within Northern Ireland.

[2] The obvious exception is security policy where Northern Ireland has sometimes provided a model for policing and legislation in Britain.

[3] J.S. Wabe, 'The Regional Impact of De-industrialisation in the European Community', *Regional Studies*, Vol.20 No.1, 1986.

[4] Northern Ireland Economic Council (NIEC), *Private Services in Economic Development*, Report No.30, 1982, p.33.

[5] NIEC, *Economic Assessment: April 1986*, Report No.58, 1986, p.14.

[6] P. Petit, *Slow Growth and the Service Sector*, London 1986.

[7] For a fuller analysis of the impact of the welfare state on Northern Ireland politics see L. O'Dowd, B. Rolston and M. Tomlinson, *Northern Ireland: Between Civil Rights and Civil War*, London 1980.

[8] In the late 1940s the Northern Ireland Prime Minister, Brooke, was able to claim that the Union ensured parity of social services with the rest of the UK, while his own party opposed the introduction of these measures in the House of Commons by the post-war Labour government; see O'Dowd *et al.*, op. cit., pp.17-8.

[9] Executives of incoming multinationals were much less likely to be active Unionist politicians than, for example, their local linen capitalist predecessors. Their relationship to populist Unionist politics has weakened further as they have distanced themselves from the politics of militant Loyalist protest against British policies. It is doubtful, however, if these changes have extended to radically altering their labour recruitment practices; see M. Maguire, 'Social Control and the Labour Process: A Case Study of a Northern Ireland Telecommunications Plant', unpublished PhD thesis, Queen's University, Belfast, 1985. Here industrial location and a wish to avoid sectarian divisions on the shopfloor are powerful disincentives to positive fair employment practices.

[10] Local government powers have been greatly reduced but local politicians still control a limited number of jobs directly. There have been several FEA investigations of complaints against local councils. Many Unionist authorities have refused to sign the fair employment declaration. Local politicians do not control education and health and social services although they are

represented on Education and Library and Health and Social Services Boards. Politicians lobby British ministers' civil servants on a wide range of matters dealing with security, employment, housing and social services. Since the Anglo-Irish Agreement Unionist politicians have withdrawn from the House of Commons, broken off contacts with British ministers and sought to suspend local authorities.

11 Of all the local parties, Alliance has come closest to endorsing the broad policies of British governments.

12 For a fuller discussion of British 'containment' strategies and of the different emphases of Labour and Tory governments since 1974, see L. O'Dowd, B. Rolston and M. Tomlinson, 'From Labour to the Tories: The Ideology of Containment in Northern Ireland', *Capital and Class*, No.18, 1982.

13 P. Wood, 'The Anatomy of Job Loss and Job Creation: Some Speculations on the Role of the "Producer Service" Sector', *Regional Studies*, Vol.20, No.1, 1986, p.40.

14 Northern Ireland Economic Council, *Private Services in Economic Development*.

15 E. Evason, *On the Edge: A Study of Long-Term Unemployment in Northern Ireland*, London 1985, p.29.

16 NIEC, *Economic Assessment: April 1986*, p.24.

17 NIEC, *Economic Assessment: April 1985*, Report No.50, 1985, p.19.

18 J. Marquand, *The Service Sector and Regional Policy in the UK*, London 1979.

19 See House of Commons, *Report from the Committee of Public Accounts*, 21 May 1980.

20 NIEC, *Public Expenditure Priorities: Overall Review*, Report No.42, 1984, pp.9-12.

21 No major political party in Northern Ireland, the Republic or Britain favours re-partition. The East-West divide in the province is significant enough in demographic, political and economic terms to provide a basis for re-partition emerging by default almost. Clearly, however, it would reproduce many of the problems generated by the 1920 partition of Ireland – relying for its stability on sectarian head-counts.

22 L' O'Dowd, 'The Crisis of Regional Strategy: Ideology and the State in Northern Ireland' in G. Rees *et al.* (eds), *Political Action and Social Identity: Class, Locality and Ideology*, London 1985.

23 P.A. Compton, *Demographic Trends in Northern Ireland*, NIEC Report No.57, Belfast 1986, p.165.

24 Ibid; see also, D. Eversley and V. Herr, *The Roman Catholic Population of Northern Ireland in 1981: A Revised Estimate*, Fair Employment Agency (FEA), Belfast 1985.

25 Compton, op. cit., p.34.

26 FEA, *Report of an Investigation by the Fair Employment Agency for Northern Ireland into the Northern Ireland Housing Executive*, Belfast 1985.

27 FEA, *Report of an Investigation by the Fair Employment Agency for Northern Ireland into the Non-Industrial Northern Ireland Civil Service*, Belfast 1983.

[28] R. Miller, 'Social Stratification and Mobility' in P. Clancy *et al.* (eds), *Ireland: A Sociological Profile*, Dublin 1986, pp.228-9.

[29] FEA, *A Final Report by the Fair Employment Agency for Northern Ireland on its Investigation into the Employment Practices of the Northern Ireland Electricity Services*, Belfast 1982.

[30] The Northern Ireland Office produced a consultative paper in September 1986 entitled 'Equality of Opportunity in Northern Ireland: Future Strategy Options' which suggests making government grants and contracts conditional on fair employment practices. It rules out reverse discrimination or quotas however as advocated in the MacBride Principles.

[31] Trade unions have had a measure of success in uniting Protestant and Catholic public service workers in the face of paramilitary intimidation.

[32] Single establishment firms such as large government departments East of Belfast and manufacturing firms such as Shorts and Harland and Wolff are more likely to have homogeneous Protestant workforces. Shorts have taken over a factory in Catholic West Belfast partly in response to Irish-American pressure. It remains to be seen if this is more a cosmetic response than an attempt to implement employment equality via locational decisions.

David Canning, Barry Moore and John Rhodes

Economic Growth In Northern Ireland: Problems and Prospects

Introduction

The economic problems of Northern Ireland, though greater in scale, are similar to those of the other peripheral regions of the United Kingdom.[1] It is a mistake to blame these economic problems on the troubles. Indeed it could be argued that while the troubles have led to a loss of manufacturing jobs, their net effect on the regional economy has been positive, due to the induced expansion of public sector expenditure and employment. Political violence has played a relatively small role in the increase in unemployment experienced by the province during the 1970s and early 1980s; a regional policy aimed at renewed economic growth may succeed even if the troubles continue.

While a successful economic policy could be carried out without an end to the troubles, the reverse is not the case. The political problem in Northern Ireland is not primarily economic, but a political solution will have to involve a lessening of economic inequality if it is to be more than cosmetic. The difficulty is not so much the high unemployment rate, over 25 per cent on average for men, as the differential between Catholics and Protestants, 40 as opposed to 20 per cent.[2] Narrowing this and other economic differentials will be much easier against a background of economic growth; if Catholic jobs are created at the obvious expense of Protestant workers, political stability will be next to impossible.

However, while a successful economic strategy does not require a political dimension, economic growth is likely to

211

increase the pressure for constitutional change. One of the major arguments for continuing the present constitutional arrangements is the large subvention paid by Britain to Northern Ireland. Gibson details this argument in considering the economic viability of an independent Northern Ireland or a united Ireland, and the economic evidence given to the New Ireland Forum stresses the problems the Republic of Ireland would have in taking over responsibility for this transfer.[3] Economic growth in Northern Ireland would lessen the need for a fiscal transfer from Great Britain and in doing so would reduce the main economic obstacle to political change. Economic success in Northern Ireland is therefore more likely to be an accompaniment to, and not a substitute for, political agreement.

Even if economic growth is viewed as desirable, both in itself and for its implications, the problem of bringing it about still remains. This essay is devoted to an examination of this problem and the prospects for a successful economic strategy. We concentrate on the labour market and the prospects for growth in employment. The main argument we develop is that the problems associated with low incomes, and the other measures of social and economic deprivation in the province, are important but cannot be cured directly; they will only be effectively alleviated by renewed growth in the regional economy.

The Economic Problem in Northern Ireland

The root of the economic problem in Northern Ireland is that the growth rate of employment generated by existing industry is insufficient to cope with the increase in the labour force brought about by the high birth rate and increasing levels of participation in the labour market. This gap must be filled by either creating additional jobs or by forcing some of the workforce to migrate out of the province, otherwise these excess workers must simply be added to the dole queue. It is vital to understand that this is a dynamic problem and that unemployment and low wages are the consequences of this demographic momentum.

The dynamic nature of the problem becomes clear if we consider what would happen if a policy of creating jobs was implemented for all those currently unemployed in the region.

Figure 1: Labour Market Flows in Northern Ireland, 1971-81

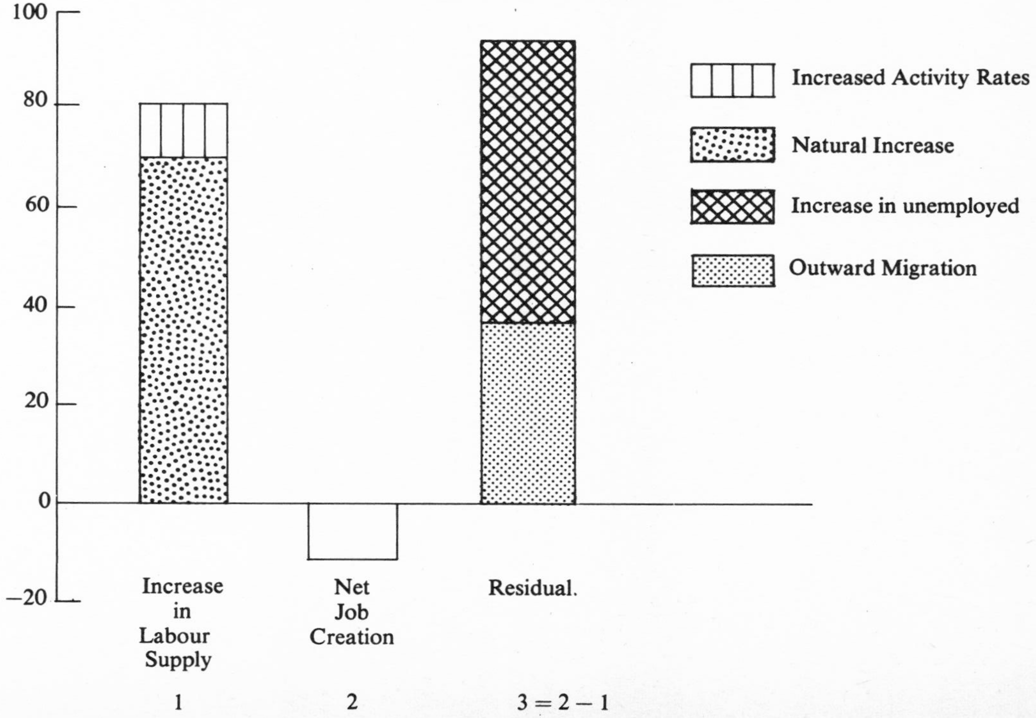

The short-run effect of such a policy (assuming that the underlying employment growth potential, currently around zero, remains constant) would, of course, be no unemployment. But in the longer term outward migration would fall, due to the ready availability of jobs. With no outward migration, and with zero underlying employment growth potential, all the future natural increase in labour supply due to the expanding population would become unemployed. This rapid expansion of unemployment would continue until the numbers unemployed become so large that employment prospects would fall sufficiently to encourage a rate of outward migration equal to the rate of population growth. Once this occurs unemployment would stabilise.

If the underlying employment growth potential remains unchanged the level at which unemployment stabilises would necessarily be the same as before. It follows that job creation in the province will only have long-term effects if it alters the future rate of growth of employment opportunities, and any jobs that are promoted should therefore have long-term growth prospects. Moreover, increasing the underlying rate of employment growth reduces the need for high unemployment and low wages as equilibriating mechanisms (to force sufficient outward migration) in the future.

We now consider the dynamics of the Northern Ireland Labour Market. Figure 1 which shows the labour market flows in Northern Ireland for the period 1971-81, makes it clear that the major factor in the rising unemployment over the period was the inflow of new workers into the labour market: job losses played a fairly small part. This inflow, some 80,000 workers over ten years, represented an increase of about 13 per cent in the total labour force. To absorb this increase (even allowing for some continued outward migration when unemployment is reduced), about 6,000 new jobs a year were needed, an annual growth rate of 1 per cent. This would have removed most of the dynamic job shortfall, but many more jobs are now required to reduce the stock of unemployed workers, which currently stands at over 120,000. A target of 30,000 unemployed by 1997, an unemployment rate of about 5 per cent, would require the creation of 15,000 jobs each year for the next ten years.

The second feature made clear by Figure 1 is that unemployment has played a large role in absorbing the excess labour supply. In principle wages could adjust to keep the labour market in equilibrium. This would require a wage rate permanently lower than that in Great Britain to give enough investment in Northern Ireland and sufficient outward migration, to equalise the actual growth rates of labour demand and supply.

But the idea that wages will adjust to clear the labour market in Northern Ireland is not borne out by the evidence. The lack of any impact of local unemployment on wage change at the regional level is common throughout the UK. While unemployment has little effect on wages, employment growth and job vacancies have been shown to be significant in determining wage levels.[4] Regression analysis suggests that a 10 per cent rise in employment in Northern Ireland is associated with a 9 per cent increase in average wages in manufacturing, implying that a policy of employment creation is likely to harm manufacturing through pushing up the general wage level. Indeed it seems that most of the wage convergence between Northern Ireland and Great Britain in the 1960s and 70s was due to policy-induced employment growth. Fortunately the effect of wage increases on employment growth seems insignificant.

The main difference between the economies of Northern Ireland and Great Britain appears to lie in their different rates of increase in population of working age, 1 per cent a year in Northern Ireland as opposed to 0.1 per cent in Great Britain. While both have similar rates of employment growth, indeed since 1960 Northern Ireland's employment growth has been better than that of Great Britain, the province suffers a continual large imbalance between actual and required job creation. Getting unemployment down in Northern Ireland is bound to be a lengthy and arduous task.

The Pattern of Employment From 1951 to 1983

Figure 1 has shown that the change in employment during the 1970s was relatively small, a loss of some 12,000 jobs leaving a total of 485,800 in employment in 1981, a decline of less than 2.5 per cent. While the change in total employment was small, it masks very large changes in the pattern of employment over the period. Between 1971 and 1983 74,000 jobs were lost in the manufacturing sector in Northern Ireland. In addition over 10,000 jobs were lost in the construction industry. The reason for the small fall in total employment has been the rapid expansion of the public sector and an increase of about 30,000 in private services.

Examining historical trends in employment growth in Northern Ireland highlights this sectoral change. Table 1 shows the changing composition of employment between 1951 and 1983.

Table 1: The Structure of Employment in Northern Ireland, 1951-83

Sector	Employees in Employment as a Percentage of total employment	
	1951	1983
Primary (extractive industries)	7.4	2.7
Manufacturing	40.9	21.6
Construction	7.1	5.4
Private services	27.5	32.4
Health and education	5.5	22.5
Other public services	11.1	15.8

Source: Census of Population.

Table 1 excludes large numbers of workers in the construction and primary sectors (especially farming) who are either employers or self-employed; if these workers were included the primary sector would look more important as a source of employment, but the overall trends shown in the table would remain the same. The most significant aspect of Table 1 is the decline of manufacturing as against public sector employment, particularly in health and education. This pattern of change is similar to, but goes further than, that in the rest of the UK.

Table 2 shows the Northern Ireland proportion of employment relative to the Great Britain proportions for the four main sectors. This highlights the decline of manufacturing in Northern Ireland relative to Great Britain while public sector

Table 2: Northern Ireland Proportions of Employment by Sector Relative to Great Britain Proportions

Sector	1951	1983
Manufacturing	108	81
Private Services	100	88
Health and Education	85	142
Other Public Services	88	127

Source: Authors' calculations.

employment, which started from a base of considerably lower relative size, has become much more important for the Northern Ireland economy. It is worth noting that while private service employment in Northern Ireland has grown both in absolute terms and as a proportion of total employment, this growth has not been as fast as that in the rest of the United Kingdom.

Figure 2 shows actual minus expected manufacturing employment in Northern Ireland (excluding shipbuilding which is very volatile due to the nature of its output). 'Expected' employment is calculated by applying GB growth rates in employment to manufacturing employment in Northern Ireland, and the graph therefore shows changes in Northern Ireland's manufacturing employment relative to Great Britain allowing for Northern Ireland's industrial structure. If employment in each industrial sector in Northern Ireland grew at exactly the British rate in a particular year the graph would be flat in that period. Any slope in the graph shows that some sectors in Northern Ireland are doing better, or worse, than their British counterparts, indicating a differential, regionally specific, effect on employment.

Differential employment growth in Northern Ireland due to specific regional effects goes through three distinct phases. Firstly, the period 1950-61 gives a relatively flat portion indicating little differential growth after allowing for industrial structure. This indicates that the falling manufacturing employment in Northern Ireland during the period, against a background of an expansion at the national level, can be almost

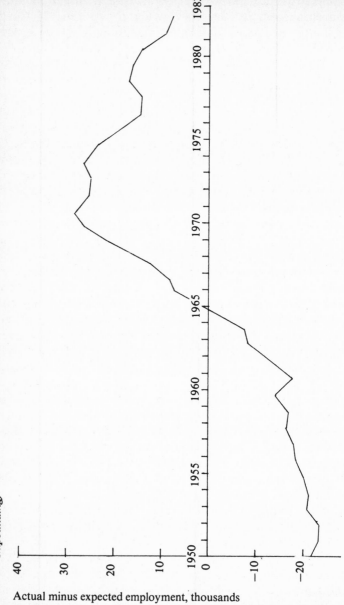

Figure 2: Actual minus Expected Employment in Manufacturing Industry in Northern Ireland 1950-1983 (excluding shipbuilding)

Actual minus expected employment, thousands

completely accounted for by Northern Ireland's adverse industrial structure. Secondly, in the period 1961-71 Northern Ireland gained about 50,000 manufacturing jobs over and above what would have been expected had each sector simply followed British trends. Finally, in the period between 1971 and 1983 Northern Ireland suffered a differential loss in manufacturing of about 20,000 jobs.

The improvement in manufacturing performance in the 1960s was associated with the strengthening of UK regional policy in this period.[5] This policy included a wage subsidy, the Regional Employment Premium (REP), and the Industrial Development Certificate (IDC), (a system of refusing planning permission for industrial plant in more prosperous regions), as well as a policy which provided capital grants and loans. The reversal of Northern Ireland's manufacturing performance in the 1970s can be attributed to the political troubles, the weakening of regional policy (removing the REP and IDC systems), and the slow growth of the world economy and national demand.

Estimating the effects of these forces seperately is difficult. The method used was to estimate what would have happened in Northern Ireland in the absence of the troubles by considering the behaviour of the other assisted areas of Great Britain over the same period. It turns out that for the 1960s the effectiveness of regional policy in Northern Ireland coincides with the pattern predicted for the effectiveness of the policy in Scotland, Wales and the North of England. Assuming that this relationship would have remained stable during the 1970s in the absence of the troubles, an estimate can be formed of what the effect of regional policy in Northern Ireland would have been in these circumstances. This calculation suggests that 40,000 jobs were lost in manufacturing due to the troubles. This is the top of the likely range, as we are attributing to the troubles all the job losses we cannot explain using the other factors we have considered.

We can now account for the observed changes in manufacturing employment for the post-war period in Northern Ireland in terms of a number of key factors. Table 3 identifies these factors and the orders of magnitude of their contribution. The first column gives the actual change in manufacturing employment in Northern Ireland in each of the three periods.

Table 3: The Contribution of Selected Factors to the Change in Manufacturing Employment in Northern Ireland, 1950-83.

	Actual Change	Estimated Contribution of			
		National Growth	Industrial Structure	Policy	Troubles
1950-51	−13	+17	−34	0	0
1961-71	+9	−9	−22	+33	−1
1971-83	−74	−51	−2	+17	−40

Source: Authors' calculations.

The second column is derived by simply applying aggregate employment change in Great Britain to the Northern Ireland stock in a pro rata way. This is what we would expect to have happened in Northern Ireland if it were a completely 'average' region reflecting only national employment trends. To calculate the third column we apply the growth rates in employment for Great Britain to the Northern Ireland stock of employment, at the beginning of the relevant period, after performing an industry disaggregation exercise; the difference between these calculated expected changes and the straightforward method used for column one gives our estimated effect of industrial structure. This industrial structure effect comes from Northern Ireland's concentration in poorly performing industries relative to the British industrial structure. Any effect due to both being overly concentrated in declining industries (relative to the rest of the world) will come through in the 'national growth' column.

The policy and troubles effects are estimated as set out above. Note that the policy effect is a net figure; in addition to those jobs created directly by regional policy the figure takes into account the positive multiplier effects of increased local demand and the negative displacement effects due to the policy-induced jobs either producing products which compete with existing firms or driving up the general wage level. The policy effect for the final period indicates the number of jobs which would have been created in the absence of the troubles. The fact that many of these jobs were not in fact created is included in the figure giving the cost, in jobs, of the troubles.

In the early period what stands out is that the adverse industrial structure figure overwhelms the positive contribution coming from national economic growth. About two-thirds of this structural component comes from the decline of the linen industry. The unexplained residual for this first period (some 4,000 jobs) may be attributable to the weak regional policy in operation. The dominant feature of the second period (1961-71) is the large differential growth in Northern Ireland's manufacturing employment after allowing for its industrial structure. We attribute this primarily to the greatly strengthened regional policies of the period; the IDC seems to have been particularly effective while the REP had little measurable impact.[5] However, despite this successful regional policy, actual employment only increased by 9,000 because of persistently adverse structural effects, and the beginning of the secular decline of manufacturing in the UK as a whole.

In the final period, the 1970s and early 1980s, two factors combined to produce a precipitous fall in manufacturing employment – the national decline of manufacturing and the intensification of the troubles. The national economy, and with it the domestic demand for manufactures, has grown relatively slowly, and while productivity increases in industry have been sufficient to cause job loss they have been insufficient significantly to increase exports through greater competitiveness. The troubles have had a considerable effect on manufacturing: existing employment is some 40,000 less than it would have been. Note that this does not imply that 40,000 jobs were actually lost through redundancy, but most of this 'loss' comes from a lower level of inward investment and job creation.

The Public Sector

Despite the decline in manufacturing in Northern Ireland, total employment has remained remarkably stable. This has been the result of a large increase in public sector employment. In order to compare what happened in Northern Ireland with events in Great Britain we calculate actual minus expected employment in the public sector for Northern Ireland; the results are shown in Figure 3. What stands out is the change which took place around 1970. Before this date there is little deviation of actual

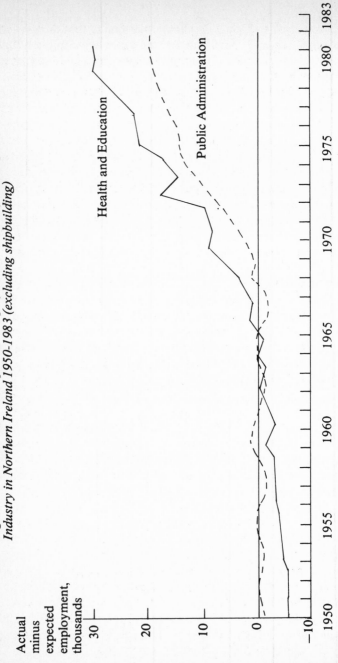

Figure 2: *Actual minus Expected Employment in Manufacturing Industry in Northern Ireland 1950-1983 (excluding shipbuilding)*

from expected employment change, indicating that the growth of the public sector in Northern Ireland was very similar to that in Great Britain. Since 1970 about 50,000 jobs have been created in the public sector over and above what would have been expected given national trends. Since 1980 however, the curves have flattened out, indicating that differential employment growth has ceased in this sector. The public sector is now the biggest employer in Northern Ireland. By 1983 employment in health, education and public administration accounted for over 38 per cent of total employment, compared with only 25 per cent in 1971 and 16 per cent in 1951. In contrast the share of manufacturing sector employment fell from 41 per cent in 1951 to 22 per cent in 1983. One important feature of this structural change is that female employment has risen while male employment has fallen, against a background of roughly constant total employment. In the period from 1960 to 1981 male employment fell by 29,000 while female employment rose by 39,000, so that by 1981 women accounted for 45 per cent of the total workforce. This highlights the fact that creating jobs in one sector to offset the decline of another frequently leads to structural unemployment; unskilled male manual workers cannot easily be turned into clerks, nurses or teachers.

Public sector employment growth has been associated with an increase in public sector expenditure. The principle which has conventionally governed the planning of public service provision in the UK is that central government funds should be distributed so that each geographical area can provide public services up to a common level. So long as this principle holds, areas with above average needs, or below average ability to pay taxes, will automatically experience a fiscal transfer, an excess of government expenditure on services over its tax revenues. The question we now address is whether this level of fiscal transfer is justified by Northern Ireland's needs using the conventional criterion of equality of public service provision.

Overall government expenditure per capita in Northern Ireland exceeded that in Great Britain by 24.9 per cent in 1981-82 and by 27.3 per cent in 1984-85. By 1983 only 54 per cent of this government expenditure could be financed by tax revenue from Northern Ireland. To decide if Northern Ireland's special circumstances require public expenditure, and the implied fiscal transfer, on this scale we need a detailed examination of each service provided, comparing actual expenditure with the levels required to bring standards in Northern Ireland up to British levels. For some programmes this is relatively easy; in the case of the social security programme, for example, the needs assessment is built in to many classes of expenditure; actual and expected expenditure must therefore be the same. Other programmes require more judgement; in health services, for example, not only the provision of doctors and hospital beds should be considered, but also the age structure of the population (as the very young and old require more services) and the relative incidence of illness.

From our estimates, overall expected expenditure exceeded actual expenditure by £84 million or 2.3 per cent in 1981-82, in 1984-85 actual exceeded expected expenditure by the same amount. Given the difficulties in assessing needs not too much significance should be read into small differences between one year and another. The basic message is clear. During the 1980s actual expenditure in Northern Ireland has been very close to that which would be expected from an assessment of expenditure needs applying British standards. The main area in which there is still a significant difference is housing; this difference could easily be made up given the very poor quality of Northern Ireland's housing stock.

The increase in public sector expenditure and employment in the 1970s is best seen as a catching up process, rather than taking Northern Ireland beyond a point which would be justified by its needs, and the employment growth in the public sector has been a welcome benefit of this process. The argument for further public sector expansion to create employment rather than to establish equity, ought to rest on grounds of relative cost. While this is a sensible policy in the short run if it provides jobs cheaply relative to subsidised private sector employment, it lacks long-run growth potential. There must come a time when public sector employment ceases to grow, and the public sector spending constraint bites. When this happens the basic problem, the differential growth rates in labour supply and demand, will reappear.

In order to get an overall measure of the effect of the troubles on employment in Northern Ireland we need to take account of their impact on service sector employment as well as on manufacturing. The troubles have led to the creation of about 24,000 security-related jobs in the public and private service sectors. We take the effect on other private sector employment to be negligible, as this is mainly determined by local demand, though the troubles, through the need for increased security may have raised costs.

It is a matter for debate whether or not the expansion in non-security related employment in the public sector should be attributed to the troubles. After the introduction of direct rule in 1972 the link between tax revenues and public expenditures in the province was broken. Before that date discretionary public spending in Northern Ireland was constrained by local tax income. Only automatic spending on social security was subsidised because equal benefit rates with Great Britain were accepted as national policy and financed by a transfer from the national insurance fund. Since the introduction of Direct Rule, government spending has been related to need, using British standards, with no constraint imposed by local revenues. It is by no means certain that this fiscal transfer would have occurred without the troubles. Assuming that without the troubles fiscal policy would have remained devolved and a balanced budget had been required, some 50,000 fewer public sector jobs, and any induced local service sector jobs, would have been created.

More concretely, our calculations suggest that the 'direct' effect of the troubles, on manufacturing and security related employment, amounts to a net loss of about 16,000 jobs. This is roughly the same as the figure calculated by Rowthorn.[7] However if we attribute the expansion of public sector spending in the province to the troubles we must add a positive effect of perhaps 35,000 jobs (about 15,000 of the public sector employment expansion already being counted as security related). This gives a net positive effect for the troubles of about 19,000 jobs.

A Policy for the Future

Four policy options are considered, and although we treat them separately they are by no means mutually exclusive: firstly, to continue the strategy followed in recent years; secondly, to cut real wages in the province relative to those in Great Britain; thirdly, to stimulate employment growth through the public sector; finally, to concentrate aid on selected industrial sectors.

(i) Continuation of present policies

The main features of this option would be to hold public expenditure at existing levels, which are broadly consistent with the province's special needs, and to apply a variety of small-firm, regional and manpower policies, albeit a little more generously in Northern Ireland than in other British assisted areas. Many national policies, for example towards agriculture, would continue to be applied equally, if not more sympathetically in the province. There is in addition industrial derating and a subsidy towards the high electricity generating cost in the province which could be continued. Such a strategy met with some success in the 1960s, mainly through the attraction to the province of British and foreign multinational companies. Some 34,000 manufacturing jobs were created by regional policy up to 1971 and this, along with a small expansion in the public sector, reduced the unemployment rate relative to Great Britain while keeping the net outward migration flow within bounds, at between 8,000 and 10,000 per annum.

Two events undermined this strategy. The first was the outbreak of the political troubles in 1969 and their continuation for almost two decades. The second was the oil crisis of the early 1970s, which sparked off a deep world-wide recession. Northern Ireland has experienced the full force of this recession: it reduced the flow of mobile investment into the province, encouraged the rationalisation of older, particularly heavy, industries, and hastened the closure of branch plants. In spite of the maintenance of a strong regional policy in Northern Ireland, these adverse conditions have resulted in the loss of some 74,000 manufacturing jobs, a decline of 44 per cent.

To a large extent the decreasing effectiveness of traditional industrial regional policies in Northern Ireland over the last fifteen years has been masked by public sector expansion. Now that this expansion has come to an end the inadequacies of present regional policies will become more apparent. The shortcomings of the present policies are numerous: they are passive: government agencies wait for firms to apply for grants; they rely more on attracting incoming firms than on indigenous firms; civil servants, who have little industrial experience, dominate decision making; short-term job creation, not long-term development, is the main target; there are no well developed views on selectivity between sectors; there is a lack of co-ordination between different job creating bodies, particularly those who create public sector jobs and those which promote private sector employment.

These failings suggest that there needs to be a departure from present policies, and the construction of an alternative strategy which is more likely to be successful.

(ii) Reducing real wages

The theoretical proposition, based on neo-classical theory, is that if wages in Northern Ireland fell, indigenous firms would be more competitive in external markets, new firms would be attracted to the province and firms serving domestic markets would become more labour-intensive in their production processes as people 'priced themselves into jobs'. We have no wish to deny the presence of these effects, but for theoretical and practical reasons wage-cutting does not provide a viable economic development programme for Northern Ireland.

If real wages were reduced labour turnover would rise as firms employing skilled, technical and professional staff lost these workers to firms in Britain and overseas. Indeed, it is unlikely that employers in such firms would allow wages to fall. There is ample evidence that firms using skilled labour prefer to pay high wages despite the presence of a large pool of unemployed, ready to work at subsistence rates.

If private firms are reluctant to cut real wages for fear of losing skilled workers how are wage cuts to be brought about in practice? There are three possibilities – a wage cut in the public sector, the reduction or abolition of unemployment benefits, or steps to restrict outward migration.

Cutting wages in the public sector would, in the short run, put downward pressure on wages in the private sector. However the main effect would be large-scale outward migration of those skilled workers who could most readily obtain employment elsewhere. The only real benefits of this measure would be the reduction in public spending due to the lower wage bill.

At the lower end of the skill hierarchy, a severe cut in unemployment benefit would bring about a reduction in wages. If migration remained possible there would be a sharp increase in the movement of unemployed to Britain. This diversion of the unemployed from one region to another cannot be considered a solution. This policy would create some low paid jobs in the province, but at the cost of substantial poverty and hardship.

The policy most likely to be successful is that of restricting outward migration. The speedy build-up of unemployed workers would force wages down while firms would not be worried about losing trained employees because of the relatively high wages outside the province. Essentially, this divorces the labour market in Northern Ireland from that in Britain, allowing its wage to follow its own path. While this policy would be the most effective of the three it seems impossible to implement from a practical point of view, not least because of EEC legislation on the rights of all workers to work in any member state.

The real argument, no matter in what way the wage cut was brought about, is whether low wages would lead to a higher rate of employment growth in the province due to inward investment by foreign capital and increased competitiveness in existing producers. If this did not happen the wage cut might lead to a removal of the unemployment problems but the underlying difficulty, the differential growth rates of labour demand and supply, would remain. In this case wages would have to fall indefinitely, so that employers absorbed the increased labour supply, or, if migration were permitted, wages fell low enough relative to outside levels to force sufficient workers to leave the province. Without economic growth, cutting wages simply substitutes one form of hardship, low incomes, for another, unemployment. It is not clear which is preferable, particularly as incomes may have to be very low to have the same effect on migration as high unemployment.

If low wages did lead to a rapid increase in investment and expansion of existing firms, creating a dynamic manufacturing base in the province, it would be a viable long term economic policy. However, inter-regional wage differentials are seldom an argument in locating new plant. Again firms would have reservations about being able to attract workers of good quality at low wages, and if wage costs were small compared with total costs even large wage differentials might be insufficient to overcome other competitive disadvantages suffered by the province. In the 1950s when there was relative political stability, and wages in Northern Ireland were as much as 30 per cent below those in England, there was no large flow of capital from Britain to Northern Ireland until an active regional policy was introduced. The same is true of the Republic of Ireland.

One variant of the wage-cutting strategy which avoids many of these problems is a wage subsidy as part of regional policy, so workers' take-home pay does not fall while firms face reduced labour costs. The REP provided a 7 per cent wage subsidy to British assisted areas and Northern Ireland between 1967 and 1976. Our evaluation of this policy is that while some jobs were created, it was much less cost-effective than other forms of employment promotion; for the UK as a whole the cost per job created by the REP was about three times as much as for job creation by investment grants. Studies of the relative effectiveness of different types of regional policy in the UK have found that wage subsidies tend not to be cost effective because: they apply to all jobs, not just those they help create; there are 'leakages' of the subsidy into higher pay and profits rather than extra employment; firms discount such subsidies in long term planning for fear of their abolition; the effect of changes in regional competitiveness on employment is distinctly disappointing.[8]

We are therefore only a little more optimistic about wage subsidies than about actual wage cuts.

(iii) Expansion of the public sector

The assumption underlying this strategy is that due to its political and geographical situation, Northern Ireland is not the most efficient location for most types of manufacturing activity. Manufacturing industry in the province should not therefore be supported by government subsidies: maximum national output would be achieved by allowing firms to go to those parts of

Great Britain in which they can operate most efficiently. These national output gains, from the concentration of manufacturing in the most efficient locations, could then be redistributed back into the regions that have foregone development in their manufacturing sector, in the form of higher public expenditure.

Theoretical analysis supports this idea in terms of maximising overall national welfare. The main advantages are a more efficient manufacturing sector, and a lower public sector borrowing requirement (because of a lower cost per job in creating public sector employment in Northern Ireland than by subsidising manufacturing industry). Conventional regional policy has cost more than £10,000 per job year (we divide the cost of each job created by the number of years it lasts for comparison with direct public sector employment) in Northern Ireland which exceeds the cost of employing a worker in services such as health or education.

The disadvantage of this strategy is that it is essentially short-term. Public service provision can grow further, but eventually a saturation point will be reached. The point is that, unlike a dynamic manufacturing sector, a large public sector is not likely to lead to a self-sustaining, and self-financing, growth in employment. Public sector employment would have to be financed indefinitely by government spending, continuing the dependence of the province on a fiscal transfer.

However, there is a strong case for using public sector employment as a short-term strategy, particularly over the next ten to fifteen years, for this is the cheapest way of alleviating the unemployment problem in Northern Ireland. There are certainly tasks that need to be done: the housing programme could be given more emphasis, while there is some evidence that environmental services, transport and communication have relatively low levels of government spending at the moment. Using the public sector in this way is essential if we wish to remove the pressure on industrial policy to create short-term employment, and to allow a longer-term view. Furthermore, any additional public spending which helps industry by reducing costs, for example through efficient transport facilities, will aid the long-term aim of an industrial recovery.

(iv) Regenerating manufacturing industry

The fourth option involves a shift away from the traditional passive form of regional industrial policy to a more active and interventionist approach. Our view is that the only long-run prospect for economic success in Northern Ireland is a policy which, over a period of time, changes the industrial structure sufficiently to give Northern Ireland a steady high rate of employment growth. This requires a more selective type of industrial policy, and regional policy in Northern Ireland is already moving in this direction. The Industrial Development Board (IDB) has published a new five year strategy which gives a higher priority to sectorally orientated initiatives, with the emphasis on improving the performance of indigenous firms.[9] The major problem with this strategy is whether the IDB staff can change from using a fairly rigid set of criteria for giving grants to deciding, on their own initiative, what type of assistance should be given and which firms should get it.

It is essential that the staff making these decisions is of sufficient quality and expertise. The IDB's support and use of the new programme in International Business and Industrial Development at the University of Ulster is a step in the right direction, but more thought needs to be given to staff recruitment and training. In particular we would advocate ending the current practice of using civil servants transferred for relatively short periods (three or four years) from other branches of government. While good at administrating policies, they are unlikely to have the background necessary for more direct involvement in industry. A more self-contained organisation, with increased recruitment from the private sector, inside and outside the province, would be much more effective when using a discretionary approach to policy.

The Scottish Development Agency (SDA) already has many of the features we are advocating for an improved IDB in Northern Ireland. It employs able management staff and uses specialised consultants on a large scale. Instead of merely administering grants and subsidies, it takes a much more active role and concentrates on specific sectors including high technology, oil, textiles, food, forest products and printing, and gives them assistance by identifying new markets, new production processes and management needs, as well as helping fund projects.[10] Overall it emphasises its close 'partnership' involvement with industry, rather than the traditional method of arm's-length support.

While arguing that the IDB could adopt some of the features of the SDA we consider it necessary and desirable to go further in establishing an agency which can co-ordinate and channel the efforts of the public sector, private firms, the universities, management consultants and technologists to create economic expansion. To do this the agency would need to be responsible for the overall development strategy, and have the power to decide which sectors should be supported and which should not. This might cause friction in the short term, for currently support to industry is dispensed amongst different government agencies. But these administrative impediments should not be allowed to hinder the establishment of an integrated single agency.

A new single agency should be responsible for establishing an integrated strategy for economic development which would identify potential growth industries; encourage firms in these industries to invest in new projects, process and product innovation; promote private sector funding through joint ventures and establish close contact with private sector sources of capital; ensure the provision of consultancy advice on management, new technology, new products and marketing; facilitate labour recruitment by ensuring government training schemes are appropriate to the long-term strategy; encourage research, innovation and marketing skills within existing companies and help forge links between local firms and financial institutions.

Perhaps the distinguishing feature of the strategy proposed here is the degree of agency discretion. The agency ought to be able to decide on the balance between automatic and discretionary funding, between small and large firms, between incoming and indigenous firms, between sectors, on the cost per job limits in different areas, and most importantly on the distribution of support to different parts of the overall strategy.

Many of the initiatives suggested here may take a long time to come to fruition. Building up a modern industrial base is bound to be a slow and, on occasions, a painful process. During the early period there may be little job creation, indeed there may be job losses, as funds are withdrawn from supporting declining industries to support new initiatives. This restructuring is a necessary stage of economic recovery. Burdening the agencies concerned with short-run job creation targets delays this restructuring and is not the most cost effective way of creating employment. If modern industries are to exist in ten or twenty years' time, emerging from the indigenous resources of the province, a serious start has to be made now.

There are several reasons why this strategic policy option is preferable to existing policies. Firstly, different industries in Northern Ireland have responded to conventional policies in different ways. Some industries, notably textiles and chemicals, have provided significantly fewer jobs than the average for the amount of public funding they have received. This suggests that a policy of greater selectivity could yield improved cost effectiveness. Secondly, the new policy option relies less on incoming firms and concentrates more on the development of indigenous firms and resources. Given the reduction of internationally mobile investment, this policy appears more realistic at present. Moreover, it has the advantage of generating the possibility of a self-sustained expansion in some sectors, with the fruits of success being contained in the region.

Thirdly, the strategy is aimed at growth rather than retrenchment, that is, propping up declining industries. It gives the possibility of a successful future while the current policy only hopes to mitigate the extent of the disaster. Fourthly, a shift from industry to the public sector as provider of jobs in the short term will be more cost effective, and will allow the industrial agencies to concentrate their energies on the long-run strategic aims of the policy.

There is no magic wand to wave at the industrial problems of Northern Ireland, indeed we can give no guarantee that the policies outlined above will in fact solve the problem. Under any policies the behaviour of the world economy will have a crucial role to play in determining the fortunes of manufacturing industry in Northern Ireland, but at least we are proposing to try to solve the problem and put the province in the best possible position to take advantage of any growth in particular sectors of the world economy which may occur. The assumption underlying the conventional policy is rapid world growth, making the attraction of outside capital relatively easy; those days have gone and we must adapt our policies.

Conclusion

The main conclusion of this essay is that the only long-term solution to the economic problem in Northern Ireland is to alter the industrial structure of the province in such a way that employment growth averages around 1 per cent per annum, approximately the rate of population growth. This requires that regional policy concentrates on those sectors that have long-term growth potential. This potential can either come from growing world demand, or because Northern Ireland can achieve a competitive advantage and a larger market share in some sectors. A realistic strategy for achieving this will require some twenty years, but this long time scale should not breed complacency. Central to the strategy is the regeneration of manufacturing employment in Northern Ireland; the longer the delay in beginning this process the more difficult it will become as the existing base shrinks further.

Given the long time scale of this plan it seems essential that the public sector takes the responsibility for short-term job creation. Public sector employment is much cheaper to create than subsidising manufacturing jobs and, in addition to any gain in employment, also helps in providing public services. One of the great handicaps of present industrial policy in Northern Ireland is the emphasis on short-run job creation; the removal of this type of short-term target will allow the agencies responsible for the manufacturing sector to concentrate on achieving the long-term goal of a dynamic, self-perpetuating and secure industrial base.

While an expansion of public sector employment is necessary in the short run, it must be seen as a temporary measure during a period of restructuring. There is a natural limit to employment growth in public services, while in manufacturing there is the prospect of long-term expansion, providing an engine of growth to power a self-sustaining economic recovery. The importance of concentration on sectors with long-term growth potential in regional policy cannot be overemphasised. Aid to industries in terminal decline and to industries with little growth potential should be lumped together with funds used to expand public sector employment and considered only as a method of relieving the short-run symptoms of the economic problem.

Changing the political or constitutional position of Northern Ireland is unlikely to improve the economic situation a great deal. In the short run an end to the troubles will lead to a large job loss in security-related services. In the longer term, even with an end to the troubles, a large fiscal transfer, either from Great Britain or some other source, will be required until a successful economic recovery occurs. It is possible to pursue a realistic economic policy in Northern Ireland aimed at long-run economic recovery despite the troubles; such a strategy should be seen as a necessary part of any plan for a solution of the political problem which does not envisage Northern Ireland remaining poor and dependent both politically and economically, on some outside body.

Notes

[1] The research for this essay was funded by the ESRC.

[2] Bob Rowthorn, 'Unemployment; the Widening Sectarian Gap', *Fortnight*, 16 December 1985.

[3] N. Gibson, 'Some Economic Implications of the Various Solutions to the Northern Ireland Problem' in J. Vaizey (ed.), *Economic Sovereignty and Regional Policy*, Dublin 1975.

[4] Barry Moore and John Rhodes, 'The Convergence of Earnings in the United Kingdom' in R. Martin (ed.), *Regional Wage Inflation and Unemployment*, London 1982.

[5] Barry Moore and John Rhodes, 'Evaluating the Effect of British Regional Economic Policy', *Economic Journal*, Vol.83, 1973, pp.87-110 and 'A Quantitative Analysis of the Effects of the Regional Employment Premium and Other Regional Policy Instruments' in A. Whiting (ed.), *The Economics of Industrial Subsidies*, London 1976.

[6] Barry Moore and John Rhodes, 'A Quantitative Analysis ...'

[7] Bob Rowthorn, 'Northern Ireland: An Economy in Crisis', *Cambridge Journal of Economics*, Vol.5, 1981, pp.1-32.

[8] A. Whiting, *The Economics of Industrial Subsidies*, London 1986 and B. Moore, J. Rhodes and P. Tyler, *The Effects of Government Regional Economic Policy*, London 1986.

[9] Industrial Development Board, *Encouraging Enterprise, A Medium Term Strategy for 1985-1990*, Belfast 1985.

[10] Scottish Development Agency, *Annual Report 1984*.

Notes on Contributors

Paul Bew is Reader in Political Science at the Queen's University of Belfast; he has written extensively on Northern Ireland with Henry Patterson, most recently *The British State and the Ulster Crisis* (1985). He is also author of a number of works on Irish history, including *Conflict and Conciliation in Irish Nationalism 1890-1960* (1987).

David Canning is a Research Fellow at Pembroke College, Cambridge, working on mathematical and monetary economics; he is co-editor (with Frank Hahn) of a forthcoming book on the latter.

Frank Gaffikin is Lecturer in Social Policy at the University of Ulster; co-author, with Stephen Nickell, of *Job Crisis and the Multinationals* (1984), he has also written on social deprivation in Northern Ireland.

Peter Mair, Lecturer in the Department of Government, University of Manchester, has written numerous articles on Irish and European politics; his book *The Changing Irish Party System* is forthcoming.

Barry Moore is a Research Fellow at Downing College, Cambridge; he has written widely on regional policy and regional economics with John Rhodes, with whom he is writing a book on regional economic analysis.

Mike Morrissey lectures in Social Policy at the University of Ulster and has written on poverty and social policy in Northern Ireland; he is currently working on a trade union economic policy for the province with the Irish Congress of Trade Unions.

Liam O'Dowd is Senior Lecturer in the Department of Social Studies at the Queen's University of Belfast; he is co-author of *Northern Ireland: Between Civil Rights and Civil War* (1980) and co-editor of a number of studies of the sociology of Ireland.

Brendan O'Leary is Lecturer in Political Science and Public Administration at the London School of Economics, author of a number of articles on Northern Ireland, and co-author, with Patrick Dunleary, of *Theories of the State: The Politics of Liberal Democracy* (1987).

Henry Patterson is Senior Lecturer in Politics at the University of Ulster; co-author, with Paul Bew and Peter Gibbon, of *The State in Northern Ireland* (1979), he is also author of *Class Conflict and Sectarianism* (1980).

John Rhodes is a Research Fellow at St Catherine's College, Cambridge, and has written extensively on regional economics with Barry Moore.

Bill Rolston is a Senior Lecturer at the University of Ulster and is author of numerous works on the Northern Ireland 'crisis'. He is co-author, with Ronnie Munck, of *Belfast in the Thirties: An Oral History*, (1987).

Bob Rowthorn is Reader in Economics at Cambridge University. His *Capitalism, Conflict and Inflation* (1980) won the Isaac Deutscher Prize; he is joint editor, with Ron Martin, of *The Geography of De-industrialisation* (1987).

Paul Teague is a Research Fellow at Cranfield Institute of Technology; he is author of numerous articles on European industrial and employment policy, and of *Labour and Europe: The Response of British Trade Unions to Membership of the European Community* (forthcoming).

Index